Roadways to Success

fifth edition

Roadways to Success

James C. Williamson
Agape Senior

Debra A. McCandrew
Florence-Darlington Technical College

Charles T. Muse
Florence-Darlington Technical College

PEARSON

Boston • Columbus • Indianapolis • New York • San Francisco • Upper Saddle River
Amsterdam • Cape Town • Dubai • London • Madrid • Milan • Munich • Paris • Montreal • Toronto
Delhi • Mexico City • São Paulo • Sydney • Hong Kong • Seoul • Singapore • Taipei • Tokyo

Editor-in-Chief: Jodi McPherson
Acquisitions Editor: Katie Mahan
Development Editor: Jennifer Gessner
Editorial Assistant: Clara Ciminelli
Executive Marketing Manager: Amy Judd
Senior Production Editor: Gregory Erb
Editorial Production Service: Electronic Publishing Services Inc.
Manufacturing Buyer: Megan Cochran
Electronic Composition: Jouve
Interior Design: Electronic Publishing Services Inc.
Photo Researcher: Annie Fuller
Cover Designer: Diane Lorenzo

Photo credits: pp. 1, 25, 45, 69, 93, 113, 139, 163, 195, 215, 237 © Shutterstock.

Library of Congress Cataloging-in-Publication Data

Williamson, James C.
 Roadways to success / James C. Williamson, Debra A. McCandrew, Charles T. Muse.—5th ed.
  p. cm.
 ISBN-13: 978-0-13-231745-0 (pbk.)
 ISBN-10: 0-13-231745-1 (pbk.)
 1. Success—Psychological aspects. I. McCandrew, Debra A. II. Muse, Charles T. III. Title.
BF637.S8W5216 2013
378.1'70281—dc23

2011043789

10 9 8 7 6 5 4 3 2 1

ISBN 10: 0-13-231745-1
ISBN 13: 978-0-13-231745-0

Jimmie lovingly dedicates this fifth edition to his family and friends, who have been constant sources of love and support: his wife, Kim Williamson; his sons, Jordan and Jake Williamson; his mother, Louise Williamson; his brother, David Williamson; and his friend and colleague, Scott Middleton.

Debi lovingly dedicates this book to her father, James. Thank you for your constant support, belief in me, and love.

Charles dedicates this book to his wife, Susan, for her support and always being there with her love and supportive nature, and to his sons, Thomas, Alex, and Matthew, who round out a very loving and caring family. Charles also dedicates this book to Dr. Edgar Boone, Professor Emeritus, North Carolina State University, who has been a true friend and mentor for over thirty years. His support and advice are greatly appreciated.

James C. "Jimmie" Williamson joined the administration of Agape Senior in January 2008 and has worked in various aspects of higher education for 26 years. Prior to his association with Agape, he most recently served as president of Northeastern Technical College, beginning in 2003. Dr. Williamson has extensive experience in higher education, having served as a faculty member or administrator at four community colleges and three universities in South Carolina. He also served as president of Williamsburg Technical College. Dr. Williamson has been published in the *Community College Review* and has received the South Carolina Governor's Award for Two-Year College Educational Champion of the Year. Academically, Dr. Williamson's doctoral cognate in gerontology and his study of senior adults—their learning styles and participation in learning-in-retirement centers—uniquely qualify him for his newest career.

Dr. Williamson holds a bachelor of visual arts and a master's in education from Winthrop University and a PhD from the University of South Carolina with a cognate in gerontology. He has served as president of the Cheraw Rotary Club and currently serves as assistant district governor of Rotary. Dr. Williamson is extremely involved in his community, having served as chairman of the Greater Cheraw Chamber of Commerce, a member of the Chesterfield County School Board, and a member of various economic development boards in and around the state. He has been honored by Winthrop University with a Professional Achievement Award and the Citizen of the Year Award from the Williamsburg Hometown Chamber of Commerce. He is also a two-time recipient of the Educational Champion of the Year award, from the South Carolina Department of Education.

Debi McCandrew is the department head for mathematics and computer technology at Florence-Darlington Technical College. She has a BS in education from Penn State University, a MEd from the University of South Carolina, and 18 graduate hours in mathematics from Francis Marion University. Ms. McCandrew is also a graduate of the South Carolina Technical College Leadership Academy. She has earned the following awards: the South Carolina's Technical Educator of the Year; the South Carolina Governor's Distinguished Professor of the Year; Florence-Darlington Technical College's Faculty Member of the Year; a Certificate of Merit from the National Academic Advising Association; and the NISOD Excellence Award for distinguished performance in teaching. Ms. McCandrew serves on the Florence-Darlington Technical College SACS Leadership Team, chairs the QEP Oversight Committee, and co-chairs the Palmetto Teaching and Learning Institute. Ms. McCandrew has made many professional presentations on academic success at the local, state, and national levels.

Charles T. Muse, Sr., retired as the vice president for academic affairs at Florence-Darlington Technical College in 2008 and is currently the executive director of the National Robotics Training Center, a division of Florence-Darlington Technical College. Dr. Muse also retired from the U.S. Marine Corps at the rank of colonel with 31 years of active and reserve duty. He received his DEd degree from North Carolina State University, majoring in adult and community college education, his MBA from East Tennessee State University, his AB degree from Catawba College, and his AAS degree in accounting from Coastal Carolina Community College.

Dr. Muse has received numerous academic, civic, and military awards, including Administrator of the Year, Distinguished President while serving as president of the Darlington Rotary Club, Distinguished Alumni Award from Catawba College, and the Legion of Merit Medal from the president of the United States. He has authored and co-authored more than 50 articles and 4 textbooks. His textbooks include *The Prentice Hall Planner: A Time Management System for Student Success* (Prentice Hall, 2003) and *A Planner for Student Success* (Pearson, 2011). He is a nationally known curriculum development specialist in the robotics (unmanned systems) manufacturing industry and has presented at national and international professional associations. He is an innovator in online curriculum development and endeavors to provide the environment for students to succeed.

CONTENTS

chapter three
TIME MANAGEMENT 45
PLANNING TO REACH YOUR DESTINATION ON TIME

chapter four
RECOGNIZING YOUR POTENTIAL AND BUILDING SELF-ESTEEM 69
FINE-TUNING YOUR VEHICLE

chapter five
INFORMATION PROCESSING AND LEARNING STYLES 93
SIGHTS, SOUNDS, AND SENSATIONS

chapter six
COMMUNICATIONS 113
SCANNING THE RADIO

chapter seven
THE PROCESS OF NOTE TAKING   139
CHARTING YOUR JOURNEY

chapter eight
LEARNING HOW TO STUDY   163
DRIVER TRAINING

chapter nine
TEST-TAKING STRATEGIES 195
GETTING YOUR LICENSE

chapter ten
HEALTH AND WELLNESS: MIND, BODY, SPIRIT 215
EXTENDING YOUR WARRANTY

chapter eleven
CAREER PLANNING, MARKETABILITY, AND DIVERSITY 237
REACHING YOUR DESTINATION

An open letter to the students who will benefit from this book: You have no doubt begun a journey of education that will take you far. The roadway you have chosen will not always be clear, for there are bumps, twists, and turns that no one can anticipate. Maybe you have started this journey before, or maybe this is your first venture into higher education. Whatever your destination and regardless of your starting point, hope abounds.

 ## NEW TO THIS EDITION

This fifth edition of *Roadways to Success* is a student-centered book that is readable and understandable by today's diverse students. Each chapter is presented in a logical sequence and organized to meet the needs of new-to-campus students or students returning to school after an absence.

Roadways to Success presents relevant material following a unique format that aids students in learning the concepts and skills they need when they need them and that will lead to their success in college. There is no busy work in *Roadways!* Every chapter activity is relevant and has a clear purpose that supports each concept presented.

Each chapter begins with a case study and a self-assessment that prepares students for the chapter material and activities. Incentives are built into each chapter to encourage students to move forward with a positive attitude. For example, when students complete the self-assessment at the end of each chapter, they are motivated by how much they have learned by following through with the activities and exercises and how much better they feel about the chapter content and themselves. New chapter features that address the needs of today's students include Help! I Need a Job, Social Media…Making Connections, and Math— The Four-Letter Word!

To help students learn material, chapters are the appropriate length for presenting specific concepts and providing effective exercises, activities, and threaded features. For example, Getting There on Time provides students with a more meaningful experience that will enhance their college experience.

In *Roadways,* there is no "fluff," like what is found in many student success textbooks—no "busy" charts, tables, and exercises that sometimes frustrate and confuse instructors. *Roadways* provides a smoothly sequenced table of contents that instructors may follow and that will meet the needs of today's college-bound students.

NEW FEATURES TO THIS EDITION

- **Help! I Need a Job!** Interviews with top-level, experienced recruiters from different businesses and industries demonstrate the importance of getting a quality education, identifying the needs of a prospective employer, realizing what an employer expects of a prospective employee, and presenting oneself in the best way possible during the application and interview process. By providing recruiters' own words, this feature is designed to give students insight into what employers from various career areas look for in the application and interview process.

- **Social Media . . . Making Connections:** This feature presents the world of social media to the new, as well as the experienced, social media traveler. Benefits and problems are addressed, along with ways to use social media for a successful college experience. Students are introduced to effective applications that apply specifically to the educational environment. This feature is designed to provide insight into social media and how its use can be an asset and lead to student success. Habitual use and the addictive nature of social media are also discussed.

- **Math—The Four-Letter Word!** This feature provides a thread that traces how math affects every aspect of our lives. Recognizing that students are often intimidated by math and mathematical concepts, each chapter provides an activity that explores the impact of math on real-life success.

- **Tips for Success:** This feature summarizes chapter concepts and suggests specific steps to take to succeed in those specific areas.

- **Addiction: Alcohol, Drugs, Food, Caffeine, and Tobacco:** This new section explores addiction in a nonthreatening way and provides self-assessment activities for students or their friends. Working through these materials helps students gain insight into compulsive behavior and what leads to addiction.

- **Stress:** Stress is problematic for many students. This new section helps students understand stress and how they can use use it in a positive way.

Roadways to Success is intended to guide you in your journey by providing practical, tried, and proven techniques that will make you a better student. The book will challenge you and ask you to examine your assumptions about studying and your ability to study. Although it is intended to be a guide, it will *not* answer all of your questions. Much of what you will learn will occur through self-discovery and self-analysis.

It is our hope that you will be better able to manage your time and your life after reading this text. Throughout this edition, we have used the case study method to assist you in understanding how the ideas in this book can be applied to real life. Read the case study at the beginning of the book carefully. You will refer to it after you have read each chapter. Additionally, this book will help you maneuver through a technologically challenging landscape.

Good habits take time to develop, and you will no doubt become discouraged somewhere along the way. Stay the course, keep on track, and make your dreams and goals your reality. We wish you well on your journey and trust that you will receive practical information here that will ultimately help all of your "roadways" lead to success!

ACKNOWLEDGMENTS

The authors wish to acknowledge the contribution of each of the following individuals:

Jennifer Gessner is a development editor at Pearson Education. Jennifer's guidance and suggestions made this edition even more useable and topical than previous editions. Her insight was valuable, and we appreciate the time, energy, and suggestions she put forth.

Clara Ciminelli is an editorial assistant in the area of Student Success and Career Development at Pearson Education. Clara provided ongoing support and kept us on track and on time. Keeping up with three authors is difficult, and we appreciate Clara's diligence, loyalty, and hard work.

Amy Judd is executive marketing manager in Student Success and Career Development at Pearson Education. Amy brought new life to the marketing effort of this book. Her keen awareness of both marketing trends and new ideas are greatly appreciated.

Supplemental Resources

INSTRUCTOR SUPPORT –
Resources to simplify your life and support your students.

Book Specific

Online Instructor's Manual – This manual is intended to give professors a framework or blueprint of ideas and suggestions that may assist them in providing their students with activities, journal writing, thought-provoking situations, and group activities. The test bank, organized by chapter includes: multiple choice, true/false and short-answer questions that support the key features in the book. This supplement is available for download from the Instructor's Resource Center at www.pearsonhighered.com/irc

Online PowerPoint Presentation – A comprehensive set of PowerPoint slides that can be used by instructors for class presentations or by students for lecture preview or review. The PowerPoint Presentation includes bullet point slides for each chapter, as well as all of the graphs and tables found in the textbook. These slides highlight the important points of each chapter to help students understand the concepts within each chapter. Instructors may download these PowerPoint presentations from the Instructor's Resource Center at www.pearsonhighered.com/irc

MyTest Test Bank – Pearson MyTest offers instructors a secure online environment and quality assessments to easily create print exams, study guide questions, and quizzes from any computer with an Internet connection.
Premium Assessment Content
  • Draw from a rich library of question testbanks that complement the textbook and course learning objectives.
  • Edit questions or tests to fit specific teaching needs.
Instructor Friendly Features
  • Easily create and store questions, including images, diagrams, and charts using simple drag-and-drop and Word-like controls.
  • Use additional information provided by Pearson, such as the question's difficulty level or learning objective, to help quickly build a test.
Time-Saving Enhancements
  • Add headers or footers and easily scramble questions and answer choices all from one simple toolbar.
  • Quickly create multiple versions of a test or answer key, and when ready, simply save to Word or PDF format and print!
  • Export exams for import to Blackboard 6.0, CE (WebCT), or Vista (WebCT)!
    Additional information available at www.pearsonmytest.com

MyStudentSuccessLab – Are you teaching online, in a hybrid setting, or looking to infuse technology into your classroom for the first time? It is an online solution designed to help students build the skills they need to succeed for ongoing personal and professional development at www.mystudentsuccesslab.com

Other Resources

"Easy access to online, book-specific teaching support is now just a click away!"
Instructor Resource Center – Register. Redeem. Login. Three easy steps that open the door to a variety of print and media resources in downloadable, digital format, available to instructors exclusively through the Pearson 'IRC'. www.pearsonhighered.com/irc

"Provide information highlights on the most critical topics for student success!"
Success Tips is a 6-panel laminate with topics that include MyStudentSuccessLab, Time Management, Resources All Around You, Now You're Thinking, Maintaining Your Financial Sanity, and Building Your Professional Image. Other choices are available upon request. This essential supplement can be packaged with any student success text to add value with 'just in time' information for students.

Supplemental Resources

Other Resources

"Infuse student success into any program with our "IDentity" Series booklets!" - Written by national subject matter experts, the material contains strategies and activities for immediate application. Choices include:

- Financial Literacy (Farnoosh Torabi)
- Financial Responsibility (Clearpoint Financial)
- Now You're Thinking about Student Success (Judy Chartrand et.al.)
- Now You're Thinking about Career Success (Judy Chartrand et.al.)
- Ownership (Megan Stone)
- Identity (Stedman Graham).

"Through partnership opportunities, we offer a variety of assessment options!"

LASSI – The LASSI is a 10-scale, 80-item assessment of students' awareness about and use of learning and study strategies. Addressing skill, will and self-regulation, the focus is on both covert and overt thoughts, behaviors, attitudes and beliefs that relate to successful learning and that can be altered through educational interventions. Available in two formats: Paper ISBN: 0131723154 or Online ISBN: 0131723162 (access card).

Robbins Self Assessment Library – This compilation teaches students to create a portfolio of skills. S.A.L. is a self-contained, interactive, library of 49 behavioral questionnaires that help students discover new ideas about themselves, their attitudes, and their personal strengths and weaknesses. Available in Paper, CD-Rom, and Online (Access Card) formats.

"For a truly tailored solution that fosters campus connections and increases retention, talk with us about custom publishing."

Pearson Custom Publishing – We are the largest custom provider for print and media shaped to your course's needs. Please visit us at www.pearsoncustom.com to learn more.

STUDENT SUPPORT –
Tools to help make the grade now, and excel in school later.

"Now there's a Smart way for students to save money."

CourseSmart is an exciting new choice for students looking to save money. As an alternative to purchasing the printed textbook, students can purchase an electronic version of the same content. With a CourseSmart eTextbook, students can search the text, make notes online, print out reading assignments that incorporate lecture notes, and bookmark important passages for later review. For more information, or to purchase access to the CourseSmart eTextbook, visit www.coursesmart.com

"Today's students are more inclined than ever to use technology to enhance their learning."

MyStudentSuccessLab will engage students through relevant YouTube videos with 'how to' videos selected 'by students, for students' and help build the skills they need to succeed for ongoing personal and professional development. www.mystudentsuccesslab.com

"Time management is the #1 challenge students face."

Premier Annual Planner - This specially designed, annual 4-color collegiate planner includes an academic planning/resources section, monthly planning section (2 pages/month), weekly planning section (48 weeks; July start date), which facilitate short-term as well as long term planning. Spiral bound, 6 x 9.

"Journaling activities promote self-discovery and self-awareness."

Student Reflection Journal - Through this vehicle, students are encouraged to track their progress and share their insights, thoughts, and concerns. 8 1/2 x 11. 90 pages.

MyStudentSuccessLab

Start Strong. Finish Stronger.

www.MyStudentSuccessLab.com

MyStudentSuccessLab is an online solution designed to help students acquire the skills they need to succeed for ongoing personal and professional development. They will have access to peer-led video interviews and develop core skills through interactive practice exercises and activities that provide academic, life, and professionalism skills that will transfer to ANY course.

It can accompany any Student Success text or be used as a stand-alone course offering.

How will MyStudentSuccessLab make a difference?

Is motivation a challenge, and if so, how do you deal with it?

Video Interviews – Experience peer led video 'by students, for students' of all ages and stages.

How would better class preparation improve the learning experience?

Practice Exercises – Practice skills for each topic - leveled by Bloom's taxonomy.

What could you gain by building critical thinking and problem-solving skills?

Activities – Apply what is being learned to create 'personally relevant' resources through enhanced communication and self-reflection.

MyStudentSuccessLab

Start Strong. Finish Stronger.
www.MyStudentSuccessLab.com

As an instructor, how much easier would it be to assign and assess on MyStudentSuccessLab if you had a Learning Path Diagnostic that reported to the grade book?

Learning Path Diagnostic

- For the **course**, 65 Pre-Course questions (Levels I & II Bloom's) and 65 Post-Course questions (Levels III & IV Bloom's) that link to key learning objectives in each topic.

- For each **topic**, 20 Pre-Test questions (Levels I & II Bloom's) and 20 Post-Test questions (Levels III & IV Bloom's) that link to all learning objectives in the topic.

As a student, how much more engaged would you be if you had access to relevant YouTube videos within MyStudentSuccessLab?

Student Resources

A wealth of resources like our FinishStrong247 YouTube channel with 'just in time' videos selected 'by students, for students'.

MyStudentSuccessLab Topic List -

1. A First Step: Goal Setting
2. Communication
3. Critical Thinking
4. Financial Literacy
5. Information Literacy

6. Learning Preferences
7. Listening and Taking Notes in Class
8. Majors and Careers
9. Memory and Studying
10. Problem Solving

11. Professionalism
12. Reading and Annotating
13. Stress Management
14. Test Taking Skills
15. Time Management

MyStudentSuccessLab Feature set:

Learning Path Diagnostic: 65 Pre-Course (Levels I & II Bloom's) and 65 Post-Course (Levels III & IV Bloom's) / Pre-Test (Levels I & II Bloom's) and Post-Test (Levels III & IV Bloom's).

Topic Overview: Module objectives.

Video Interviews: Real video interviews 'by students, for students' on key issues.

Practice Exercises: Skill-building exercises per topic provide interactive experience and practice.

Activities: Apply what is being learned to create 'personally relevant' resources through enhanced communication and self-reflection.

Student Resources: Pearson Students Facebook page, FinishStrong247 YouTube channel, MySearchLab, Online Dictionary, Plagiarism Guide, Student Planner, and Student Reflection Journal.

Implementation Guide: Grading rubric to support instruction with Overview, Time on Task, Suggested grading, etc.

ALWAYS LEARNING

PEARSON

Pearson Success Tips, 1/e

ISBN-10: 0132788071 • ISBN-13: 9780132788076

Success Tips is a 6-panel laminate that provides students with information highlights on the most critical topics for student success. These topics include MyStudentSuccessLab, Time Management, Resources All Around You, Now You're Thinking, Maintaining Your Financial Sanity, and Building Your Professional Image. Other choices are available upon request via our www.pearsoncustomlibrary.com program, as well as traditional custom publishing. This essential supplement can be packaged with any student success text to add value with 'just in time' information for students.

Features

- **MyStudentSuccessLab** — Helps students 'Start strong, Finish stronger' by getting the most out of this technology with their book.
- **Time Management** — Everyone begins with the same 24 hours in the day, but how well students use their time varies.
- **Resources All Around You** — Builds awareness for the types of resources available on campus for students to take advantage of.
- **Now You're Thinking** — Learning to think critically is imperative to student success.
- **Maintaining Your Financial Sanity** — Paying attention to savings, spending, and borrowing choices is more important than ever.
- **Building Your Professional Image** — Students are motivated by preparing for their future careers through online and in person professionalism tips, self-branding, and image tips.
- **Additional Topics** — Topics above are 'default.' These topics include MyStudentSuccessLab, Time Management, Resources All Around You, Now You're Thinking, Maintaining Your Financial Sanity, and Building Your Professional Image. Other choices are available upon request via our www.pearsoncustomlibrary.com program, as well as traditional custom publishing. This essential supplement can be packaged with any student success text to add value with 'just in time' information for students.

Topic List

- MyStudentSuccessLab*
- Time Management*
- Resources All Around You*
- Now You're Thinking*
- Maintaining Your Financial Sanity*
- Building Your Professional Image*
- Get Ready for Workplace Success
- Civility Paves the Way Toward Success

- Succeeding in Your Diverse World
- Information Literacy is Essential to Success
- Protect Your Personal Data
- Create Your Personal Brand
- Service Learning
- Stay Well and Manage Stress
- Get Things Done with Virtual Teams
- Welcome to Blackboard!

- Welcome to Moodle!
- Welcome to eCollege!
- Set and Achieve Your Goals
- Prepare for Test Success
- Good Notes Are Your Best Study Tool
- Veterans/Military Returning Students

NOTE: those with asterisks are 'default' options; topic selection can be made through Pearson Custom Library at www.pearsoncustomlibrary.com, as well as traditional custom publishing.

Introducing CourseSmart, the world's largest online marketplace for digital texts and course materials.

A Smarter Way for Instructors

▶ **CourseSmart saves time.** Instructors can review and compare textbooks and course materials from multiple publishers at one easy-to-navigate, secure website.

▶ **CourseSmart is environmentally sound.** When instructors use CourseSmart, they help reduce the time, cost, and environmental impact of mailing print exam copies.

▶ **CourseSmart reduces student costs.** Instructors can offer students a lower-cost alternative to traditional print textbooks.

▶ **"Add this overview to your syllabus today!"**
REQUIRED COURSE MATERIALS - ALTERNATE VERSION AVAILABLE:

CourseSmart is an exciting new choice for students looking to save money. As an alternative to purchasing the printed textbook, students can purchase an electronic version of the same content. With a CourseSmart eTextbook, students can search the text, make notes online, print out reading assignments that incorporate lecture notes, and bookmark important passages for later review.

A Smarter Way for Students

▶ **CourseSmart is convenient.** Students have instant access to exactly the materials their instructor assigns.

▶ **CourseSmart offers choice.** With CourseSmart, students have a high-quality alternative to the print textbook.

▶ **CourseSmart saves money.** CourseSmart digital solutions can be purchased for up to 50% less than traditional print textbooks.

▶ **CourseSmart offers education value.** Students receive the same content offered in the print textbook enhanced by the search, note-taking, and printing tools of a web application.

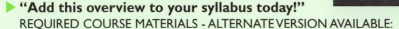

CourseSmart is the Smarter Way
To learn for yourself, visit www.coursesmart.com

This is an access-protected site and you will need a password provided to you by a representative from a publishing partner.

ALWAYS LEARNING

PEARSON

 INTRODUCTION TO THE CASE STUDY

Throughout this edition of *Roadways to Success,* you will be asked to refer to the case study found below. It tells the story of a typical community college student (we have named her Gwen) who faces obstacles and challenges as she tries to make a better life for herself and her family by continuing her education. You may be able to identify with Gwen in some ways.

Be sure to read and understand this story fully. You will be asked to refer to it at the conclusion of each chapter. There, you will be given an opportunity to examine what you have learned in each chapter and to apply those principles to Gwen's life. (Hint: You may want to "tab" or "dog ear" this page, so it will be easy to find when you are asked to refer back.)

We hope that you will see the practical applications to the theories and principles in each chapter. Once you can distinguish how these principles apply to Gwen's situation, you should be able to apply them to your own life, as well.

 THE CASE STUDY

Gwen is a 28-year-old single parent of two beautiful children. Both of her children are in elementary school and active in sports—specifically, soccer and baseball. Gwen's oldest daughter, Kristen, is 9 and in the fourth grade. Her youngest child, Randy, is 6 and in the first grade. Randy has special needs and attends a special school. Both children are technically savvy and can maneuver around a computer quite well. Gwen lives with her mother, who helps out with the children.

Gwen has been working minimum-wage jobs since she dropped out of high school at age 16 with a tenth-grade education. She is very bright but did not take advantage of the opportunities afforded her in high school, and now her higher-education alternatives are limited. She works at a local restaurant during the day as a cook and for a cleaning company on the weekends.

Some afternoons, it is easy for Gwen to get that sinking feeling, so she always keeps a ready supply of Red Bull on hand for a pick-me-up. Gwen does not eat well and rarely gets enough sleep. Because of her responsibilities as a mother, an employee, and now a student, she has little time for what she considers unimportant things like sleep.

A few years ago, Gwen realized the only way she could make a better life for her family was by getting an education. Although she had never been crazy about school, she enrolled in an adult education program and earned her general equivalency diploma (GED). It was while taking courses in the adult education program that Gwen began to realize the power of the Internet and got hooked on social media. A friend at adult ed suggested that she set up a Facebook page, and before long, Gwen was spending hours on the computer after work, chatting with friends and getting involved in meaningless conversations.

Gwen spent so much time on Facebook that she had to extend the time needed to earn her GED. In the limited time Gwen could find for herself, she allowed her Facebook and Twitter accounts to distract her during the day. She was at risk of being asked to leave the adult education program if she did not complete modules in a timely manner. Gwen knew this was her last chance for an education, and she did not want to mess it up. So, she deleted her social media accounts and now uses the computer only for research. "There will be time for that later," she wisely told herself.

After earning her GED, Gwen knew she wanted to work in a health field. She made an appointment with the admissions office at a local community college. Gwen began the process of applying to the college and eventually took the placement exams. She was feeling good about her progress until she learned the result of her math placement exam and the courses she was approved to take: Psychology 201, English 101, Music 105, and Remedial Math. Taking the remedial course seemed to help Gwen with her math anxiety, which had been a problem for her since middle school. She had always thought of herself as being a poor math student and could make herself physically ill just thinking about taking a math exam.

Gwen's feeling of initial success quickly vanished as she faced several challenges. She realized she had to become a master at time management. She could no longer function on four hours of sleep per night. She needed to be awake and alert in class to be able to take advantage of the opportunity before her.

When Gwen took her first exam in English 101, she failed it. She did not understand what had happened on the test. She had tried to study, as best she knew how. After the next class, she asked the instructor for assistance and was referred to the Success Center, where she could practice her writing and English skills with the help of a peer tutor. Her grades gradually improved, and she ended the term with a C in each class.

During the semester, Gwen also faced other challenges she had not expected. As mentioned earlier, time management was quite a challenge. She had to learn to balance classroom time, work time, and time caring for her children with study time and rest time. She did not have much time available to see her friends, and so she had to explain that her temporary absence in their circle was due to balancing long-term goals and objectives.

School has also been a challenge for Gwen because she has encountered some professors who come from backgrounds different from hers. To Gwen, they talk funny and have different ideas.

And financially speaking, things could not have been worse. Gwen's hours at work were reduced, and as a consequence, her take-home pay was also reduced.

Everything seems to be stacked up against Gwen as she tries to make a better life for herself and her family. But she is determined *not to quit*.

Read through this textbook, and find out what skills and techniques Gwen can use to be academically successful this time around. Also find out how she can recognize that math is not the monster she thinks it is. She took a class like the one you are enrolled in now, followed the techniques outlined in this text, and became successful. Just like Gwen, you can find success, but you must apply what you learn in this course and with this text.

Best wishes for *much* success!

Roadways to Success

chapter 1

CONNECTING WITH YOUR CAMPUS RESOURCES

STOPPING TO ASK FOR DIRECTIONS

Emil's high school experiences had never taken him from his home campus to the local community college campus. As a result, when he arrived for orientation, he was overwhelmed, not only by the various departments but also by the sheer number of buildings on campus! How would he ever find his way around, much less navigate a sea of people and key places? Emil soon realized that much of what he needed could be found in the materials given to him when he applied: the college catalog, handbook, and brochure. Emil enrolled in a course designed to help him maneuver the college experience and soon was able to use the library, the computer lab, the financial aid office, and the career services office to his advantage.

Emil was also unfamiliar with the concept of *professor*, which seemed different from *teacher*. Taking the new class enabled him to understand the differences and engage his professors on a more sophisticated level. Emil liked his new environment, and by using the campus resources available to him, he soon became a proficient student. ■

This chapter is designed to help you understand what resources are typically available on a college campus. Colleges vary in the types of resources and services they offer students, based on where they are located, what kinds of students they serve, and the proportion of commuter to residential students. In addition, this chapter is devoted to helping you understand your professors and to making sense of this new world you have entered. ■

Objectives

AFTER READING this chapter and completing the exercises, you will be able to do the following:

- Identify tangible and intangible resources.
- Understand what resources are typically available on college campuses.
- Discuss campus resources, such as the library, computer labs, and special-needs labs (writing, math, reading, etc.).

- Use the resources available on your campus.
- Understand the role of a professor.
- Understand the concept of *academic freedom.*
- Understand what makes a good student.
- Understand basic classroom etiquette.

TANGIBLE VERSUS INTANGIBLE RESOURCES

> The real object of education is to give students resources that will endure as long as life endures; habits that time will not destroy; occupations that will render sickness tolerable, solitude pleasant, life more dignified and useful, and death less terrible.
>
> —Sidney Smith

Before having a discussion about resources, a discussion about tangible resources versus intangible resources is necessary. *Tangible* resources are things you can see, feel, taste, hear, or smell. Tangible resources are things such as money for tuition, books to learn from, computers to use for producing papers, and so on. *Intangible* resources, on the other hand, cannot necessarily be touched or seen. In a college setting, intangible resources are things in place to support your overall education. These resources take the shape of services and include things such as tutoring, counseling, help with academic subjects, and advice from your professors. All resources, both tangible and intangible, are important, and all play a major role in helping you become a successful student.

In the space below, list some tangible and intangible resources you are aware of on your campus.

TANGIBLE RESOURCES

_____

_____

_____

_____

INTANGIBLE RESOURCES

_____

_____

_____

_____

Milestones

Where Are You Now?

Before you begin reading this chapter, take a few moments to complete the Milestones checklist. The statements are designed to determine what you already know about the resources and people available at your college.

Answer each statement by checking "Y" for Yes, "N" for No, or "S" for Sometimes.

1.	I know how to use the college catalog.	Y	N	S
2.	I know how to find services I need.	Y	N	S
3.	I am aware of the computer options available to me on the campus.	Y	N	S
4.	I know where to find my academic advisor.	Y	N	S
5.	I know where to go to get help with my classes.	Y	N	S
6.	I am aware of campus organizations and clubs.	Y	N	S
7.	I understand the concept of *academic freedom*.	Y	N	S
8.	I know how to find my professors' offices.	Y	N	S
9.	I know how to approach my professors in their offices.	Y	N	S
10.	I know all of my professors' office hours.	Y	N	S

If most of your responses were "No," don't despair. This chapter is designed to help you get familiar with the "road," so your "journey" will be easier and more worthwhile.

THE "OWNER'S MANUAL": YOUR COLLEGE CATALOG

Just as you receive an owner's manual when you purchase a new car, you will receive a college catalog when you are accepted to your institution. All colleges are obligated to provide you with a catalog after you enroll. This college catalog may be either a hard copy or an electronic copy on the college's website.

Today, most colleges are not printing catalogs because of the cost. Colleges have created a catalog or catalog archive section on the website that contains the current-year catalog and several past years' catalogs. It is an "owner's manual" for your time in college.

SOCIAL MEDIA . . .

Making Connections!

Numerous resources are available to students. Essentially, no question should go unanswered with all of the search engines now available. Today, a student can search for available jobs, check out corporate and college websites, and write cover letters and draft résumés from templates—all without ever leaving the computer.

For this activity, search the classified section of a local or state newspaper for a job you might be interested in.

*What level of education does the position require?*_____

*Search your college's website. Can you get the required educational experience at this college?*_____

_____

Pretend that you have completed the appropriate level of education and that you have the required amount of experience to be able to apply for this job. Search for the company's website.

*Does the company provide a mission statement?*_____

*Are other available jobs listed on the site?*_____

*Does the website give any of the company's history?*_____

*Is there an online application for employment?*_____

Now, pretend you are going to apply for a position with the company. Search the Web to find sites that can help with writing a cover letter and résumé. Take the time to draft your own résumé and write a fictitious cover letter for the job you found that interested you. Have an instructor or friend look at the résumé and cover letter. In his or her opinion, would you get the job?

Now, using social media sites such as LinkedIn, Facebook, and Twitter, explore the variety of professional opportunities available in your field. You might, for example, search on Facebook for a corporate page to "like."

And here's a word of caution: Numerous employers report that they now check Facebook regularly before offering positions to potential employees. If your Facebook page has language or photos that portray you in a less than professional and dignified way, you should probably delete them before applying for a job.

It is important that you keep this document as you move through your educational experience. Many requirements may change during your enrollment. Colleges typically "grandfather" in the old rules, so they still apply to students already enrolled. Your college catalog should offer answers to questions such as "What are the graduation requirements for this institution?" and "What courses are required in my major for me to graduate?"

For this next exercise, pick a major you might be interested in (even if you have not declared a major). In the space provided, write the name of your major, the degree you will receive, and the page number from the catalog on which the course requirements are listed. Here is an example:

Major: Machine tool technology

Degree: Associate of applied science

Page: 43

*Major:*_____

*Degree:*_____

*Page:*_____

Also, to complete this exercise and to record this work for the future, you may wish to prepare a Graduation Checklist.

Review the courses required for you to graduate in your major. How many hours (semester or quarter) will be required for you to graduate?

Write down the number of hours required to graduate in your major.

_____

Doing some simple division, estimate the number of semesters or quarters that will be required for you to complete your degree. For example, if 60 semester hours are required to complete the degree, 15 hours must be completed each semester, which comes to 4 semesters or 2 years.

_____

This is your *projected completion time*—the time after which you can reasonably expect to graduate. Of course, if you are able to take fewer or more hours per semester or quarter, this schedule will differ. Students with families and/or full-time jobs may limit themselves to nine hours per semester, for example. Determining your projected completion date will help you put your college experience in perspective. Now, take a look at the courses required for your particular major. Check the catalog to see if any of these courses has a prerequisite. A *prerequisite* is a course or other requirement that must be completed before another course can be taken. Do any of your courses have prerequisites? If so, what are some of the prerequisites?

List some of the courses with prerequisites, and write out what the prerequisites are.

_____

College catalogs are wonderful resources for answering many questions that arise. For example, if you want to know the policy on repeating courses, just turn to the catalog's index, and it will refer you to the page for the answer. Often, college catalogs list professors' complete names and the schools from which they earned their degrees. In addition, the college catalog explains how to become involved in student activities and lists the hours of operation for the student bookstore, student union, and so on. In short, the

Catalog Scavenger Hunt

Now, take a moment to discover more about your college by exploring your college catalog. Complete the following Catalog Scavenger Hunt:

1. My college was founded in _____.

2. My college president is _____.

3. My college offers _____ degrees.

4. The department chairperson for the major I have selected is _____.

5. The college mission statement is on page _____.

6. Information about student records is provided on page _____.

7. A map of the campus is on page _____.

8. My college has _____ campuses.

9. College fees are listed on page _____.

10. The withdrawal/expulsion policy is on page _____.

11. I will be put on academic probation if my grade-point average (GPA) falls below _____
_____.

12. The policy for plagiarism is found on page _____.

13. My campus mailing and Internet addresses are _____.

college catalog should be your best friend as you go through the process of earning your degree. *Keep the catalog, and refer to it often!*

Knowing where to find particular items in the catalog is important. The catalog is the "road map" of your educational journey, and being able to read it is important. Spend some time getting to know your catalog.

Equally as important is knowing how to access your campus website. Generally, information listed in the catalog is also listed on the website, and any changes, additions, or deletions to the information may be reflected on the website in a more timely manner.

 THE **LIBRARY**

If the classroom is the "heart" of the college, then the library is the "brain." The library is a wonderful resource, and using it will enable you to get the most out of your educational journey. The library is one place on campus that houses numerous resources, such as academic and scholarly works, usually under one roof.

Library Scavenger Hunt

1. Who wrote *Gone with the Wind?* _____

2. Find an article on computers. Write down the title of the magazine or newspaper, plus the article title and author. _____
_____

3. Locate a book dealing with human behavior. Write down its title and author. _____
_____

4. For how long can you check out a book? _____

5. What is the overdue fee? _____

6. What is the head librarian's name? _____

7. What is the first line of Shakespeare's play *Hamlet?* _____

8. What is the call number for the *Dictionary of Occupational Titles?* _____
_____

9. What did Carl Sandburg win a Pulitzer Prize for? _____

10. What was the lead story in a newspaper published the day you were born? _____
_____

In completing the exercise above, you could find many of the answers using a search engine. Resist the urge to look up the answers electronically. Instead, make it a point to use the library and become familiar with the variety of resources provided there.

The library is best used as a daily tool—whether as a quiet place to study or as a place in which to "get directions" and find out more about "points of interest" throughout your journey. Take time to complete a library tour. You will likely be glad you did. If you are still unclear about where a particular item is located or how to use a special piece of equipment, *ask!* Librarians will not do your work for you; however, they are a resource. Use their knowledge and time wisely.

COMPUTER RESOURCES:
A TRIP ALONG THE INFORMATION SUPERHIGHWAY

Nearly all colleges and universities today are required to include computer literacy as part of the program of study they offer students. The definition of a well-rounded student today includes computer literacy. Using computers is a way of life today. Most colleges and universities offer Internet services to their students; take advantage of this service, if it is offered to you.

Using computers can also help you be a better student. Today, there are software packages to help you with math, writing, and grammar. Check with your library or tutoring center to see what software packages are available to help with various subjects.

ALTERNATIVE ROUTES:
DISTANCE EDUCATION AND OTHER NONTRADITIONAL FORMATS

A number of colleges now use nontraditional formats for course delivery, such as the Internet, videotaped courses, and interactive video courses. The course content can vary for each format, and students are expected to be motivated and able to work independently.

Taking these courses can be exciting and challenging but also overwhelming for students who are academically less prepared. Often, these courses have strict deadlines for completing assignments, and they require the students to be very self-disciplined. Before you register for a course such as this, consult your academic advisor.

MAKING A "PIT STOP":
LEARNING RESOURCE CENTERS

Occasionally, your academic journey can be a little bumpy. Maybe you turned in a paper and did not receive the grade you had expected. Maybe you took a math test and did not do as well as you hoped you would. Do not despair! On most campuses, help is available in learning centers, often referred to as the "math center," the "reading center," or the "writing center."

These centers employ students and professional tutors that can assist you with academic problems. For instance, if you are having a problem with fractions, someone from the math center will show you how to add, subtract, multiply, and divide fractions. Maybe he or she can go through your homework or class assignments and then show you a videotape or DVD that covers fractions. The same would be true if you were having problems with adverbs. Help would be available in the writing center.

Often, these centers can give you practice work and let you work on specific academic problems while you are there.

*On your campus, what is the name of the tutoring center?*_____

*Where is it located?*_____

*What is its phone number?*_____

*What are its hours of operation?*_____

TRAVELING COMPANIONS: YOUR FRIENDS

A discussion about resources is not complete without mentioning one of the most valuable resources: your friends. Friends can make your journey easier, help you understand difficult material, and even quiz you before exams. Supportive friends can keep you going and help you understand your options when you feel like giving up.

Friends are valuable resources, but they can also be big problems. When choosing friends, choose carefully. If someone is making you get behind in your schoolwork, think about whether you want to be friends with that particular person. Don't let someone else rob you of your chance to be a more educated person.

COUNSELING SERVICES

There are times in almost all of our lives when we need a little help dealing with a variety of problems. Sometimes, we just need to talk to someone who can look at our situation with an open mind and help us work toward a solution.

On a college campus, these services can take the form of emotional counseling, academic counseling, and career counseling. The best advice is to seek out someone on campus you feel comfortable with and then talk with him or her. It probably is not wise to let the situation fester. These services are free to you and may make your days as a freshman easier.

Some students feel embarrassed or ashamed to seek counseling, but the fact is that many students need and seek advice every day on everything from money problems to relationship breakups.

FINANCIAL AID SERVICES

Even the most well thought out plans are sometimes disrupted by financial problems. Many students wait until it is too late to seek financial counseling and apply for financial aid. It may be that your funds are running low and you have to temporarily withdraw for a year or a semester. Wait! Before you make that decision, talk to a financial aid counselor. These counselors are trained to help students find scholarships, jobs, and federal, state, and local aid. You may not need to interrupt your studies after all.

Learn about and take advantage of the services offered on your campus, including counseling, financial aid, learning centers, and others.
Source: ACE STOCK LIMITED/ALAMY

MATH —the four letter word!

Math certainly plays a part in your overall college experience and the resources available to you. The practical applications of math include determining the total cost of your education, being able to cover your educational expenses through financial aid or finding part-time work (you have to be able to produce revenue greater than the costs of the education), determining how many hours it will take you to graduate, and so on. Additionally, this chapter is all about connecting you to the resources available to you. Should you be a student who needs extra assistance in math, the simple exercise for this portion of the book is to find those resources: tutoring services, math labs, and so forth.

Examine/identify the many campus resources available to assist you when taking a math class:

1. The best resource is always your math instructor. If you are taking a math class this semester, write down your math instructor's office hours and contact information.

   _____

   _____

2. On your college campus, identify where math tutoring services are located, who provides the services, and when are they open.

   _____

3. Many college campuses provide workshops for students on a variety of topics. Contact your college's student services department, and ask if it offers "math anxiety" workshops, calculator workshops, and so on. List the services provided by your college.

   _____

   _____

The most obvious type of financial assistance is federal and state financial aid. These programs have been in place for many years and are the staple of many college students. The following types of aid are available from the federal government: Pell grants, direct loans, Federal Family Education Loans (FFEL), Federal Supplemental Educational Opportunity Grants (FSEOG), and Federal Work-Study (FWS). To determine which type of aid is available at your school, contact the financial aid office.

According to *The Student Guide* published by the US Department of Education, here is how each form of aid is defined:

- **Loans.** Borrowed money that you must repay with interest.
- **Grants.** Money that you do not have to repay.
- **Work study.** Money earned for work you do at the college.

As an undergraduate, you may receive all three types of assistance.

Student Eligibility for Federal Financial Aid

To receive aid from the major student aid programs, you must meet these criteria:

- Have financial need, except in some special instances
- Have a high school diploma or GED, pass an independently administered test approved by the US Department of Education, or meet the standards established by your state
- Be enrolled as a regular student working toward a degree or certificate in an eligible program (You may not receive aid for correspondence or telecommunications courses unless they are a part of an associate, bachelor, or graduate degree program.)
- Be a US citizen
- Have a valid Social Security number
- Make satisfactory academic progress
- Sign a statement of educational purpose
- Sign a statement of updated information
- Register with the Selective Service, if required

Source: *The Student Guide*, U.S. Department of Education.

One of the biggest mistakes students make when thinking about financial aid is forgetting about scholarships from private industry and social/civic organizations. To find out more about all types of financial aid, examine the following publications: *Free Dollars from the Federal Government* (Prentice Hall), *Winning Scholarships for College: An Insider's Guide*, 3rd ed. (Marianne Ragin), *Peterson's 4-Year Colleges* (Peterson's), *Paying for College Without Going Broke* (Princeton Review and Kalman Chany), *How to Get Money for College* (Peterson's), and *College Financial Aid: How to Get Your Fair Share* (Lauren Zo).

You should also research the following: your college catalog, your place of employment, your parents' or spouse's place of employment, social and civic groups, and the Internet.

 HEALTH SERVICES

Most college campuses have some type of health or physical services. It is important to know where these facilities are located and what services are available to you. Some colleges offer students a health insurance policy.

The health services on campuses vary drastically. In the spaces provided, record what types of health services are available on your campus.

The health service office is located at _____

The phone number is _____

What type of insurance plan does your college offer? _____

_____

What is the price of this insurance? _____

 THE LIFE OF A PROFESSOR

Although it may seem that your professors have lives of leisure with lots of free time, the opposite is true. For professors to keep up with what is happening in their fields, they must *constantly* read, study, and learn about the latest developments. Great professors are always trying to improve what they bring to their students. Because of this, professors spend a great deal of time doing research for courses and for publishing articles and books. Publishing is extremely important to most professors, and they are very proud of the works they have published. In addition, professors are asked to present their research at conferences and to give workshops and seminars. Professors also provide assistance to students as academic advisors.

Ranking, or seniority, is very important to a professor. Because this is so vital, a professor will spend many hours trying to become a better teacher or researcher and thus be ranked at a higher level. Generally, ranking follows this order: instructors are often beginning professors, instructors become assistant professors, assistant professors become associate professors, and associate professors become professors (sometimes referred to as "full" professors).

> 'To teach is to learn twice.
> —Joseph Joubert

ACADEMIC FREEDOM AND WHAT IT MEANS TO YOU

The right of a professor to teach subject matter that is considered controversial or that might be viewed as different or uncommon is known as *academic freedom*. As long as the basic ideas of a course are taught, colleges and universities usually leave the method of instruction to the professor.

Basically, academic freedom allows professors to approach the subject matter in whatever manner they choose. For students, academic freedom gives them the opportunity to experience many different approaches to learning. Students may be asked to write a paper in one class, put together a group presentation in another class, and recite a reading in yet another class.

Controversial subject matter can be discussed within the framework of academic freedom, and so the subject matter can be quite different from what you encountered in high school. Subjects that might be viewed as taboo in high school can be discussed, debated, and deliberated in college, all because of academic freedom.

Academic freedom makes the U.S. system of higher education unique. It allows students to experience a wide variety of approaches and can make the college experience richer and more rewarding.

List several assignments or projects you had to complete earlier in your education.

_____

_____

Which assignment did you like the most?

_____

Why did you like this particular assignment?

_____

_____

Which assignment did you like the least?

_____

Why did you not like this particular assignment?

_____

_____

Examine the teaching style of your favorite professor. What is his or her dominant style? Is it the lecture method? Do you like this style?

Many teachers use both so-called left-brain and right-brain approaches to teaching. Using both approaches is appropriate for all types of learners. Some teachers present information using only an analytical, or left-brain, approach. Their instruction usually includes a lot of explanation and visual aids, with specific, detailed directions and lots of tests. Teachers who use a global, or right-brain, approach might introduce a lesson with a joke or short story. This kind of teacher encourages students to think for themselves and uses group learning or discovery as an important part of teaching. The professor who uses this kind of approach may test using presentations, charts, games, and so on.

As a student, you should be able to recognize these differences in professors and be able to learn from either the left-brain or right-brain approach and possibly other techniques. Just as you have preferences in the way you like to learn, professors have preferences in the way they like to teach. Being a successful student means being able to identify a professor's method or style and then changing your study habits to adapt to it.

Examine the teaching style of one of your current professors. Describe it.

_____

_____

Do you like this particular style? Why or why not?

_____

_____

UNDERSTANDING WHAT
THE PROFESSOR WANTS

Your professor will give you a syllabus on the first day of class. The syllabus outlines specifically what he or she expects from you during the course. It is a contract that assures you that course requirements will not change in the middle of the term. On the syllabus, you may be able to find out when tests will be given, what other work will be required for the course (papers, book reviews, etc.), and how much each test and assignment will count toward your final grade. You will probably also see the attendance policy for the course on the syllabus. Some professors also include important dates during the semester, such as the last day to withdraw from a course, the last day to add a course, and so on.

What you might not find out by reading the syllabus is what the professor expects of you. One of the best ways to find that out is to ask! Ask the professor how you should prepare for class each day. He or she will be impressed that you cared enough to find out what is expected of you, and you will begin to understand more about what he or she expects.

Questions to Ask Other Students about Professors

1. How much outside reading does the professor require?
2. Are the tests multiple choice, true/false, or essay?
3. How closely does the professor follow the grading scale?
4. What grade did you receive? Do you feel you earned this grade?
5. What would you change if you had to take the course again?
6. Would you take another course from the professor?
7. Did you learn a lot?

Above all else, *ask, ask, ask!* If you do not ask the instructor or some of your peers, you are dealing with an unknown.

WHAT MAKES A GOOD STUDENT?

A survey of professors around the United States asked, "What makes a good student?" Additionally, professors were asked what they liked most about today's students and what they liked least about them. Here are some of the professors' answers:

- "The biggest difference in students of today has to do with the fact that students of today are more opinionated and more verbal."
- "Students of today are better prepared academically."
- "Students of today face a limited job market and so they are more focused."

The survey also asked the professors another question: "Beyond the information that you give daily, what is the most important message that you want to leave with your students?"

- "I hope that I can instill in my students the ability to look *beyond* and not simply accept that a problem will automatically have an answer that is black or white, right or wrong, good or bad. . . . I also want my students to be able to deal with change and to *like learning!*"

Finally, professors were asked what they thought made a good student.

- "A 'good' student is . . . one who is self-motivated and . . . *wants* to understand and apply concepts."
- "A good student is . . . one who wants to learn, explores the boundaries of information, is not passive but rather active in pursuing knowledge."
- "A 'good' student accepts academic responsibility."

To summarize, professors seem to like students who (1) want to learn, (2) are self-motivated, (3) question what they are learning and try to relate it to real issues, and (4) have a sense of why they are in school.

WHAT MAKES A GOOD PROFESSOR?

Just like professors, students were also surveyed and asked to respond to questions. The first question was "What is the biggest difference between your college professors and your high school instructors?" Here are some of the students' responses:

- "College professors require more from you than high school instructors."
- "College professors go into detail on almost everything, they are very specific and are not easily strayed off of the subject."
- "College professors make you think more."

The second question asked of students was "What do you like most about your college professors?" and the third question was "What do you like least about your college professors?" Students' answers included the following:

- "What do I like most about college professors? They are *demanding.*"
- "College professors are passionate about what they teach—they have a real interest in the subject."
- "College professors set higher expectations with little direction, which forces you to become more responsible and devoted to your schoolwork."

In summary, college students expect college professors to be more demanding, and they are. College professors expect students to be able to keep up with the pace of their classes.

Agape Senior is a company that focuses on integrated health care for senior adults in a faith-based atmosphere. With 12 facilities in South Carolina (both assisted-living and skilled-nursing homes), the company employs more than 1,300 employees. Agape provides services for senior adults that include housing, pharmacy, therapy, hospice, ambulance, durable medical equipment, insurance, and real estate.

Here are Scott Middleton's (founder and CEO of Agape Senior) comments on employment with Agape Senior.

1. WHAT DOES AGAPE LOOK FOR IN AN EMPLOYEE?

"Learn how to communicate well. Verbal and written communication are important to Agape and can tip the scale in the decision of 'who is the best candidate for this position.' Employees are expected to develop a team spirit and work with others to ensure we meet our goals. Agape looks carefully at the attitude of each job candidate."

What can you do to be the prospect Scott is looking for in an employee?

_____

_____

2. WHY WOULD YOU HIRE ME?

"Research the company before you apply. Answer these questions: What can I do to add value to this company? What do I have to offer? Why is this a good fit for me and for the company? Where is this company going, and how can I assist in meeting their goals?"

What can you do to make Scott want to hire you?

_____

_____

3. HOW CAN I GAIN A COMPETITIVE EDGE?

"Apply your knowledge. Volunteer, work part-time jobs, perform an internship, and work in your area of expertise.

"Agape is interested in hiring employees who have taken the necessary steps to understand their culture and who are able to add value to their vision, mission, and goals.

"Our website (www.agapesenior.com) will tell you who we are and how we differ from similar companies in the health care industry. It also outlines our mission, our vision, and our goals."

What can you do to gain the competitive edge for an Agape Senior job?

_____

_____

_____

_____

4. WHAT ROLE WILL YOUR EDUCATION PLAY IN BEING ABLE TO GET A JOB AT AGAPE?

"Take your education seriously. This is the time to learn the competencies that will be valued in your future career. Education is not only what you learn in the classroom and read in the textbook, but it is also how you apply your knowledge."

How can you demonstrate that your education is relevant and competitive?

_____

_____

_____

_____

5. WHAT VALUES DO YOU SEEK IN YOUR EMPLOYEES?

"Develop a positive, can-do attitude. Find ways to stretch yourself and go above and beyond what is expected. Strengthen your self-esteem by becoming an expert at something that is important to you. Be proud of your accomplishments, and share them enthusiastically with Agape."

How can you convince Scott that you would be a valuable Agape employee?

_____

_____

_____

What would you include in your résumé that will address Scott's comments about prospective employees?

_____

_____

_____

How could you use your résumé's cover letter to demonstrate your strengths relative to the job description?

_____

_____

_____

Your college instructors are likely to ask you to think more and do more than your high school teachers did.
It is a professor's job to challenge you intellectually.
Source: SHUTTERSTOCK

CLASSROOM ETIQUETTE

Classroom *etiquette,* or knowing how to properly conduct yourself in a college lecture or class, is very important as you begin your journey. One of the key things about being a good student is realizing that you are not the only person in the room. There may be times when you are not interested in what is being said, but the person next to you may be interested. Being a responsible student means having respect for the other students in your class, as well as for the instructor.

Think about the following ways you can respect the instructor and the other students:

1. If you are late for class, do not make a lot of noise when you enter the room. Never walk in front of the instructor as you enter the room. Take the seat closest to the door.

2. Eating, drinking, and using tobacco products in a classroom setting is rude, unless the professor has given you permission to do so.

3. If you must leave class early, be sure to tell the professor before class. If you know you will have to leave class early once or twice a week, have your counselor arrange for you to take another section.

4. Do not start to pack up your materials and begin to rustle through your books and papers before your professor has dismissed the class.

5. Do not start a conversation with another student during a lecture, regardless of the subject matter. Use the time before and after class to discuss topics with other students.

6. When visiting a professor's office, try to make an appointment instead of simply showing up. If you must go to the professor without an appointment, never enter his or her office without knocking. Have your questions lined up *before* you knock on the door. Also ask if the time is convenient for the professor.

7. If you disagree with a grade you have received, make an appointment to talk with the professor and ask him or her to go over the specifics of the grade. Try not to be defensive. Professors like students to be interested enough in their work to question and probe, as long as they do so diplomatically!

You should extend the same amount of courtesy to your professors and fellow students that you expect from them.

READING THE PROFESSOR'S SCHEDULE

As you begin to learn where your professors' offices are located, you will also notice that most professors post their schedules outside their doors. A typical professor's schedule might look something like the one shown in Figure 1.1.

Looking at the schedule shown in Figure 1.1, when would you try to make an appointment with Dr. Doe?

_____

To get to know your professors better, copy the Professor Information record that follows, and use it for each professor you have. Check the schedule of each professor, and make an appointment with him or her. During your conversation with the professor, fill out the information sheet. Hopefully, doing this activity will allow you to see your professors as real people and foster relationships with them outside class. But if you understand a little more about their backgrounds, you might find it easier to understand their views while you are in their classes.

Figure 1.1 A Typical Professor's Schedule

Dr. John Doe — Office 237–B

	MON	TUES	WED	THURS	FRI
8:00	Eng 101		Eng 101		Eng 101
9:00	Eng 102	Office	Eng 102	Office	Eng 102
10:00	Office		Office		Office
11:00	Eng 201	Office	Eng 201	Office	Eng 201
12:00	Lunch	Lunch	Lunch	Lunch	Lunch
1:00		Eng 202		Eng 202	
2:00	Office		Office		Office

Professor Information

Professor's name: _____

Professor's office location: _____

Professor's office phone: _____

Where did the professor go to school?

   Undergraduate: _____

   Graduate: _____

   Graduate: _____

   Postgraduate: _____

How long has the professor taught at this school?

_____

If the professor is ranked, what is the rank?

_____

_____

Does the professor have any special research interests?

_____

If so, what are they?

_____

What are the professor's hobbies?

_____

What advice can the professor give you about being a successful student?

_____

_____

 # THE NEXT STEP

Now that you have become more aware of the tangible and intangible resources available on college campuses, it is time for you to do an inventory of what is available on your college campus. An *inventory* is simply a list. Using Exercise 1.1, make a list of all of the resources available on your college campus. Use your college catalog to help you complete this exercise.

Exercise 1.1   Resources Available to Me

Academic: _____

_____

Financial: _____

_____

_____

_____

Social: _____

_____

Physical: _____

_____

Career: _____

_____

Religious: _____

_____

Milestones

Now That You Are Here . . .

Now that you have completed this chapter, revisit the Milestones checklist.

Answer each statement by checking "Y" for Yes, "N" for No, or "S" for Sometimes.

1.	I know how to use the college catalog.	Y	N	S
2.	I know how to find services I need.	Y	N	S
3.	I am aware of the computer options available to me on the campus.	Y	N	S
4.	I know where to find my academic advisor.	Y	N	S
5.	I know where to go to get help with my classes.	Y	N	S
6.	I am aware of campus organizations and clubs.	Y	N	S
7.	I understand the concept of *academic freedom*.	Y	N	S
8.	I know how to find my professors' offices.	Y	N	S
9.	I know how to approach my professors in their offices.	Y	N	S
10.	I know all of my professors' office hours.	Y	N	S

How did you do on this inventory after reading the chapter? If you would like to be a more successful student, you must first know what is available to you to assist in this endeavor. A variety of resources are available to you on campus, if you ask for help.

TIPS FOR SUCCESS
In order to effectively apply for financial aid, you need to . . .

- Never miss a deadline.
- Read all instructions before beginning the process.
- Fill out the application completely, and have someone proofread your work.
- Submit all required documentation according to the instructions. Do all that the application asks you to do.

- *Never lie* about your financial status.
- Talk to the financial aid officer at the institution you will attend.
- Always keep a signed copy of your tax return for *each* year!
- Apply for everything possible.

APPLYING WHAT YOU KNOW

Now that you have completed this chapter, refer to the Case Study about Gwen at the beginning of this book. Based on Gwen's situation, answer the following questions:

1. What campus resources did Gwen utilize?

2. Were they helpful to her? If so, how?

3. If you were faced with some of the problems Gwen faced (such as not doing well in her English class, having financial difficulty, not understanding her professor), what might you do?

GETTING THERE ON TIME

1. How does knowing your professors' schedules assist you in managing your time?

   _____

   _____

   _____

   _____

   _____

2. Explain how the effective use of campus resources can assist you in managing your time.

   _____

   _____

   _____

   _____

   _____

   _____

   _____

3. What is the result of not meeting financial aid deadlines?

   _____

   _____

   _____

   _____

4. What is the result of not meeting academic deadlines?

   _____

   _____

   _____

   _____

Using campus resources effectively can aid you tremendously in managing your time. Be sure to use the resources available to you, both on campus and off campus, wisely. Your time as a student is valuable. Utilize all available resources to make the most of your time and your education.

JOURNAL

The purpose of this journal exercise is to give you a chance to think about what you have learned from this chapter about campus resources. Consider what you have learned about locating resources, finding out about the life of a professor, and financing your education. List the steps you are going to take to implement this new knowledge. Also, complete this phrase as it relates to this chapter:

As a result of reading this chapter and in preparing for my journey, I plan to . . .

chapter 2

GOAL SETTING AND MOTIVATION

MAPPING YOUR JOURNEY

In the earlier part of [the twentieth] century, a friend's grandfather came to America from Europe. He arrived by ship in the harbor of New York, passing by the Statue of Liberty. After being processed at Ellis Island, he went into a cafeteria in New York City to get something to eat. He sat down at an empty table and waited for someone to take his order. Nobody ever came to his table. Finally, a man with a tray full of food sat down opposite him and told him how things worked in a cafeteria setting. "Start at the end of the line," he said to the old man, "and just go along and pick out what you want. At the end of the line, they'll tell you how much you have to pay for it."

"I soon learned that's how everything works in America," Grandpa told his friend. "Life is a cafeteria here. You can get anything you want as long as you're willing to pay the price. You can even get success. But you'll never get it if you sit at a table and wait for someone to bring it to you. You have to get up and get it yourself."

—from *Bits and Pieces (Vol. 1)* ■

In Shakespeare's play *King Lear*, the king tells his daughter, "Nothing will come of nothing." This statement rings true, doesn't it? If there is no plan, there will be no action. If there is no action, there can be no success.

This chapter is intended to help you visualize where you hope to be in one, five, and even ten years. The exercises in this section are designed to examine your abilities in goal setting and to determine your motivational level. Many people have plans and goals, but they do not have the most important things needed to achieve success: They do not have clear objectives, and they do not have motivation. ■

Objectives

AFTER READING this chapter and completing the exercises, you will be able to do the following:

- Identify the fears that could hinder you in reaching your goals.
- Define your long-term goals and short-term goals.
- Write down your long-term and short-term goals.

- Write down specific steps or strategies for reaching your goals.
- Identify barriers that destroy goals and decrease motivation.
- Understand what you value most in life and where you are going.

> *Far better is it to dare mighty things, to win glorious triumphs even though checkered with failure, than to take rank with those poor spirits who neither enjoy much nor suffer much because they live in the gray twilight that knows neither victory nor defeat.*
>
> —Oliver Wendell Holmes

WHAT DO THESE PEOPLE HAVE IN COMMON?

Albert Einstein was 4 years old before he could speak and 7 before he could read a word. Yet he went on to become one of the world's greatest scientists.

A newspaper fired Walt Disney because he had "no good ideas." Disney later developed animated cartoons and motion pictures. He also designed and developed both Disneyland and Disney World.

Abraham Lincoln dropped out of grade school, ran a country store and went broke, and took 15 years to pay off his bills. As a politician, he lost a race for the state legislature at the age of 32, lost two races for the House of Representatives, and lost two races for the U.S. Senate. He later ran for president and won, but he was hated by half of the country. Yet eventually, he became one of the most famous leaders in history.

Malcolm X was abandoned as a child and grew up quite poor. As a young adult, he spent time in prison. He later became one of the most powerful speakers and leaders of the civil rights movement of the 1960s.

What did these people have in common? Luck? A tooth fairy? A genie in a lamp? No. They all had . . .

Goals! Objectives! Motivation!

Milestones

Where Are You Now?

Using the Milestones checklist, take a few moments to determine where you stand in relation to goal setting and motivation.

Answer each statement by checking "Y" for Yes, "N" for No, or "S" for Sometimes.

1.	I use goals to guide my actions.	Y	N	S
2.	Having goals is important to me.	Y	N	S
3.	I often set goals.	Y	N	S
4.	I write down objectives that shape my goals.	Y	N	S
5.	I face my fears head on.	Y	N	S
6.	I take responsibility for my life.	Y	N	S
7.	I know where I want to be in three to five years.	Y	N	S
8.	Having more than one goal is important to me.	Y	N	S
9.	When I reach a goal, I celebrate.	Y	N	S

You should not be too concerned if you have more "No" and "Sometimes" answers to these questions. This chapter will help develop and focus on your goals and objectives and will help you learn how to develop motivation.

 **ELIMINATING FEAR**

Two Fears That Hinder Growth and Stifle Motivation:
The Fear of Failure and the Fear of Change

Beginning your journey means realizing that every fear you have is learned. That's right, learned! You are born with only two fears: the fear of loud noises and the fear of falling. The rest are learned. Many times, your progress and success are limited, because you are afraid to move forward, afraid to take chances, or afraid to set goals beyond what you already know how to do.

The famous artist Vincent Van Gogh once said, "The way to know life is to love many things." And the way to love many things—and in the end, to know life better—is to take chances, set goals, be motivated, and expand your comfort zone.

HELP!
I Need A Job!

Paul McDuffee is the Vice President for Flight Operations and Commercial Business Development at Insitu, Incorporated. Insitu is a leading global provider of unmanned aircraft systems (UAS) solutions that meet a wide range of customer needs.

The following numbered items present Paul's thoughts about prospective employees. After reading each of Paul's thoughts and comments, answer the questions addressed to you as a prospective employee.

1. WHAT DO YOU LOOK FOR IN AN EMPLOYEE?

"We look for someone who possesses the skills, knowledge, and ability necessary to be successful. More importantly, does the individual share our values? You can train a person in a skill. You can't shape their passion and values quite as easily."

What can you do to be the kind of employee Paul is looking for?

_____

_____

_____

2. WHY WOULD YOU HIRE ME?

"If you can positively contribute to our organization, share our passion and values, in all likelihood, you'll get a chance. An applicant needs to demonstrate just how they would be a good fit in our company by providing examples of how they have conducted themselves professionally and socially. Can they express their ideas clearly? Can they compete in a high-energy, intense work environment with minimal supervision? Our company has been successful because we trust our employees to 'do the right thing.' Again, it gets back to sharing values. Anyone with a jaded background and lacking moral integrity need not apply."

What can you do to make Paul want to hire you?

_____

_____

_____

3. HOW CAN I GAIN A COMPETITIVE EDGE?

"We are primarily a high-tech, engineering-oriented company. We also market and deploy our products around the world. To get attention from us, a prospect will have to bring examples of past accomplishments that clearly demonstrate an ability to make a real difference in our company performance. An applicant should know all they can absorb about our company, its history, its customer base, and anything noteworthy we have accomplished."

What can you do to gain the competitive edge for a job at Insitu?

_____

_____

4. WHAT ROLE WOULD MY EDUCATION PLAY IN BEING ABLE TO GET A JOB WITH YOU?

"It would be important but not the only factor. We would be interested in what kind of practical experience an individual has just as much as their pedigree. In absence of experience, the educational background takes on more weight. Where did you go to school? What did you study? What outside activities were you involved in? All important questions for a first-time job applicant with little experience."

How can you demonstrate that your education is relevant and competitive?

_____

_____

5. WHAT VALUE CAN I BRING TO YOUR COMPANY?

"You tell me! An applicant needs to sell themselves. Can this person add value to our operation? We'll dig until we get an answer to that question. If we can't, the interview is over. Caution, when selling yourself, don't overreach. Humility and honesty are appreciated. Don't 'puff.' One last thing: the ability to obtain a security clearance is of real value to us. A person with a checkered past will have difficulty."

How can you convince Paul that you would be a valuable Insitu employee?

_____

_____

What would you include in your résumé that will address Paul's comments about prospective employees?

_____

_____

How could you use your cover letter to demonstrate your strengths relative to the job description?

_____

_____

This sounds easy, doesn't it? Actually, many people have goals, but they are afraid to move forward or do not know how to move forward. The first fear you should conquer is the fear of failure. Having goals is meaningless if you are afraid to go after them. Now, you have to ask yourself, "Is it better to try and fail or never to try at all?" The answer, once again, is quite simple. Failure is part of growth.

Some of your strength comes from difficult situations in which your comfort zone was stretched. You may have a few failures. We have all been there, haven't we? Just remember this old saying: "That which does not kill us makes us stronger."

The fear of change is another thing that can rob you of your hopes and dreams. Humans are creatures of habit, and in that light, change is neither natural nor desired. Change causes a great deal of frustration and physical reaction. However, when planning your goals, it is helpful to realize that change is one of the few things in this world that is guaranteed. The most successful people in the world are those who have learned how to deal with change and accept it as a part of life. For us to learn how to communicate with new people, feel comfortable in new situations, and develop new ideas, we must undergo change.

In answering the following questions, take a moment to reflect on your life and what situations cause you fear and possibly hinder you from growth.

> Change is never easy.
> Change is almost always met with resistance.
> The person who brings about change is usually not very well liked.
> Change creates unfamiliar ground.
> Change takes courage.

List three activities you feel comfortable doing.

1. _____
2. _____
3. _____

List two activities you would like to do but are afraid to try. Explain why you are afraid to try each one. Explain what would encourage you to do this activity.

1. _____

I am afraid because

_____
_____

What would make you do this activity?

_____
_____

2. _____

I am afraid because

_____

What would make you do this activity?

_____

_____

List two people you feel comfortable with, and indicate why.

1. _____

    *Because*_____

2. _____

    *Because*_____

List two people you do not feel comfortable with. Explain why you are uncomfortable and what it would take to make you spend time with each person.

1. _____

    *Because*_____

    What would make you spend time?

    _____

    _____

2. _____

    *Because*_____

    What would make you spend time?

    _____

    _____

Review your answers. You may have even written statements such as "I've never done this activity before" and "I just don't know this person very well."

A major part of your education involves learning how to expand your horizons through people, places, and things. Fear can play a major role in keeping your comfort zone small and stagnant. Follow these words of advice:

- ■ Don't be afraid to fail.
- ■ Don't be afraid to change.

> If you want to make good use of your time, you've got to know what's important and then give it all you've got.
> —Lee Iacocca

A major part of your education involves learning how to expand your horizons through new people, place, interests, and activities.
Source: SHUTTERSTOCK.

- Don't be afraid to take chances.
- Don't be afraid to go beyond what you know and feel at this moment.

WHAT IS A GOAL?

Many dictionaries define a *goal* as the purpose toward which effort is directed. Have you ever wanted a new car, a new DVD player, or a new outfit? If you have, then you have had a goal—the goal of getting one or all of these physical, material things. Goals are simply statements about the things you want and what you are willing to do to get them.

Goals should be obtainable and realistic. An obtainable, realistic goal is well defined, well planned, well organized, and well within your reach, considering the resources, skills, talents, and time you have to devote to it. In other words, you need to have a carefully developed plan to reach a goal.

Goals also have timelines. You can have short- and long-term goals. Short-term goals may be things such as the following:

- I want to purchase a new wide-screen TV.
- I want to make an A on my next English test.

Long-term goals are more elaborate and planned:

- I want to be a doctor.
- I want to get married and have three children.

Years ago, Dr. Albert Einstein was traveling on a train headed west. During the early part of the trip, he looked up and saw the train's conductor coming down the aisle, asking passengers for their tickets. Dr. Einstein began looking for his ticket. He looked in his coat pockets, he looked in his pants pockets, and he looked around his seat, but he was unable to find his ticket. When the conductor approached him, Dr. Einstein stated that he could not find his ticket, at which point the conductor said that he knew who he was and it was no problem. Nevertheless, Dr. Einstein continued to look for his ticket. The conductor assured him several times that he knew who he was and that it was okay if he could not find his ticket. Finally, Dr. Einstein said to the conductor, "Young man, I know who I am, but I don't know where I am going."

SOCIAL MEDIA . . .

Making Connections!

Have you started using social media? If not, why? The how and why of social media is presented in a short article at http://sarahmerion.com/philosophy/how-why-students-use-social-media/. Sarah Merion discusses the opportunities for adding value, connecting with people online, and learning from others. In addition, she states that using social media is fun and provides a way to update your status. Check it out at the website just mentioned.

Let's look at the how of social media in a little more detail. To get you started, read the specific yet simple step-by-step instructions provided in an article by writergirllinds, eHow Member, How to Use Social Networking | eHow.com, www.ehow.com/how_5847180_use-social-networking.html. What do you need? That is simple. All you need to get started is e-mail and a computer or a smart phone.

Start with one social networking site. Spend at least two weeks at that site before trying to add a second site. Also update your site on a regular basis. Do not provide too much information in your updates. More is not always better, and interacting with others on the site is the best way to make new friends.

Follow these steps to start on your road to social media communities. If you are already using one of these social media sites and you have the time, explore a second one by following these steps.

1. *Pick one site to start. Concentrate only on that site, so you are not overwhelmed from the beginning. Here are some examples:*

   Facebook—A friend-based social networking site. You can share as little or as much information as you would like. Networks are formed based on your school, neighborhood, and work groups.

   Twitter—Twitter is a short, 140-character-based platform. You use these short "tweets" to discuss current events, social topics, your life or business, and pretty much anything else you can think of discussing.

   LinkedIn—LinkedIn is used more for business connections. This social networking site helps get your business known in more than 200 countries. You build a virtual contact network to help increase your business contacts.

2. *Sign up for an account, which is usually easy. It requires you to set up a username and Web address for your social networking page.*

3. *Set up your profile, which can be easy or difficult, depending on the social network you choose. Try to keep things simple in the beginning by adding just some basic information, a profile picture, and so on.*

4. *Start increasing your friends. The key to learning social networking is to continue to grow your friend lists. Here are some tips for growing your friend base:*

   Facebook—The easiest way to gain friends on Facebook is by finding people you know. As you continue to update your page, you will likely find more and more people you know or who are in your network of friends.

   Twitter—It is more important to have others follow you than to have you follow hundreds of people on Twitter. The key to gaining followers on this social networking page is to continually have useful or entertaining updates. It is also important to interact with your fellow "Tweeple."

   LinkedIn—This site is based on the principle "It's who you know." You have to actually know a contact or be introduced to a contact before he or she will be added to your network.

Both long-term and short-term goals are important. Achieving goals takes sacrifice, planning, and a great deal of hard work. But without goals, your life would become aimless.

HOW TO WRITE A GOAL

Goal setting seems rather easy, doesn't it? Actually, it may take some time and thought and preparation for goals to come true. An obtainable and realistic goal statement should have the following qualities:

1. *An action statement:* A statement that includes an active verb.
2. *Objectives:* Activities or tasks that need to be accomplished in sequence.
3. *Target dates:* Deadlines that provide the timing of each objective.

However, the goal statement is the third part of a four-part process. This four-part process is as follows:

- *Values:* What do you value most in life?
- *Purpose/Focus/Direction:* Where are you going in life?
- *Dreams/Goals:* How are you going to get there?
- *Objectives/Activities:* What specific steps are you taking to achieve your goals?

You must start with values and focus before you can get serious about writing goals and objectives. After you have defined your values and your focus or direction in life, you can start writing down goals. Exercise 2.1, the Goal Setting Sheet, is a valuable tool for helping you plan for your future.

The example that follows illustrates how this process moves from life values to direction to goals to specific objectives with deadlines. Your values and direction can, but do not necessarily need to, be repeated each time you complete a Goal Setting Sheet. Each Goal Setting Sheet should begin with one value. That value should be followed by one direction or focus for your life. That focus leads to one obtainable, realistic goal that is followed by a specific list of objectives or steps that you need to take to reach your goal within a specific deadline.

> The greater danger for most of us is not that our aim is too high and we miss it, but that it is too low and we reach it.
> —Michelangelo

Goal Setting: Example

VALUES. What do you value most in life?

Having a meaningful career in a health care profession.

PURPOSE/FOCUS/DIRECTION. Where are you going in life?

My life's career will be to become a successful registered nurse.

DREAMS/GOALS. How are you going to get there?

By obtaining a college degree in nursing.

OBJECTIVES/ACTIVITIES. What specific steps are you taking to achieve your goal?

Sequence	Objective/Activity	Deadline
1.	Register for college	August 8
2.	Meet academic advisor	August 9
3.	Select courses to take	August 9
4.	Obtain financial aid	August 11
5.	Attend first class	September 5

Exercise 2.1 Goal Setting Sheet

Values. What do you value most in life?

_____

_____

_____

_____

Purpose/Focus/Direction. Where are you going in life?

_____

_____

_____

_____

Dreams/Goals. How are you going to get there?

_____

_____

_____

_____

Objectives/Activities. What specific steps are you taking to achieve your goal?

Sequence	Objective/Activity	Deadline
____	____	____
____	____	____
____	____	____
____	____	____

MATH —the four letter word!

Having math skills is as important in the goal-setting process as it is in other decision-making processes. For example, earlier in this chapter, "I want to purchase a new wide-screen TV" was listed as a short-term goal. The most economical way to make a purchase of this type is to save the money and pay cash, instead of putting it on a credit card. By putting this type of purchase—a major home appliance—on a credit card and having in-terest added each month, you will end up paying sometimes twice as much as the original cost.

How much would you need to save each month, over a year, to have the cash to purchase a new wide-screen TV? There are least three things to consider mathematically: the amount to save each month, the effect of compound interest on the amount you are saving, and the length of time (12 months).

How much do you need to save each month for a year to accumulate $1,500 to purchase a new wide-screen TV?

The equation to determine the required monthly saving amount is compound interest future value, or $FV = P(1 + r/n)^{Yn}$, where FV = future value, P = principal, r = interest rate, Y = years, and n = compound n times per year.

Let's look at an example. The amount you want to save, or the FV, is $1,500. The amount you plan to save each month, or the P, is $120. $120 is a good estimate. The interest rate, or r, is 5 percent. The number of years, or Y, is 1, and interest will be compounded each month, or n = 12.

$FV = P(1 + r/n)^{Yn}$

$FV = 120(1 + .05/12)^{1^{12}}$

$FV = 120(1 + .0042)12$

$FV = 120(1.0042)12$

$FV = 120(12.05)$

$FV = \$1,446$

The future value of money for $120 saved monthly compounded each month at 5 percent or 12 times for one year is $1,446. Your goal is $1,500. Therefore, you need to save a little more than $120 a month to reach your goal. If the interest is compounded daily, as it is at many financial institutions, the results will be higher.

Is monthly interest compounding better than daily compounding interest? _____

What is your one-year savings goal? _____

What equation will you use? _____

How much do you need to save each month to reach this goal? _____

Use an interest rate of 1 percent, compounded monthly.

Solve the equation. _____

_____

_____

_____

_____

What is your answer? Is it a realistic answer? To check your answer, use one of the many compound interest calculators online or one of the apps on your smart phone. Here are some online sites for compound interest calculators.

www.moneychimp.com/calculator/compound_interest_calculator.htm

http://www.webmath.com/compinterest.html

www.thecalculatorsite.com/finance/calculators/compoundinterestcalculator.php#results

Remember that a goal must be something that can be measured. In other words, you must be able to prove that it was completed. Here is an example:

GOAL 1: I will save (the action statement) $100 by putting back $10 a week (the objective). I will have $100 dollars by January 31 (target date).

This goal is obtainable and measurable. You can measure it by having $100 in the bank on January 31.

WHAT IS AN OBJECTIVE?

Objectives can be called the "road map" for achieving a goal. They are the strategic plan by which you can get the new DVD player, the iPod, the new wardrobe, or the new car. They chart the course you can follow to graduate from college.

Look at a goal and work through a few objectives for achieving the goal.

GOAL: I want to purchase a new wide-screen TV.

OBJECTIVE(S):

1. Find a part-time job.
2. Save $10.00 a week.
3. Save my income tax refund.
4. Shop around for an affordable wide-screen TV.
5. Buy the wide-screen TV.

All goals require objectives and plans. Wide-screen TVs are never purchased without goal setting, planning, and hard work.

ROADBLOCKS TO SUCCESS: BARRIERS TO ACHIEVING YOUR GOALS

Regardless of how hard we try, how much we struggle, and how many objectives we plan, we will experience times when roadblocks arise that threaten to destroy our goals and motivation.

Create a list of barriers that could keep you from achieving your goals.

1. _____

2. _____

3. _____

You may have listed money, time, family, transportation, or lack of motivation.

Using your list, talk with some of your friends and create ideas of where you can go to find assistance in overcoming these barriers.

Create a list of college and community resources that can assist you in overcoming your barriers.

I can find help _____

_____

_____

Campus and Community Resources

Financial aid office	Student organizations
Veterans' office	Hall or residence counselors
Mature student (nontraditional) services	Professors
Minority student services	Staff members
Disabled student services	Campus library
Career counseling office	Campus health services
Academic assistance center	Community drug and alcohol center
Peer tutoring center	Community organizations
Personal counseling center	Churches, synagogues, mosques, temples
Computer assistance center	Family and friends
Campus religious organization	Former high school teachers or counselors

You may have listed some of the places and people identified in the box on page 38. Review this list, because it may give you some ideas of where to find help that you and your group did not consider.

Now that we have discussed goal setting, objectives, and roadblocks, you are ready to begin planning a goal and working toward it. Exercise 2.2 is a goal-setting exercise that will assist you in plotting your course and setting goals. Use this exercise to develop the skill of goal setting.

> *It ain't enough to get the breaks, you gotta be willing to use 'em.*
> —Huey P. Long

TRAVELING THE ROAD ON YOUR OWN: MOTIVATION

What Is Motivation?

Motivation is a *force*, the driving force that causes you to do something—to *act!* Without motivation, you will achieve little. You not only have to write goals and set objectives, but you also have to work at becoming a motivated person.

Why Is Motivation Important?

For many of you, college will be the first time in your life that you are on your own. For others, going to college may be one of the most exciting things you have ever done. You may be living at school, renting an off-campus apartment, or having a home of your own. Others of you may have your first full-time or part-time job. For some students, this may be the first time you have left your child in the care of someone else.

At this point in your life, many people may be *pulling* at you, but perhaps no one is *pushing* you. No one is around to wake you up and put you on a bus or drag you to the car so that you can make it to class on time. More often than not, your professors *will* care if you come to class. Many professors *do* take class roll, and *will know* your name. So, it is very important that you not adopt the attitude that it is okay not to attend class. The motivation to go to class and do well in school will have to come from within you.

> Nothing in this world can take the place of persistence.
> Talent will not;
> nothing is more common than unsuccessful people with talent.
> Genius will not;
> unrewarded genius is almost a proverb.
> Education will not;
> the world is full of educated derelicts.
> Persistence and determination alone are eternal.
> The slogan "press on" has solved and always will solve the problems of the human race.
> —Calvin Coolidge

List the things that motivate you in your life.

_____

_____

You may have listed such things as these:

Family	Religion or spirituality	Learning
Friends	Money	

Exercise 2.2 Goal Setting

For practice, use the spaces provided to describe a short-term and a long-term goal. Once you are comfortable with this process, use copies of the Goal Setting Sheet, found in Exercise 2.1, to record and track your progress on each of your goals.

Write a short-term goal.

_____

_____

Why is the goal important to you?

_____

_____

List the objectives:

_____

_____

Target date: _____

Barriers to overcome:

_____

_____

Write a long-term goal.

_____

_____

Why is the goal important to you?

_____

_____

List the objectives:

_____

_____

Target date: _____

Barriers to overcome:

_____

_____

Milestones

Now That You Are Here...

Now that you have had the opportunity to think about what you value most in life, to determine where you are going in life and to write goals and specific steps or objectives for reaching your goals, complete the Milestones checklist again to see how much you have improved.

Answer each statement by checking "Y" for Yes, "N" for No, or "S" for Sometimes.

1.	I use goals to guide my actions.	Y	N	S
2.	Having goals is important to me.	Y	N	S
3.	I often set goals.	Y	N	S
4.	I write down objectives that shape my goals.	Y	N	S
5.	I face my fears head on.	Y	N	S
6.	I take responsibility for my life.	Y	N	S
7.	I know where I want to be in three to five years.	Y	N	S
8.	Having more than one goal is important to me.	Y	N	S
9.	When I reach a goal, I celebrate.	Y	N	S

How did you do this time on the self-analysis? You should have more "Yes" answers this time and should be more self-confident and more motivated. In addition, you should have a written plan of where you are going and how to get there.

TIPS FOR SUCCESS

To be successful in the goal-setting process and to stay motivated, you need to . . .

- Carefully examine your life to determine what you value most.
- Determine where you are going in life.
- Seek advice from people who have achieved the same goal.
- Set realistic goals that can be measured.
- Find something that motivates you, and stick with it.
- Not let setbacks cripple you. Look at failure as a lesson and move on.
- Think positively. Good things come to those who wait—and work hard.

APPLYING WHAT YOU KNOW

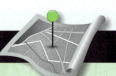

Goal setting is a difficult task for many people. Some fear is often involved, along with a commitment of time and energy to accomplish an obtainable, realistic goal.

Refer to the Case Study about Gwen at the beginning of this book. Based on Gwen's situation, answer the following questions:

1. What goal-setting and motivational strategies or techniques should Gwen utilize?

_____

_____

_____

_____

_____

_____

2. How can Gwen use the Goal Setting Sheet, presented in Exercise 2.1, to assist her in achieving her goals?

_____

_____

_____

_____

_____

_____

_____

_____

_____

_____

_____

_____

_____

_____

GETTING THERE ON TIME

A logical and effective way to track your goals and your Goal Setting Sheets is to file and reference them to your planner—the one that came with your textbook or your personal planner. You can also save them as Word documents on your computer. But please understand that this is only the first step in effectively tracking your goals.

Once you have determined what you value most, where you are going, and what goals and means to achieve those goals you have, then you must add specific objectives and set deadlines for the accomplishment of each objective. The best place to record and track your deadlines is in your planner's to-do list. Naturally, you will need to write this objective on the date that it is due. Taking this systematic approach will ensure that you stay on track; that you do not forget any reports, projects, or papers; and that you meet your objectives and goals.

To try using this system of filing and tracking goals and objectives, pick a goal you want to accomplish this semester and complete the following five-step plan:

1. Complete a Goal Setting Sheet using the form presented in Exercise 2.1.

2. Establish a completion date within the semester for your goal.

3. Make sure you have listed realistic, measureable objectives.

4. Record each objective in your planner in the to-do list on the due date that leads to the goal completion date.

5. Finally, execute this plan by completing the objectives listed each day on your to-do list, or carry them forward in your planner to be completed on the next day. Endeavor to successfully complete this goal by its completion date.

JOURNAL

The purpose of this journal exercise is to give you a chance to think about what you have learned from this chapter about goal setting and motivation. Consider what you have learned by completing the various exercises, and comment on your newly found knowledge. List the steps you are going to take to implement these new goal-setting and motivational skills.

As a result of reading this chapter and in preparing for my journey, I plan to . . .

chapter 3

TIME MANAGEMENT

PLANNING TO REACH YOUR DESTINATION ON TIME

John is almost always late for class and "a dollar short" when it comes time to pay his bills each month. At 25 years of age, he is in his sixth year working for a local manufacturer and is never late for work. But many times, he is late getting to his college classes and completing his class assignments. He works the first shift and attends college at night four nights a week. He and his wife, Susan, have started a family with their first child, a son named John Jr.

John's lateness to class has cost him a letter grade in one class and a warning of administrative withdrawal in another class. John can no longer risk being late for classes or college assignments. He needs a better plan to manage his time and his daily activities. ■

Two of our most important resources are our time and our money. Time is unique, because we all have the same allocation of time each day: 24 hours.

Money management is similar to time management, in that many tools, techniques, and skills can be learned and practiced by college students to put them on the road to debt-free living and financial success. A more detailed discussion of money management may be shared with you by your professor. It is found in the Instructor's Manual.

The management of time—knowing how to "get things done"—seems to confuse students who have not yet mastered this technique. The process of time management can be quite simple, yet if undeveloped, it can cause major problems. Few people have enough time, yet everyone has all that is available. Everyone has 24 hours each day, 168 hours each week, 52 weeks each year—no more, no less. The real problem is not with *time* but with what *you* choose to do with the time you have available to manage. The last statement—that *you* choose what to do with your time—is crucial. ■

> I am definitely going to take a course on time management . . . just as soon as I can work it into my schedule.
> —Louis E. Boone

 # A DAILY TIME ANALYSIS

An easy way to understand where your time goes, how much *discretionary*, or free, time and *nondiscretionary*, or required, time you have, and other questions about your daily activities and the use of a 24-hour day is to complete a daily time analysis.

Several very effective daily time assessments can be used for this exercise. The easiest and least time consuming is the "wheel" approach. The "wheel" is a circle that is divided into 24 equal parts, like a large pie with 24 slices. Each slice represents an hour of the day.

Milestones

Where Are You Now?

Using the Milestones checklist, take a few moments and determine where you stand in relation to time management.

Answer each statement by checking "Y" for Yes, "N" for No, or "S" for Sometimes.

1.	I know how to prioritize my responsibilities.	Y	N	S
2.	I manage my time effectively.	Y	N	S
3.	Completing daily goals is important to me.	Y	N	S
4.	I make a daily to-do list.	Y	N	S
5.	Writing down all of my assignments helps me.	Y	N	S
6.	I use short-term and long-term planning.	Y	N	S
7.	I understand discretionary time, or free time, versus nondiscretionary time.	Y	N	S
8.	My friends do not control my time.	Y	N	S
9.	I am in control of my time.	Y	N	S
10.	I understand that time management helps me to become a better student.	Y	N	S

You should not be too concerned if you have more "No" and "Sometimes" answers to these questions. Few students have more "Yes" answers. If you follow the principles and complete the exercises presented, you should have all "Yes" answers when you complete this assessment at the end of this chapter.

Exercise 3.1 offers a personal daily time analysis. Completing this analysis should take about 20 minutes. Its purpose is to open your eyes to the realization that there are only 24 hours in a day and that most students do not really know where all the hours go. A completed "wheel" daily time analysis is presented in Figure 3.1 for your reference as you conduct your individual assessment.

To complete Exercise 3.1, follow these three steps:

STEP 1. Choose a particular day of the week that you want to analyze—for example, a Monday. After you have chosen a day, review the list of daily activities that are common to most students, and write in the corresponding number of hours spent on each activity. You may also want to add one, two, or more activities that are pertinent to your daily life.

STEP 2. Using a pencil, shade and mark sections of the "wheel," or pie, that represent the same number of hours you spend in that activity each day.

> Time is the scarcest resource and unless it is managed, nothing else can be managed.
> —Peter Drucker

Exercise 3.1   The Wheel-Daily Time Analysis

Choose a particular day of the week (e.g., Monday) and write the number of hours you spend that day next to each activity listed. Add any activity that is associated with this particular day. Using a pencil, shade and mark slices of the pie or wheel that represent the same number of hours that you spend doing that activity. Analyze your results. What was your total number of hours for that day?

Sleep	_____ hours
Classes	_____ hours
Study	_____ hours
Work	_____ hours
Meals	_____ hours
Family	_____ hours
Spiritual	_____ hours
Exercise	_____ hours
Commuting	_____ hours
TV	_____ hours
Computer	_____ hours
Cell phone	_____ hours
_____	_____ hours
_____	_____ hours
TOTAL	_____ hours

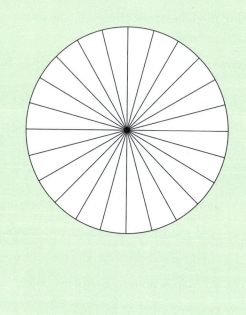

Figure 3.1   A Daily Time Analysis

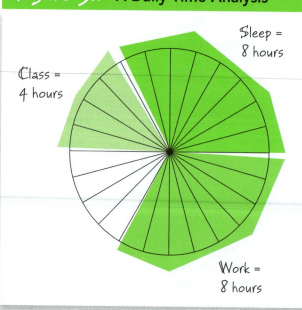

Sleep = 8 hours

Class = 4 hours

Work = 8 hours

You will need to average some activities as you complete the "wheel." In our example, sleep is usually computed at between six and eight hours per day, depending on individual needs. Thus, the "wheel" in our example has eight slices shaded and marked to represent eight hours of sleep. Classes or class time is about four hours a day and has been shaded and marked, as well. Note that our example has a total of 20 hours of activities, which nearly completes the shading of the "wheel," and only three activities have been listed.

STEP 3. The final step in this process is to analyze your results. What was the total number of hours for your sample day? Did you exceed 24 hours for that day?

What does this exercise tell us? First, most students exceed 24 hours in a day in doing this activity. Many compute 26, 27, or more hours. What an eye-opener!

Do we really know where our time goes? Without an effective time-management system or planner that includes a daily plan and to-do list, it is very difficult to know where your time goes and what you have truly accomplished for any particular day. This exercise also assists us in determining how much discretionary time we have in any given day. Discretionary time is the amount of free time you have to yourself each day. It is time to do what you wish. Unlike nondiscretionary time—that is, time spent in class or at work—discretionary time is time that you plan and control. How much free time do you have each day? How do you spend that time? Is your free time productive?

Successful time management will help you accomplish your goals and tasks more successfully and with less stress.
Source: SHUTTERSTOCK

IF I WERE YOUNG, I WOULD FORM GOOD HABITS

In *The Book of Virtues,* William Bennett quotes Aristotle as saying that good habits formed in youth make all the difference in life. Some 50 years earlier, Clovis G. Chappell, in his book *If I Were Young,* devoted a whole chapter to choices and the forming or developing of good habits. Chappell was a Methodist minister and evangelist who concentrated much of his time, energy, and writing to the development of moral, spiritual, and educational growth in young people. "I'd Form Good Habits" is the title of the first chapter in *If I Were Young,* in which he uses Jesus as an example of a man with good habits, living a good life.

To paraphrase Chappell, habits make the person. If you are a person of bad habits, you are not living a full life. If you are a person of good habits, you are living a better life. For this reason, it is of the highest importance that all of us give earnest and eager attention to forming the right kinds of habits.

The choices we make day by day gradually form our habits. It is therefore important to have a systematic approach that emphasizes your goals and provides a logical way to make daily choices that move you toward the accomplishment of goals.

Often, when students make a wrong choice, they tend to repeat that choice. That wrong choice may thus become a habit. To be successful or to do our best educationally, we need desire, discipline, and execution. To have a balanced life, we need to make the right choices in all areas of life. If you make the right kinds of study choices, they will lead to developing good study habits.

If you always do what you have always done, you will always get what you have always gotten.
—Leo Buscaglia

'Tis easier to prevent bad habits than to break them.
—Benjamin Franklin

 ## SUCCESSFUL TIME MANAGEMENT

There are three keys to effective time management. Daily quiet or planning time is the first essential *key* of successful time management. Planning time is that time of day during which you review the current day's activities and

HELP!
I Need A Job!

Joe Dyer is a retired U.S. Navy admiral and the president of the Government & Industrial Robots Division of iRobot, Incorporated. iRobot designs and builds robots that make a difference. In 2009, iRobot generated more than $298 million in revenue and employed more than 500 of the robot industry's top professionals, including mechanical, electrical, and software engineers and related support staff. Here are Joe's thoughts about prospective employees.

As you read Joe's comments, list the things that you need to do to be a competitive candidate for a position with iRobot.

1. WHAT DO YOU LOOK FOR IN AN EMPLOYEE?

"We look for innovators that can accelerate new technology and speed product from lab to end users. We look for work ethic, education, energy and a sense of 'systems engineering.' "

What can you do to be the prospective employee Joe is looking for?

_____

_____

_____

2. WHY WOULD YOU HIRE ME?

"Education, experience, and a proven track record are very important, as is your willingness to prove yourself before expecting a promotion and higher pay. Your leadership ability will set you apart from other candidates. Can you get others to follow you, and do you have the knowledge to lead them in the right direction?"

What can you do to make Joe want to hire you?

_____

_____

_____

3. HOW CAN I GAIN A COMPETITIVE EDGE?

"You need to be bright, hard working, well educated, have a strong 'need to achieve,' and have a record of accomplishment."

What can you do to gain the competitive edge for an iRobot job?

_____

_____

_____

4. WHAT ROLE WILL MY EDUCATION PLAY IN BEING ABLE TO GET A JOB WITH YOU?

"Education puts tools in your toolbox. It also demonstrates your ability to achieve and to complete and finish a major goal. Your grades are an indicator of your standing vis-à-vis others. If you don't have top grades, you need to have other offsetting strengths."

How can you demonstrate that your education is relevant and competitive?

_____

_____

_____

5. WHAT VALUE CAN I BRING TO YOUR COMPANY?

"You should bring hard work, honesty, and an ability to deal with ambiguity. You also need the energy and confidence to be a self-starter."

How can you convince Joe that you would be a valuable iRobot employee?

_____

_____

_____

What would you include in your résumé that will address Joe's comments about prospective employees?

_____

_____

_____

How can you use your cover letter to demonstrate your strengths relative to the job description?

_____

_____

_____

tasks, assess your accomplishments, and plan for the next day. The second *key* to successful time management is a to-do list. Daily planning and a prioritized to-do list go hand-in-hand with effective time management. A time-management system or planner, the third *key*, is the glue that holds time management together. It is the place for your calendar, your daily plan, your to-do list, and your notes and files. A planner is easy to use and is one of the most effective time-management tools available for students today.

Identifying Time-Management Strengths and Weaknesses

Are you an effective planner? What are your goals? Do your goals have any impact on your motivation? Do you believe self-esteem is a building block for success? These and other questions are included in the second exercise we will use to identify your time-management strengths and weaknesses. This assessment will take about 20 minutes.

Exercise 3.2 is a three-step exercise:

1. Read each question, and assign it a score of 1 to 5 (with 5 being the highest).
2. After responding to each question, add together all the numbers to compute an overall score.
3. Transfer or record the individual question scores from the first page to the corresponding question numbers on the second page. For example, transfer the score for question 1 to 1 under the "Self-Esteem" column. Transfer the score for question 2 to 2 under the "Goal Setting & Planning" column, and so on. Once you have identified your strong and weak areas, how do you go about improving in those areas?

Solutions

The first and simplest approach to solving identified problems is to go back to the original 25 questions. These 25 questions are based on the most effective practices of time management and student success. For example, question 2 and every fifth question thereafter represents an effective goal-setting or planning principle. If you scored low in goal setting and planning, questions 2, 7, 12, 17, and 22 provide effective practices of time management that, when implemented, will improve your time-management skills.

The effective use of a time-management system, setting priorities, and developing a study plan will go a long way in helping you solve your time-management problems. Completing the next series of exercises and examples will assist you in developing and fine-tuning your time-management skills. It will also assist you in developing and implementing an effective study plan.

A Time-Management System: A Planner for Student Success

After identifying your strengths and weaknesses and determining possible solutions and ways to build on your strengths and to improve on your weaknesses, the next step is to find a planner you can use on a daily basis to increase your productivity.

Please refer to your regular planner or the one that you purchased for this class. We will take you through a systematic approach to time management and the effective use of a planner. In addition, we will explain how a planner

> If you don't plan it, it won't happen.
> —Anonymous

> Anything less than a conscious commitment to the important is an unconscious commitment to the unimportant.
> —Stephen Covey

Exercise 3.2 Identifying Time-Management Strengths and Weaknesses

Answer each of the following questions by writing in a score of 1 to 5, with 5 being the highest.

_____   1.   Do you have high self-esteem?

_____   2.   Do you have a written plan of the goals you plan to achieve?

_____   3.   Are you on time for class, work, appointments, and so forth?

_____   4.   Do you know what _active listening_ is?

_____   5.   Do you use a study plan?

_____   6.   Are you a positive person?

_____   7.   Do you write a daily list of tasks you plan to do?

_____   8.   Can you quickly find things that you have filed or stored?

_____   9.   Do you know what _passive listening_ is?

_____ 10.   Do you schedule time to study?

_____ 11.   Do you often think about your future?

_____ 12.   Do you meet college and work deadlines?

_____ 13.   Are your home and work areas clean and orderly?

_____ 14.   Do you continue to listen when you don't agree?

_____ 15.   Do you know how to read a textbook?

_____ 16.   Are you serious about your future?

_____ 17.   Do you have a quiet time or planning time each day?

_____ 18.   Do you have an effective filing system?

_____ 19.   Do you know how to get others to listen to you?

_____ 20.   Do you know how to highlight a textbook?

_____ 21.   Are you a risk taker?

_____ 22.   Do you prioritize items on your to-do list?

_____ 23.   Do you keep college and work supplies where they are easily accessible?

_____ 24.   Do you continue to listen when you don't like the speaker?

_____ 25.   Do you have a suitable place to study?

_____   **Total Score**

A score of 100 to 125 is outstanding and indicates very effective time-management habits and skills. A score below 75 indicates that one or more areas may need improvement. But which areas are strong and which are weak? The chart on the following page will provide you with an indication of your strong areas, where you have effective time-management skills, and your weak areas, where you need some improvement.

(continued)

SELF-ESTEEM	GOAL SETTING & PLANNING	ORGANIZING	LISTENING	STUDYING
1. _____	2. _____	3. _____	4. _____	5. _____
6. _____	7. _____	8. _____	9. _____	10. _____
11. _____	12. _____	13. _____	14. _____	15. _____
16. _____	17. _____	18. _____	19. _____	20. _____
21. _____	22. _____	23. _____	24. _____	25. _____

Total Scores

_____   _____   _____   _____   _____

A score of 20 or higher in any one of the five areas indicates strength in that area. A score of 15 or higher indicates a fairly strong area that can be improved on. A score of 14 or less indicates a weak area that needs improvement. How do you address or solve these weaknesses or problems?

can be used to build on your strengths, improve your weaknesses, and help you to become an effective student and to succeed in all areas of your life. If you use this system correctly, it will become an integral part of your life.

When you first open your planner, you should come to an information page. This page is for your own personal use and information. Your name, mailing address, and phone number(s) are important, as is the note that states *"Reward Offered If Lost and Returned."* In most cases, your planner will be returned if you misplace it.

Most planners also display reference calendars in the first several pages. Reference calendars are just that: They may be used to refer to last year, next year, or as a quick reference for any particular month of the current year.

MONTHLY PLANNING. The monthly calendar is an important planning document. All appointments, class schedules, work schedules, meetings, and other activities or events should be entered here first. Using a monthly calendar properly will provide you with week-at-a-glance and month-at-a-glance planning documents. You can see all the activities or events for any week or month. Why do you need such a tool? Used properly, you will be better able to schedule your classes and other events without double scheduling or scheduling events too close together, which can be frustrating and time consuming.

The monthly calendar should never be used as a to-do list. Having a to-do list, class schedules, meetings, and the like on the same document is very confusing and can cause unnecessary stress. Most monthly calendars have a place for additional notes. This is a good place to list events or activities that may take place in a certain month but not necessarily on any particular day. For example, a friend or relative may ask you to call next month but not on any specific day. The note section is a good place to record reminders. If a friend or relative does ask you to call in August, you can record it under the note section for the month of August (see Figure 3.2).

Figure 3.2

monthly schedule

AUGUST 2012

SCHEDULE AND EVENTS

SUNDAY	MONDAY	TUESDAY	WEDNESDAY
			1
5	**6**	**7**	**8**
12	**13**	**14**	**15**
19	**20** 8 – Eng / 9 – Math / 12 – Lunch / 1 – Study / 3 – Work	**21** 8 – ⟵ Work ⟶ 5 –	**22** 8 – Eng / 9 – Math / 12 – Lunch / 1 – Study / 3 – Work
26	**27** 8 – Eng / 9 – Math / 12 – Lunch / 1 – Study / 3 – Work	**28** 8 – ⟵ Work ⟶ 5 –	**29** 8 – Eng / 9 – Math / 12 – Lunch / 1 – Study / 3 – Work

monthly schedule

AUGUST 2012

THURSDAY	FRIDAY	SATURDAY	NOTES
2	**3**	**4**	*Call Aunt Laura in early August
9	**10**	**11**	*Classes begin August 21
16	**17**	**18**	*Review August budget & develop September budget
23 8 – ⟵ Work ⟶ 5 –	**24** 8 – Eng / 9 – Math / 12 – Lunch / 1 – Study / 3 – Work	**25**	
30 9 – ⟵ Work ⟶ 5 –	**31**		

MATH —the four letter word!

To be successful in a math course or most college courses, you will need to attend class and study at least two hours a week outside of class for each one hour in class.

What does the math look like? If you are taking a three-hour math class, you will need to use this equation to determine how many hours you need to spend a week on this class:

Number of hours of the class per week + (2 x the number of hours)

= Total time, or 3 + (2 x 3)

= 9 hours per week on your math

If you are taking four three-hour courses, you will need to spend 4 x 3 + 2 (4 x 3) = 36 hours per week on these courses. This is the minimum amount of time, if you want to learn the material and pass the courses.

There are 7 days x 24 hours = 168 hours in each week. If you sleep 8 hours x 7 days = 56 hours per week and eat 3 hours x 7 days = 21 hours per week, that leaves 91 hours left to accomplish your objectives each week.

Do you have a job? Subtract those hours from the 91. Do you go shopping, take showers, have other social obligations, or spend time on social media? Subtract those hours, as well.

Refer back to the weekly time analysis you completed earlier in this chapter to get more accurate numbers. You need to think seriously about the amount of time you have each week to devote to college before you sign up for a full load of classes. Do you have an adequate amount of time to devote to college and be successful?

How much time do you need to spend on your college work each week, including class time and outside-class study time? Complete the following exercise to determine the total amount of time you need to devote to college each week this semester. Use the following example as your guide:

1. How many hours do you spend in class each week?

   Total number of scheduled class hours each week: _____

2. How many hours do you need to study each week?

   2 × total hours scheduled each week: _____

3. What are the total hours you need to devote to college each week?

   Total class hours + 2 × total class hours = Total hours devoted to college

   Example of class schedule with four three-hour courses:

   $4 \times 3 + 2(4 \times 3) =$

   $12 + 2(4 \times 3) =$

   $12 + 24 = 36$

   Determine the total hours you need to devote to college each week to be successful this semester:

   1. _____

   2. _____

   3. _____

   If you take 12 hours of classes, you need to fit your 36 hours for these classes into your week. Developing and using good time-management techniques is essential, if you are to succeed in your goal to successfully complete each class.

DAILY PLANNING. Daily planning is one of the keys to successful time management. It is the heart of a time-planner system. To see an example of a two-page-per-week daily planning concept, review the example in Figure 3.3.

The right side of the daily schedule lists your daily appointments and events. All of your activities for any given day—such as Friday, August 24—are recorded on your daily schedule. Where do these activities and events originate? When do you execute your daily plan? How do you get started?

First, set aside about 15 minutes each day for planning. If you can, set this planning time at the end of the day, when you have fewer interruptions and can reflect on what happened today and what you need to do tomorrow. Start with your monthly calendar and transfer your classes, meetings, and work schedule for that day to your daily schedule for tomorrow.

For example, if it were August 23, you would be planning for August 24, and you would transfer all classes, meetings, work hours, children's ball games, and so on from your monthly calendar to your daily schedule. After you have done that, you will have a schedule of events that you know will happen tomorrow. You also can see whether there is any discretionary time on August 24, as well.

The left side of the daily schedule is a prioritized daily to-do list. Where did the items on this to-do list originate? These items come from several different places. Some are items that you wrote on the August 24 to-do list that you knew about last week. For example, you have a test or quiz in English on Monday, August 27. Your instructor announced it on August 17. Once the assignment was made, you decided to study for that test on August 24. Two things must be accomplished at this point.

Number 1: Do you have any free time on August 24? If the answer is "yes," then block off time on your daily schedule—say, from 10:00 a.m. to 12:00 noon for study. Number 2: Write on your to-do list, "Study for English test."

Three very important things have just happened. You committed to preparing for a test by studying on a particular day, August 24. To ensure that you have time to study, you blocked off two hours on your daily schedule. Finally, to emphasize the importance of this event and to make it a part of your daily goals for that day, you included "Study for English test" on your to-do list, with a high priority of A1.

Record other items on this to-do list as you are planning for the next day. For example, you want to cash your paycheck tomorrow, which is a high priority and needs to be on your list. Or perhaps you need to talk to two classmates about a project. Tomorrow will be a good day to do that task. Again, note the amount of free time you will have on August 24.

PRIORITIES AND TO-DO LISTS. Developing and prioritizing a to-do list involves several important steps. As mentioned previously, the tasks that form your to-do list come from several sources. Naturally, the first step is to create the list. It should consist of the tasks you feel should be accomplished on any given day. Keep in mind that your to-do list should be long on days with a great deal of free time and short on days with little or no free time. For example, August 24 is a day with several hours of free time. In Figure 3.3, the student has two classes: an English class from 8:00 to 9:00 a.m. and a math class from 9:00 to 10:00 a.m. From 10:00 a.m. to 12:00 noon, there is a block of free time. Note that earlier, we filled in a two-hour study time and listed that as a task on the to-do list. Lunch runs from 12:00 noon to 1:00 p.m., if

Figure 3.3

daily schedule

MONDAY AUGUST 20, 2012

Priority/Check Off	To Do List	Time	Appointments/Events	
	1st day of classes	8:00	English	Rm 5202
		9:00	Math	Rm 7216
		10:00		
		11:00		
		12:00	Lunch	
		1:00		
		2:00		
		3:00	Work	
		4:00		
		5:00	→	

TUESDAY AUGUST 21, 2012

Priority/Check Off	To Do List	Time	Appointments/Events
		8:00	Work
		9:00	→
		10:00	
		11:00	Lunch
		12:00	Work
		1:00	
		2:00	
		3:00	→
		4:00	
		5:00	

WEDNESDAY AUGUST 22, 2012

Priority/Check Off	To Do List	Time	Appointments/Events
		8:00	English
		9:00	Math
		10:00	
		11:00	
		12:00	Lunch
		1:00	Work
		2:00	
		3:00	
		4:00	
		5:00	→

daily schedule

THURSDAY AUGUST 23, 2012

Priority/Check Off	To Do List	Time	Appointments/Events
A1	Review	8:00	Work
	August Budget	9:00	
	Develop	10:00	
A2	September Budget	11:00	→
		12:00	Lunch
		1:00	Work
		2:00	
		3:00	
		4:00	
		5:00	→

FRIDAY AUGUST 24, 2012

Priority/Check Off	To Do List	Time	Appointments/Events
A1	Study—Eng test	8:00	English
A2	Cash check	9:00	Math
A6	Call M. Black—appt.	10:00	Study
A3	Email report to Bob	11:00	→
A5	Call auto shop	12:00	Lunch
A4	Outline speech	1:00	Study
		2:00	
	Refer to Eng presentation file	3:00	Work
	Report from John Smith	4:00	
	Report from Jane Jones	5:00	→

SATURDAY AUGUST 25, 2012

Priority/Check Off	To Do List	Time	Appointments/Events
		8:00	
		9:00	
		10:00	
		11:00	
		12:00	

SUNDAY AUGUST 26, 2012

Priority/Check Off	To Do List	Time	Appointments/Events
		8:00	
		9:00	
		10:00	
		11:00	
		12:00	

you choose to go to lunch, and work starts at 3:00 p.m. Between lunch and work, you have another two-hour block of free time.

The next step is to analyze the list, identify the most important items, and assign them an A priority. This system of setting priorities was introduced by Allan Lakein in his book *How to Get Control of Your Time and Your Life*. Lakein's system is an A, B, and C system, with Cs being routine tasks that can be put off indefinitely. We have deleted Bs and Cs from our prioritizing process to allow you to concentrate on what is most important to you.

When you end up with more than one A, you have to prioritize the items. If you could only do one of your A's, which one would you do? That A becomes your A1 priority and the next, your A2 priority.

You can also create some shorthand codes for your to-do list. For example, you can use an X for a task you have completed or an → for a task you have moved forward to another day's to-do list.

Once your daily schedule and prioritized to-do list have been completed, you have a well-organized plan of action for the next day. You have what is called *closure*. You can now forget about your to-do list until tomorrow.

In Figure 3.3, at the bottom third of your to-do list, leave space for an Assignments Due section. Usually, planners have a similar space that is designed to help you track special projects at college or at work. For example, suppose that you are working on a presentation for one of your classes with two other students. Each of you has researched certain aspects of the presentation, and the three of you are going to report your findings to one another. How can you remind yourself that the other students' reports are due to you on a certain date? Simply note this detail in the Assignment Due (or similar section of your to-do list) on the correct date (see Figure 3.3). At the end of the day, when you are in your planning mode for the next day, you notice that only one of your classmates turned his report in to you. At this point, you should write on your to-do list for the next day, "Call Jane Jones, English report." Following this systematic process will ensure that you and your teammates do not miss deadlines.

CONTACTS DIRECTORY. The A–Z, or contacts, directory in most planners is designed to provide you with a quick source of information about your friends, peers, family members, and coworkers. By using the monthly calendar, the daily schedule, and the prioritized to-do list with the directory, you will have an excellent filing and retrieval system.

Look at an example to see how this retrieval system works. The presentation for your English class is a major project that requires research, note taking, and several interim reports by your project team. How can you track and file all of this information in a way that will make it available at your fingertips as you need it?

First, record the initial project due date, as well as several other deadlines, in the monthly calendar. The monthly calendar becomes a very valuable planning document. You are now in a position to look at any given week or month to see the workflow of this project. Next, move the planning process to an action process. This process is accomplished by moving tasks that originated from your monthly calendar due dates and deadlines to your daily schedule and prioritized to-do list. When you take notes as part of your project, you file them and reference that information back to your assignment due section of the prioritized to-do list. In the example (Figure 3.3), note that two reports

SOCIAL MEDIA . . .

Making Connections!

David Spinks, in a recent article on his blog at Davidspinks.com, suggests "10 Must-Try Social Media Sites for College Students." Three of these social media sites are Cramster (cramster.com), Twitter (twitter.com), and Zumeo (zumeo.com).

Cramster is described on its website as "the leading provider of online homework help for college and high school students." Students can get homework help and answers to questions in math, algebra, physics, chemistry, calculus, science, engineering, accounting, English, writing, business, humanities, and more. It also provides step-by-step solutions to the exercises in more than 300 textbooks. Students can ask any homework question and get expert homework help in as little as two hours.

Twitter allows you to connect with anyone in the world—a friend, relative, classmate, celebrity, business professional, or anyone with a shared interest. You can use Twitter to network with professionals; stay updated on current news, trends, and ideas in many different industries; and connect with businesses on a personal level. You can also use Twitter when you are looking for a job. Check out these Twitter sites to assist you in your job search: twitter.com/careerealism, twitter.com/sweetcareers, and twitter.com/findinternships.

Zumeo states on its website that it can provide students with a three-in-one professional profile, a multitheme traditional résumé, and a portfolio. It also provides a social job match, employer research, and other applications. The "Job Listing" feature is very easy to use and has a number of filters, allowing you to search for jobs based on location, your personality type, and your education. In addition, when looking for a job posting, you can click to view the company's profile, view it on a map, or go to the actual job posting, where you can apply for the job. Zumeo automatically creates an online résumé with a brief description, plus your objective, experience, skills, and education. You can also upload files to develop a portfolio.

Cramster, Twitter, and Zumeo are only three of Spinks's must-try social media sites for college students. Check out his blog, Davidspinks.com, for the full list of 10 sites he recommends.

Many students are familiar with Twitter, but some have not been introduced to Cramster or Zumeo.

To gain insight into two additional social media communities and learn more about these types of social media, follow these steps:

1. Go to Cramster with a math problem you had difficulty with or are having difficulty with now. See how successful you can be in using social media in solving math problems.

   a. What did you encounter at Cramster?

   _____

   _____

   b. Were you able to successfully solve your math problem? Why or why not?

   _____

   _____

2. Now check out Zumeo. Set up your account, and develop your résumé.

   a. What, if any, problems did you encounter with Zumeo?

   _____

b. Were you able to successfully set up your account and develop your résumé? If not, why?

_____

_____

If either website becomes inactive, go to your favorite search engine and search for similar sites that provide résumé, portfolio, and tutoring support.

---

are due from your teammates, John Smith and Jane Jones. Also, note that your notes and your research report are filed in your English Presentation File, which can be a hard copy or an electronic file. Once you receive the other reports on this project, you will file them in the English Presentation File, as well. It is also important to have consistency in your note-taking process.

YOUR STUDY TIME

Be prepared to take full advantage of the time available for studying. Be physically and emotionally prepared and use your time wisely.
Source: ANNIE FULLER/PEARSON

Time spent studying must be time for which you are physically and emotionally prepared. During this time, it is important that you not be tired or hungry. It is also important that you attempt to let go of distracting emotional issues. You will not be able to use your time wisely if you have not met the needs of your mind and body. (Another barrier to effective study time is procrastination. We will discuss that later in this chapter.)

As a student, you have to set aside a certain number of hours, _five days a week_, for studying. The amount of time spent will vary from day to day and from student to student. As a rule of thumb, for every hour spent in class, spend two hours studying for that class. For example, if your class meets three hours per week, then you should spend six hours outside of class studying for it.

This estimate is a realistic amount of time and should be used as a guide. You should try to remember that some classes will require more time and others not as much. Most students need one to three hours of outside study time (per course, per week) to be academically successful.

Of the courses you are taking now, which ones will require the most outside study time?

_____

Why?

_____

Which courses will require the least amount of outside study time?

_____

Why?

_____

These questions raise a good point for the nontraditional student: Is it realistic to be a full-time student, a full-time employee, and a parent all at once? Students who find that they are able to juggle a variety of commitments will always tell you that it is not easy. Tough decisions concerning what is urgent and what can wait must be made on a daily basis. Many successful adult students also indicate that support from family, friends, and spouses helps tremendously with the time-management problem of being a student, an employee, and a parent. Even so, try to remember that the decision to be a student carries with it a significant time commitment.

Use the monthly calendar and the daily schedule in your planner to complete the following tasks:

1. You should have already blocked out the time you are in class, at work, participating in religious/social activities, and so on.
2. Examine the time remaining, and indicate the time that could be used for studying.

Do you have free time that you can dedicate to studying?

_____

If not, what can you eliminate?

_____

_____

What can you do to prevent these situations from interfering with your study time?

_____

_____

YOUR STUDY TIME AND DAILY PRIORITIZED TO-DO LIST

At the end of each day, you should make a prioritized to-do list for the next day to help you organize your study time. This plan should enable you to get the most from your valuable time. It is important to list those assignments that are most difficult to complete first. If you save those items until the end, you will not be at your best. This could increase your frustration, and you may decide not to complete the assignment. If there are unfinished tasks on your list, transfer them to your study plan for the next day.

By developing a priority system of tasks that must be accomplished, you ensure a much more efficient use of your time. Many successful people have time-management systems that they have developed over a long period. Talk to successful students and ask them to share their techniques for using their planners. Sharing helpful tips on time management can help you as well as others.

LEADING TIME WASTERS

Time wasters are a big problem in a time-management system. Recognizing distractions and avoiding them is a major hurdle in the time-management game. Here are some of the leading time wasters:

- Cell phone calls and texting
- Television
- Virtual worlds or virtual reality games
- Computer games and the Internet
- A messy house, office, or dorm room
- Procrastination

What time wasters have you encountered?

_____

_____

How can you eliminate these time wasters?

_____

_____

PROCRASTINATION: THE ENEMY OF THE STUDENT

"I'll do that in a little while." How many times have you uttered this statement?

Procrastination, or putting off until tomorrow what you should do today, can kill the best study plan. The good news is that *you* are in control. You choose whether to complete or not complete assignments, and then ultimately, you suffer the consequences if you have procrastinated.

Volumes have been written about procrastination—its causes and possible solutions. Loren Broadus does an excellent job of addressing this subject in his book *How to Stop Procrastinating and Start Living.* He suggests that students should "prime the pump." If you spend 10 minutes on a task, the next day, you will see that you made an effort, as opposed to doing nothing at all.

> Don't put off for tomorrow what you can do today, because if you enjoy it today you can do it again tomorrow.
> —James Michener

Why do students procrastinate? Here are a few of the most often used excuses:

- I'm too tired right now. I'll take a break and then I'll do it.
- I don't have enough time to do this paper now.
- I have got to check Facebook first.
- It's too nice of a day to spend on my assignments.
- If I wait a little longer, I'll do a better job.
- I don't understand this assignment. I'll wait until the next class and ask the professor.

Are you a procrastinator? Find out by completing the questionnaire in Exercise 3.3. Read each question and answer by putting an X under "Yes" or "No." This exercise will only take a few minutes—so why put it off?

Dealing with Procrastination

Making a prioritized to-do list every day is one of the most important tasks for dealing with procrastination. Without a well-thought-out, prioritized to-do list, each day becomes a frustrating mixture of important and not-so-important tasks. Which one to do and which one is the most important? This question needs to be asked and answered during your planning time each day.

Here are some other tips:

- Refer to your college long-term and short-term goals during planning.
- Start with your number-1, A1 priority as the first thing to accomplish.
- Set and commit to all deadlines for college assignments.
- Do one small portion of an assignment just to get started.
- Do not invite interruptions! Turn your cell phone off when doing college work.
- Select the best time of day to do certain tasks.
- Be flexible in responding to interruptions and getting back on task.

Exercise 3.3 Are You a Procrastinator?

	Yes	No
1. Do you feel resentful when reminded of unfinished homework?	____	____
2. Do you feel you have too much college work to do each day?	____	____
3. Do you find yourself making excuses for not doing college assignments?	____	____
4. Do you spend time online with friends while letting homework go?	____	____
5. Do you delay class assignments so long that you're embarrassed to do them?	____	____
6. Do you use high-energy times for low-priority tasks, like Facebook?	____	____
7. Do you have a hard time deciding which class assignments to do first?	____	____
8. Do you make promises to professors or others and fail to keep them?	____	____
9. Do you agree to do an extra-credit assignment and then regret it?	____	____
10. Do you fail to list class projects on your to-do list?	____	____
11. Do you think you work better the night before a big project is due?	____	____
12. Do you put off doing a major class project until the week it is due?	____	____
13. Do you always feel in a hurry?	____	____
14. Do you continue to work on completed class projects?	____	____
15. Do you wait until the last minute on some class projects?	____	____
16. Do you have difficulty saying "no" to classmates when asked to help them?	____	____
17. Do you think more about one bad grade than other grading problems?	____	____
18. Do you feel frustrated at college and at home most of the time?	____	____
19. Do you feel guilty when you take time off?	____	____
20. Do you forget to write down assignments that you agree to do?	____	____

Total ____

Give yourself 5 points for each "Yes" answer, and total your score. Then see what your score says about you:

0–20	Efficiency Expert
25–40	Doing Well
45–60	Room for Improvement
65–80	In Need of Help
85–100	A Full-Blown Procrastinator

How did you do? Do not be discouraged if you earned a high score. Most students have procrastination tendencies and struggle to be more time conscience and effective in daily tasks.

Milestones

Now That You Are Here . . .

At this point, you have had the opportunity to learn the principles of time management and to develop an effective calendar and to-do list. Now that you have completed this chapter on time management, take a few minutes to complete the Milestones self-analysis again.

Answer each statement by checking "Y" for Yes, "N" for No, or "S" for Sometimes.

1.	I know how to prioritize my responsibilities.	Y	N	S
2.	I manage my time effectively.	Y	N	S
3.	Completing daily goals is important to me.	Y	N	S
4.	I make a daily to-do list.	Y	N	S
5.	Writing down all of my assignments helps me.	Y	N	S
6.	I use short-term and long-term planning.	Y	N	S
7.	I understand discretionary time, or free time, versus nondiscretionary time.	Y	N	S
8.	My friends do not control my time.	Y	N	S
9.	I am in control of my time.	Y	N	S
10.	I understand that time management helps me to become a better student.	Y	N	S

You should have all "Yes" answers at this point. If not, go back over the chapter and put into practice the principles that were discussed. By following these principles, using the forms provided, and following the tips listed in the next section, you will be well on your way to more effective time management.

TIPS FOR SUCCESS

In order to become an effective time manager, you need to . . .

- Work on your hardest subjects first. Save the easiest subjects for last.

- Organize free time into usable chunks. Five minutes here and there is of little or no value.

- Make lists, prioritize the items, and follow the priorities you have decided.

- *Revise* your to-do list every night.

- Find a place that allows you to study without interruption.

APPLYING WHAT YOU KNOW

Reading this chapter on time management has given you the opportunity to determine where your time goes and how much time you spend on various activities and commitments. It has also given you an opportunity to identify your time-management strengths and weaknesses. Now that you have completed this chapter, refer back to the Case Study about Gwen at the beginning of this book. Based on Gwen's situation, answer the following questions:

1. What time-management strategies or techniques should Gwen use?

    _____

    _____

2. How should Gwen use the monthly calendar, daily plan, and to-do list to help her address the challenges she faces?

    _____

    _____

3. If faced with problems similar to Gwen's (no free time, no time for her friends, and little time for family), what would you do?

    _____

    _____

GETTING THERE ON TIME

This feature reinforces what you will learn throughout the text about time and time management. This particular exercise focuses on self-management as it relates to time management. Answer the following questions:

How organized is your life is at this moment, and how do you feel about that?

_____

_____

How do you feel when you do not have control of your time?

_____

_____

How do you deal with not having control of your time?

_____

_____

How do you feel about other things and other people controlling your time?

_____

_____

JOURNAL

The purpose of this journal exercise is to give you a chance to think about what you have learned from reading this chapter about time management. Consider what you have learned by completing the various exercises and comment on your newly found knowledge. List the steps you are now going to take to implement your new time-management skills.

As a result of this chapter and in preparing for my journey, I plan to . . .

chapter 4

RECOGNIZING YOUR POTENTIAL AND BUILDING SELF-ESTEEM

FINE-TUNING YOUR VEHICLE

I remember walking to the mailbox and getting the letter from my "college of choice." As I walked back toward the house, every dream I had of a college education passed before my eyes. "We regret to inform you that because of your SAT scores and your high school rank, your application has been denied."

I was not the best student in the world. Looking back, I was not even average. I passed senior English with the grade of D-minus. My predicted grade-point average (GPA) for college was a mere 0.07. I never knew how to study. I never asked for any assistance. I did not even know how to properly use the library. I now faced having to continue working in the textile plant instead of going to college.

Two days later, another letter came to me from the college. It was signed by the director of the Summer Prep Program. They offered me a second chance. Their letter stated that if I would come to the summer session and make at least a B average, I would be admitted as a temporary student. The weight of the world was on my shoulders. How could I, a D-minus high school student, take four classes in college and score a B? Quickly—and I mean very quickly—I learned how to ask for help. I went to the Assistance Lab, and the first thing I learned was how to study. I studied and I studied and I studied. At the end of four weeks, I had three A's and a B. I had made it!

Those four weeks were the easy part. I had changed and I knew that I could never go back. I had a thirst for something that could only be quenched in college . . . a thirst for knowledge.

Dr. Robert Sherfield, a faculty member at the College of Southern Nevada in Las Vegas, wrote this passage. He learned that his dreams could be realized by assuming responsibility for his future and learning how to study. ∎

Life is about change and about movement and about becoming something other than what you are at this very moment. —Unknown

This book is intended as a guide for how to assume responsibility for your own learning. The primary concern at this moment is to develop the basic skills that will allow you to graduate and move into the world of work, get that promotion, or move on to a four-year degree.

How do you feel about being enrolled in this course? You may be upset at this moment because you were required to take it. Many freshmen feel the same way. The First Year Experience (FYE) or College Success Course is a special program designed to aid first-year students with their transition to college. Boston University offered the first extended orientation course in 1888. In 1911, Reed College in Portland, Oregon, was the first to offer credit for such a course.

Interest in this course increased through the early part of the twentieth century, and many institutions offered a Freshman Seminar course. During the 1960s, colleges faced an increasing need to prepare a diverse student body, leading to a resurgence for the Freshman Seminar course. In 1972, the University of South Carolina introduced University 101 in an effort to build trust, understanding, and open communication among students, faculty, staff, and administrators.

Most colleges and universities offer a course with the word *success* or *experience* in the title, which teaches students how to do well in college. These courses are usually three credit hours, are required to graduate, and provide first-year students with important life and study skills. Having these skills helps students adjust to college requirements, which leads to self-mastery, a strong academic foundation, and the total concept of lifetime wellness.

Nevertheless, freshmen often do not want to "waste their time" in these types of classes! One day, a professor heard a group of students complaining about having to take a "student success" course. When she came around the corner of the hallway, the students froze with fear, knowing she had heard them talking. They were right! She had heard them. She stopped to ask how they were doing, sat on the bench with them, and told them something that made a huge difference in their lives.

"I know that you are upset for having to enroll in this student success class," she said. "But without this class, there may be no graduation for you. This program is not a punishment but an opportunity for you. So many people never get an opportunity to learn how to succeed in college, but this college cares about you. You can look at it as punishment, or you can look at it as the first day of the rest of your life. *You* have to make that decision."

Most of the students chose to take her words seriously, because they knew in their hearts that they lacked the skills to make it to graduation. After graduating from college, most students who took student success courses as freshmen will say without hesitation that study skills and student orientation courses work. Research has proven that freshmen that enroll in orientation or study skills courses graduate in higher numbers than those who do not take them (Barefoot & Gardner, 2008). Taking this course gives you a better chance at having a successful college experience. It makes today the first day of the rest of your life. ■

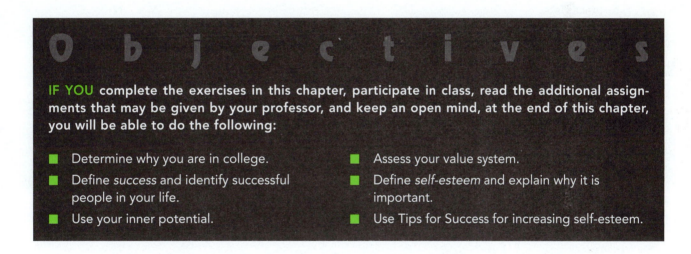

Objectives

IF YOU complete the exercises in this chapter, participate in class, read the additional assignments that may be given by your professor, and keep an open mind, at the end of this chapter, you will be able to do the following:

- Determine why you are in college.
- Define *success* and identify successful people in your life.
- Use your inner potential.

- Assess your value system.
- Define *self-esteem* and explain why it is important.
- Use Tips for Success for increasing self-esteem.

WHY ARE YOU HERE?

It does not matter if you are just starting college, are in your second semester, or in your second year. You have probably asked yourself from time to time, "How did I get here?" or "Why am I really sitting in this class?" What answers come to your mind? Your first thoughts might have included one or more of these:

- My friends came, so I did too.
- Job retraining.
- To provide a better life for my family.

The first step to success in most endeavors is deciding to take action. You have done that by enrolling in college. Second, you probably have a good idea why you are here and what you want to accomplish.

Milestones

Where Are You Now?

In the Milestones checklist, you will find 10 questions intended to make you think about your potential and self-esteem at this point in your life. Take a few moments, and answer each statement carefully.

Answer each statement by checking "Y" for Yes, "N" for No, or "S" for Sometimes.

1.	I am serious about my future.	Y	N	S
2.	I study at least two hours per week per course hour.	Y	N	S
3.	I feel better about myself when I manage my time.	Y	N	S
4.	I enjoy learning.	Y	N	S
5.	I take risks.	Y	N	S
6.	I expect a great deal from myself.	Y	N	S
7.	I often think about my future.	Y	N	S
8.	I plan for my success.	Y	N	S
9.	I have high self-esteem.	Y	N	S
10.	I am a positive person.	Y	N	S

If you happen to have more negative answers to these questions, relax! This text is designed to give you the skills to help you develop your potential and realize your goals.

Using the spaces that follow, list the reasons you have chosen to attend college.

1. _____

2. _____

3. _____

Was it hard to come up with your list, or did you jot down your thoughts quickly? Why? If it was difficult, perhaps it is because most of us spend little time actually thinking about our education and what it really means to our future. The next few questions are intended to get you thinking about college on a different level. Take your time responding to each question.

Is learning an enjoyable experience for you?

_____

Why or why not?

_____

_____

How could learning become a more enjoyable experience for you?

_____

_____

What major ideas must you consider to make learning and school more enjoyable experiences? List what you feel your school could do to make learning more enjoyable for you.

1. _____

2. _____

3. _____

List what you feel your teachers could do to make learning more enjoyable for you.

1. _____

2. _____

3. _____

Most important, list what you can do to bring about change. How can you make learning and school a more enjoyable experience?

1. _____

2. _____

3. _____

A great part of your success in college is realizing that *you* can bring about change. You have just begun by spending time evaluating your current situation. Remember that it's hard to play ball when you're not on the field.

WHERE ARE YOU GOING? AND WHAT IS SUCCESS?

The famous poet Robert Frost wrote a poem about two roads splitting in a forest and his decision to take the road less traveled. Today, you are faced with the same decision. There are two roads for you. One will be filled with

SOCIAL MEDIA . . .
Making Connections!

Using social media has a great number of benefits. Students need to understand how social media can benefit them both personally and academically.

For example, the personal and academic connections you make online can draw you into an online community that can recommend various resources, identify experts in the group, and share content within that community. Using social media sites is also free. Using them will require your time and energy but not much money. Social media also provides more rapid sharing of information and access to your professors. For example, if you are absent from a class or a lab, you may be able to get your work finished, provided that your college uses a learning management system (LMS) such as Blackboard, WebCT, or Desire2Learn, which posts assignments, quizzes, exams, and so on or your professor accepts work submitted via e-mail to his or her college account.

The message board and e-mail on LMSs enable students to interact with their professors and other students in a timely and effective manner. LMSs also facilitate group assignments and ensure that students receive their assignments based on a structured schedule. For the professor, LMSs eliminate many of the excuses students make about assignments and deadlines. For extroverts, these technologies provide another dimension or way to access friends, professors, and other students. Usually, extroverts need no encouragement to communicate with other students, professors, college staff members, and the like. However, not all students are extroverts.

For students who are more introverted or have low self-esteem, the use of social media can greatly facilitate communication. Students with low self-esteem are reluctant to introduce themselves or start conversations with other students. Social media provide a great way to make introductions and facilitate conversations. In group assignments, social media can assist you in developing rapport online with your group members, making it a great deal easier to continue communications in person. Social media can be used as a great ice-breaker opportunity to build effective working relationships and boost your self-confidence. Using these media also gives you time to think about your responses to questions or the formulation of questions you need to ask.

1. How will you use social media to jump-start your college career?

List the steps you are going to take to better utilize your college's social media community.

_____

_____

_____

_____

challenges and hard work. The other will be the road that, unfortunately, many students take: the road that avoids challenges, sidesteps opportunities, and often leads to dropping out of college.

Which road will you take? Only you can make that decision, and it will not be an easy one. Whatever your ultimate goal might be, it will be important to map out a course to get there and then learn to take the proper roadway. Success seldom happens without a plan. In the coming days, you will begin to realize that your road will look different, ride different, and feel different from that of your friends. Everyone's path to success is different, and only you can map your course.

The following questions are intended to help you develop a philosophy about success and determine what you can do to bring about success in your life.

Write your definition of success.

_____

_____

Describe one person in your life whom you consider to be successful. Why do you think this person is successful?

_____

_____

List the one accomplishment you want to achieve more than anything else.

_____

_____

Why is this so important to you?

_____

_____

How do you plan to achieve this?

_____

_____

What part does your education play in reaching this goal?

_____

_____

What do you need to do to make sure you reach this goal?

_____

_____

What part does taking this course play in reaching your goal?

_____

_____

I have learned that success is to be measured not so much by the position one has reached in life, as by the obstacles which they have overcome while trying to succeed.
—Booker T. Washington

A Definition of Success

To laugh often and love much;

To win the respect of intelligent people and
the affection of children;

To earn the approval of honest critics and
endure the betrayal of false friends;

To appreciate beauty;

To find the best in others;

To leave the world a bit better, whether by a
healthy child, a garden patch, or a
redeemed social condition;

To have played and laughed with enthusiasm
and sung with exultation;

To know even one life has breathed easier
because you have lived.

This is to have succeeded.

—Ralph Waldo Emerson

"There is a joke about a man who was asked if
he could play the violin and he answered,
'I don't know. I've never tried.' Those who have
never tried to play a violin really do not know
whether they can or not. Those who say too
early in life and too firmly, 'No, I'm not at all
musical,' shut themselves off from whole areas
of life that might have proved rewarding. In
each of us, there are unknown possibilities,
undiscovered potentialities—and one big
advantage of having an open self-concept
rather than a rigid one is that we shall continue
to expose ourselves to new experiences, and
therefore we shall continue to discover more
and more about ourselves as we grow older."

—Alfred Adler

There are probably as many definitions of *success* as there are people in the world. The definition offered by Ralph Waldo Emerson in his poem makes us think of the many ways we can succeed. Thinking positively and realizing that one failure or one setback does *not* make us unsuccessful is a step toward success. Having a setback only means that we have to try harder and concentrate on the many positive aspects of our lives. Our setbacks can help us see our potential.

DISCOVERING AND ACHIEVING YOUR POTENTIAL

One of the keys to a successful life is analyzing your potential and setting your goals. Many times, students let other people determine what they will be able to do for the rest of their lives. Because of poor math performance, you may never choose to be an architect or physicist. Math may simply not be your strongest area. This does not mean that you cannot do math. Rather, it means that you may have to try harder in this subject area. You have to look beyond what you are capable of at this very moment to discover your true potential. In other words, do not cut yourself short just because problems arise in certain areas, and do not rely too heavily on your greatest skills.

The first step to discovering your potential is deciding what you value most in your life. Is it playing the violin, becoming a physical therapist, or repairing a car? Do you enjoy working with people or numbers, indoors or outdoors? All of these endeavors are worthy, but you will be the one to make the final decision.

The exercise that follows will help you begin to evaluate your life and your potential. Some of the questions are going to be a bit difficult, because you may have never thought about them and you probably have never written down the answers. Take as much time as you need to answer these questions truthfully and completely.

List three things you expect of yourself.

1. _____

2. _____

3. _____

List three things you consider yourself capable of, interested in, or talented in.

1. _____

2. _____

3. _____

Now, explain why you consider yourself capable, interested, or talented in these things.

1. _____

2. _____

3. _____

List three things that interest you but that you consider yourself less capable of or talented in.

1. _____

2. _____

3. _____

Explain why you believe you are less capable or talented in these areas.

1. _____

2. _____

3. _____

More than likely, for the final three responses, you provided reasons such as "I do not spend enough time on it," "I am not as committed as I should be," "I am afraid of what people will say," and so forth. Many times, our potential is limited by our lack of practice, time, or commitment or our fear that we may be thought of as different.

Realizing our potential *requires* us to conduct an evaluation of our interests, our values, our dreams, and ourselves. It requires us to take risks. So often in this life, we let others tell us what to do, and we let them choose our future. It is only when we go through self-analysis that we set our goals and begin our journey toward achieving our true potential. Simply stated, when we are sure of ourselves and like ourselves and if we realize our potential and find the motivation to make our dreams come true, success will most likely follow.

HELP!
I Need A Job!

The Sunshine House®
A Tradition in Early Education

Dennis Drew is the president and founder of The Sunshine House, Inc. For 35 years, The Sunshine House—located in ten states with 110 centers—has partnered with families to give children an early foundation for a bright future. More than a day care or child care, The Sunshine House offers innovative early care and education programs to young children, ages 6 weeks to 12 years. The Sunshine House staff provides an age-appropriate curriculum, nurturing attention, and love and compassion in a setting designed with your child in mind. Here are Dennis's thoughts about prospective employees.

After reading each of Dennis's thoughts and comments, answer the questions addressed to you as a prospective employee.

1. WHAT DO YOU LOOK FOR IN AN EMPLOYEE?

"On our Sunshine House application there is a question: 'Tell us in one paragraph why you want to work at the Sunshine House.' This is usually the first thing most directors read when preparing to interview a prospective employee for a position. We are looking at grammar as well as content, as well as looking for a desire to work with children not just a desire to have a job."

What can you do to be the prospect Dennis is looking for in an employee?

_____

_____

_____

2. WHY WOULD YOU HIRE ME?

"To 'hire' for a position, the person would need to be flexible, honest, show a knowledge of child care and early child education. Attitude always plays a large part in our decision to hire or not to hire. The person has to be the right fit for our schools. Enthusiasm and a positive attitude carries so much weight in this business."

What can you do to make Dennis want to hire you?

_____

_____

_____

3. HOW CAN I GAIN A COMPETITIVE EDGE?

"A prospective employee should dress as a professional and look professional when coming for an interview. He or she should be prepared with references and documentation of their experience and training. Again, we will be looking for enthusiasm, energy, and a love for children. We expect to see and feel their desire to teach children and care for children. We want to know that child care and education is their chosen profession."

What can you do to gain the competitive edge for a job at The Sunshine House?

_____

_____

_____

4. WHAT ROLE WOULD MY EDUCATION PLAY IN BEING ABLE TO GET A JOB WITH YOU?

"Education does play a large part when making our final decision, but a person with just the education and not the experience would not automatically cement the position. Teaching and caring for children is a gift; not everyone possesses that gift. Patience is a virtue, especially with young children. Education in this field refines and amplifies those gifts and talents."

How can you demonstrate that your education is relevant and competitive?

_____

_____

_____

5. WHAT VALUE CAN I BRING TO YOUR COMPANY?

"An individual brings value to this company by his or her love for children and ability to nurture and grow these young minds and bodies so they are not only prepared to go to schools but also prepared for life. The Sunshine House succeeds as an organization and a business if every teacher (every employee is a teacher) keeps their mind on the importance of keeping the children under our care safe and growing each child through love and skill."

How can you convince Dennis that you would be a valuable Sunshine House employee?

_____

_____

What would you include in your résumé that will address Dennis's comments about prospective employees?

_____

_____

How could you use your cover letter to demonstrate your strengths relative to the job description?

_____

_____

_____

 **PERSONAL VALUES**

What do you value most in your life? A great part of discovering our potential means evaluating questions that help us see more clearly where we are going—and from where we have come. So many times, we concern ourselves with our friends, our family, or someone else, but we spend very little

When you take time to get to know yourself, you will be better able to realize your potential and find the motivation to reach your goals.
Source: SHUTTERSTOCK

time thinking about our own lives. Has this happened to you? This section in the book is designed to allow you to spend some time with yourself, your values, your ideas, and your life.

In Exercise 4.1, you will be given an imaginary $100 to use in an auction. You may spend the money any way that you choose based on your value system. You will be bidding on items that you value most according to your value system. At the end of the auction, you will compare how your values differ from those of people around you. Your professor will assist you with this exercise and will be the auctioneer. He or she will list the items to be bought on the board or just refer to The Auction section in your book that lists each item.

After the auction is over, your professor will ask you why you bid on certain items. Listen carefully to your peers and compare their reasons for bidding or not bidding on items to your reasons. You will be surprised how different—and how alike—you may be.

In the Values Auction, what item did you bid the most money on?

_____

_____

Why?

_____

_____

What item did you bid the least amount of money on?

_____

_____

Why?

_____

_____

People's value systems differ greatly, and it is only when we understand our own values that we can truly begin to appreciate the values of others. This is somewhat complicated by the fact that building self-esteem means knowing our values and ourselves, but it is almost impossible to know what we value without having positive self-esteem. We have to work on both issues at the same time and treat both with care and detail.

 ℰxercise 4.1 **The Values Auction**

Directions: Ten items are available for bidding in the Values Auction. Review the list that follows to get an idea of what you might purchase. You have $100 to spend, and you can bid in $5 increments. You may want to bid $5 on each item, $10 on ten items, or $100 on one item. You cannot spend over $100, however. If someone outbids you on an item, you can move money from any item you have not purchased.

Example: If you have a written bid of $35 on "A satisfying religion" and someone else bids $40, you can move money from any item to outbid that person, as long as you do not spend over $100. After the bidding has ended, be sure to record the top bid for which each item sold, so you can compare how your views and values may differ from those of your classmates.

The Auction

ITEM TO BE BOUGHT	MY BUDGET	TOP BID
A happy marriage and family	$ _____	$ _____
A chance to be president	$ _____	$ _____
The love of friends	$ _____	$ _____
Self-esteem and confidence	$ _____	$ _____
A healthy life	$ _____	$ _____
A world free of prejudice	$ _____	$ _____
To understand the meaning of life	$ _____	$ _____
Success in a chosen profession	$ _____	$ _____
A satisfying religion	$ _____	$ _____
Unlimited power	$ _____	$ _____

 ## SELF-ESTEEM

Another area that you will have to consider on the road to achieving your full potential is your self-esteem. Just as you are the only one who can identify and realize your own potential, you are the only one who can give yourself worth.

The way you feel about yourself also determines how you treat other people. Only strong people can be sensitive and caring. People who are weak and have low self-esteem are the ones who are cruel and insensitive.

Reread that statement and consider it carefully. Often, we think of this situation in the converse—that strong people are cruel and insensitive. However, it is only the people who love and respect themselves who can love and

> They are the weakest, however strong, who have no faith in themselves.
>
> —Christian Boree

respect others. When you begin to discover your potential, you will begin to build your self-esteem.

What Is Self-Esteem?

Much research has been done in the areas of self-esteem and self-worth. Basically, *self-esteem* is the picture or photograph that you hold of yourself in your mind. It is the value you place on who you are, what you are worth, and how you feel about yourself.

Self-esteem is learned. You learn self-esteem in your family of origin. You do not inherit it. You develop your self-esteem in part through the other people in your life.

Why Is Self-Esteem Important?

Low self-esteem has been linked to many problems in our society. The lack of self-esteem has been traced to poor performance in school, crime, homelessness, teen pregnancy, and even AIDS, to name a few social and academic problems. According to Dr. Stanley J. Gross from his article "How to Raise Your Self-Esteem" from http://psychcentral.com/lib/2006/how-to-raise-your-self-esteem/

> Low self-esteem is a negative evaluation of oneself. This type of evaluation usually occurs when some circumstance we encounter in our life touches on our sensitivities. We personalize the incident and experience physical, emotional, and cognitive arousal. This is so alarming and confusing that we respond by acting in a self-defeating or self-destructive manner. When that happens, our actions tend to be automatic and impulse-driven; we feel upset or emotionally blocked; our thinking narrows; our self-care deteriorates; we lose our sense of self; we focus on being in control and become self-absorbed.

Mohdmman Aryana's 2010 study confirmed the findings of previous studies on the relationship between self-esteem and academic achievement. He found that there was a direct relationship between self-esteem and academic achievement. In this study he found that increases in self-esteem are positively correlated with increases in academic achievement.

Developing Positive Self-Esteem

If you have low self-esteem, you are not going to be able to increase your self-esteem overnight. However, there are ways to begin to develop self-esteem that may have some immediate impact. Spend some time with these questions, and answer them truthfully.

What is the most important statement you can make about your life?

_____

_____

List the three things you like most about yourself.

1. _____

  *Why?*_____

  _____

  _____

2. _____

  *Why?*_____

  _____

  _____

3. _____

  *Why?*_____

  _____

  _____

Now, list the three things you would like to improve on or change about yourself.

1. _____

  *Why?*_____

  _____

  _____

2. _____

  *Why?*_____

  _____

  _____

3. _____

  *Why?*_____

  _____

  _____

Do you consider yourself a positive or a negative person? Why?

_____

_____

How do you think others see you?

_____

_____

_____

_____

_____

_____

Write an advertisement for you as a person. Think about your best "selling points."

_____

_____

_____

_____

_____

_____

_____

_____

> Building self-esteem comes with reclaiming that part of ourselves that we put on the sidelines because we felt we didn't deserve to be happy.
> —Robinson

How do you really view yourself? What picture of your life do you hold in your mind? Do you often tend to see the bad more clearly than the good? If you study your responses, you will find that you probably spend much of your time concentrating on the things you like least about yourself and not nearly enough time concentrating on the things that are beautiful and positive in your life.

Building positive self-esteem is mathematical. It simply requires you to subtract and to add. It requires you to subtract, or take away, those things in your life that are negative or that make you feel bad. It may mean that you have to subtract people, jobs, or even objects from your life. However, building positive self-esteem also means that you have to do some adding in your life, as well. You have to add things to your life that make you feel good and positive. You can add friends, a new job, a college education, or a new environment.

List three things in your life that make you feel good.

1. _____

2. _____

3. _____

MATH —the four-letter word!

What does math have to do with self-esteem? Many college students view themselves in terms of how they look and how people look at them. They value their lives from their outward appearances. Many people today base their first impression on what you look like as opposed to who you are as a person. We need to appreciate others for who they are and not how they look.

Overvaluing someone's outward appearance has produced a range of diet programs, many of which depend on the dieter's ability to count calories and stay at or under a daily caloric intake goal. Counting calories is a math concept.

It is important to feel good about the way you look. Your appearance is also important in establishing positive self-esteem. From a diet standpoint, you can lose weight by reducing your calorie intake. You can also lose weight by increasing the amount of time devoted to exercise as you reduce calories, but it is difficult to reduce weight by exercising without reducing calories. For example, it takes a two-mile run to burn 300 calories. Consider the fact that a simple donut contains 300 calories. If you eat one additional donut each day, you will have to run at least two miles a day to burn off those 300 additional calories.

Therefore, to follow these types of diets and count calories each day, a student will need to apply some basic math concepts. For example, you need to know what your daily caloric intake should be to maintain your current weight, how many calories to reduce each day to lose weight, and what daily plan to follow.

How Do You Calculate Calories Needed per Day?

Many college students live on a diet of 2,000-plus calories a day and gain weight. However, the actual number of calories you need to maintain your body weight will vary, depending on your activity level and current weight. Caloric intake requirements should be calculated regularly to allow for fluctuations in activity and weight loss or weight gain. A simple mathematical equation can help you determine the number of calories needed to maintain your weight.

Follow the steps outlined to determine each of the following:

1. Your daily caloric intake to maintain your current weight

2. How many calories should be derived from fat

3. Your daily caloric intake to lose weight

4. How you can lose one pound per week

To calculate your daily calorie intake, you need to consider the following information: Active males can determine the number of calories needed to maintain body weight by multiplying their weight in pounds by 15, and active females should multiply their weight by 12. Inactive males should calculate daily caloric intake by multiplying their body weight by 13, and inactive females should multiply their weight by 10. Active is defined as doing at least 30 minutes of exercise four to five times a week.

Next, determine how many calories should be derived from fat each day. The US government recommends that 30 percent of your total caloric intake should be from fat. However, we recommend that you shoot for 20 percent, if you are serious about losing weight and maintaining a healthy lifestyle. To determine the number of calories from fat, simply multiply your daily caloric intake by 20 percent, or 0.20.

(continued)

Finally, to lose one pound of weight per week, you need to reduce your caloric intake by 500 calories a day. For example, Gwen weights 165 pounds. Let's calculate what she needs to do to lose five pounds in five weeks:

1. Determine Gwen's daily caloric intake to maintain her current weight.
   Gwen is an inactive female, so the equation is:
   Weight x 10 = Daily Caloric Intake, or 165 x 10 = 1,650

2. Determine Gwen's daily caloric intake from fat.
   Daily Caloric Intake x .20 = Daily Caloric Intake from Fat
   1,650 x .20 = 330

3. To lose one pound per week, reduce daily caloric intake by 500 calories.
   Daily Caloric Intake – 500 calories = New Daily Caloric Intake Goal
   1,650 – 500 = 1,150

4. To lose five pounds in five weeks, Gwen will need to reduce her daily caloric intake from 1,650 to 1,150 each day for five weeks.

What do you need to do to lose five pounds over the next five weeks?

1. What category do you belong in: active male, inactive male, active female, or inactive female?

   _____

2. What is your required daily caloric intake to maintain your current weight?
   Weight x Your category = Daily Caloric Intake

   _____

3. Determine your daily caloric intake from fat.
   Daily Caloric Intake x .20 = Daily Caloric Intake from Fat

   _____

4. Determine your weight reduction daily caloric intake.
   Daily Caloric Intake – 500 calories = New Daily Caloric Intake Goal

   _____

5. What do you need to do to lose five pounds over the next five weeks?

   _____

   _____

To assist you with your weight-loss goal, many apps are available on your smart phone and online for access with your computer. Check out these sites to help with your goal to lose weight:

www.ehow.com/how_2146946_calculate-calories-needed-per-day.html

caloriecount.about.com/cc/calories-goal.php

nutrition.about.com/od/changeyourdiet/a/calguide.htm

If any site becomes inactive, just key "calorie calculation" in a search engine. Go online to find many helpful sites, or check out the "calorie counter" apps on your smart phone. You will also find total calories for different foods for a specific serving size. In addition, you should learn to read food labels for calories per serving size.

List three things in your life that make you feel bad.

1. _____

2. _____

3. _____

Study the lists you just created. What have you done in the past week to eliminate the bad, or negative, aspects of your life?

_____

_____

What have you done in the past week to add good, or positive, aspects to your life?

_____

_____

As mentioned earlier, children are not born with self-esteem. They learn their worth from their caregivers. Often, you learn what you can or cannot do through your association with other people, not yourself. Many times, you may be told "You'll never be able to do that" or "You're not smart enough to do that." You have probably heard the old expression "Tell a child he is dumb long enough, and he'll believe it." All too often, we believe what others tell us about ourselves and fail to listen to our inner voice, which says, "Yes, I can."

When was the last time your negative thoughts came true?

_____

_____

_____

Do you believe that others' actions or words lead you to fail?

_____

_____

_____

Building positive self-esteem is a mathematical process, requiring you to subtract negative aspects from and add positive aspects to your life.
Source: SHUTTERSTOCK

After studying the answers to these questions, you can see how negative thoughts from others or from yourself—from your inner voice—can cause your self-esteem to be lowered. Students sometimes forget they are in control of their emotions and actions. Focus on the positive aspects of your life and role as a student.

Now, let us look at ways to build positive self-esteem!

It has been said that the only way to conquer fear is to face it head on. The same is true with building self-esteem. The only way to build positive self-esteem is to note your shortcomings and do your best to correct them. The best way to correct shortcomings is to take them one at a time. For example, if you listed a fear of public speaking or a lack of public speaking skills as one of the things you would like to improve about yourself, you should develop a plan that allows you to correct the situation slowly. You need to map out a course that will raise your self-esteem in the area of public speaking. Here are some things you might try:

- Choose one person in class you do not know very well, and begin a conversation with him or her.

- Accept an invitation to a party where you will know only a few people. You will be forced to talk with others.

- The next time you have an oral report due in history, biology, or English, look at it as an opportunity, not as a tragedy.

- If you are asked to speak at church or a club meeting, accept the challenge, no matter how difficult it may seem.

- Take a public speaking course as an elective.

List an area where you would like to feel better about yourself and raise your self-esteem.

_____

_____

_____

Now, plot a course that will help you achieve your ultimate goal and make you feel better about yourself.

*Step 1.*_____

_____

*Step 2.*_____

_____

*Step 3.*_____

_____

Now That You Are Here . . .

Now that you have had the opportunity to reflect on who you are, what your values are, and how they impact self-esteem, complete the Milestones checklist again.

Answer each statement by checking "Y" for Yes, "N" for No, or "S" for Sometimes.

1.	I am serious about my future.	Y	N	S
2.	I study at least two hours per week per course hour.	Y	N	S
3.	I feel better about myself when I manage my time.	Y	N	S
4.	I enjoy learning.	Y	N	S
5.	I take risks.	Y	N	S
6.	I expect a great deal from myself.	Y	N	S
7.	I often think about my future.	Y	N	S
8.	I plan for my success.	Y	N	S
9.	I have high self-esteem.	Y	N	S
10.	I am a positive person.	Y	N	S

How did you do on this self-analysis? Do you now have a more positive outlook? Are you more positive in how you view life and your academic goals? Did you learn new ways to increase and enhance your self-esteem? If so, you are well on your journey to becoming a better and more positive student. If not, perhaps you need to spend some additional time going back over the exercises in this chapter and asking a fundamental question: How do these things affect me today and in the future?

TIPS FOR SUCCESS

To fully develop your potential and build positive self-esteem, you need to . . .

- Get **involved** in your own life. Don't let others control you!
- Take negative power **away** from your friends and family.
- Embrace the notion "I am **responsible** for my own life."
- Focus on your **potential** and your strengths.
- Control your **self-talk**, the little voice, usually negative, you hear inside your head.
- Take at least one **positive** risk per week.
- Stop **comparing** yourself to other people!
- Develop a "**victory** wall" or a "victory file," and post or file your achievements
- Surround yourself with people who **support** you.
- Keep your promises, and be **loyal** to friends, family, and yourself!
- Win with **grace,** and lose with class.
- Learn from your **mistakes,** and then move on!
- See yourself as **successful!**

APPLYING WHAT YOU KNOW

Now that you have completed reading this chapter, refer back to the Case Study about Gwen at the beginning of this book. Based on her situation, answer the following questions:

1. Gwen was going to college to improve her life and make a better life for her family. What do you hope to gain from your college experience?

_____

_____

_____

_____

_____

2. In Gwen's value system, she saw education as important to her life and to the life of her family. What does your value system tell you about your own life? How will you apply the reflection you completed in this chapter to your own life?

_____

_____

_____

_____

_____

3. Gwen was determined not to let her past educational experiences get her down. What have you learned from examining your past experiences, and how can that help you with the decision to attend college?

_____

_____

_____

_____

_____

GETTING THERE ON TIME

You can use numerous strategies to help you succeed in college. One such strategy is to plot the coming semester on a calendar. The faculty at most colleges are required to provide students with a course syllabus the first day of each class. The syllabus generally contains the course objectives, a grading scale, and dates of reports, exams, tests, and so on.

To benefit from this strategy, complete the following exercise:

1. *Take all your course syllabi for this semester and record the date of each test, exam, report, and research paper on your monthly calendar. For example, record all test dates on your monthly calendars and on your daily schedules.*

2. *Now look for blocks of time on days that precede your test dates. When you find a good date to study for an upcoming test, block out study time. Allow as much time as you can devote to studying for that test on your monthly calendar.*

3. *Make sure you record study time on your daily schedule for that day.*

Now you have a study plan in place for that particular test.

4. *Repeat this process for each test, research project, assignment, and so forth.*

A monthly calendar gives you a month at a glance, which helps you see how much schoolwork you have for that time frame and allows you to spread your study time more evenly over several weeks. A daily schedule provides you with a plan of action for each day and only needs to be executed or followed to help you meet your study goals. Your monthly calendar and daily schedule are very useful planning documents that set the stage for your study, research, and writing time.

> We are always getting ready to live, but never living.
> —Ralph Waldo Emerson

JOURNAL

The purpose of this journal exercise is to give you a chance to think about what you have learned from this chapter on building self-esteem. Consider what you have learned by completing the various exercises, and then comment on your newly found knowledge. List the steps you are going to take to develop a more positive outlook and build strong self-esteem.

As a result of this chapter and in preparing for my journey, I plan to

chapter 5

INFORMATION PROCESSING AND LEARNING STYLES

SIGHTS, SOUNDS, AND SENSATIONS

Math! How Andre hated that subject. It didn't matter how hard he studied—he didn't get it. He could remember his parents, teachers, and friends pestering him about studying. Andre did study. He even had tutors. But nothing seemed to work. He was discouraged and frustrated, and he knew he was doomed to never make a grade better than a D.

Then one day, all that changed. It was Andre's freshman year in college. He never forgot that first class with Mr. Lane, who explained that math was about to become everyone's favorite subject. Andre thought he was crazy. "That'll be the day," he thought.

Miraculously, Mr. Lane changed Andre's attitude toward math! First, he explained how important it was for students to think positively and believe that they could master numbers. Sure, some students would have to work hard, but Mr. Lane explained that to really understand math, they needed to see it, hear it, and touch it. For example, he told students to use their fingers when counting and to remove their shoes and use their toes, if they had to.

Mr. Lane was an excellent teacher. He really did show the class how to see, hear, and touch math. For the first time in Andre's life, he understood what he was doing in math. It was as if someone had unlocked a door that was blocking his way. Andre got 88 out of 100 on his first test. He even managed to pass the class with an 82! ■

Objectives

AFTER READING this chapter, completing the exercises, participating in class, reading the additional assignments that may be issued by your instructor, and keeping an open mind, you will be able to do the following:

- Explain information processing theory and learning style theory.
- Identify your preferred learning style.
- Create and use learning style strategies to learn and recall information.

- Use a global and analytical approach to processing information.
- Use mnemonic devices, or "memory tricks," to store and recall information.

> He who has no inclination to learn more will be very apt to think he knows enough.
> —John Powell

The story about Andre is quite common. Perhaps his fear of math sounds familiar to you. Many students share fear, anxiety, and frustration over math and other subjects. Fortunately, Mr. Lane was able to show this student how to master a tough subject.

Students often give up or quit learning new material, because they do not comprehend it right away. What they do not realize is that they may not have been processing information correctly. Andre's story is a perfect example of how learning involves seeing, hearing, and touching the information to understand it.

The intention of this chapter is to show you how to become a successful student by applying information processing theory and learning style theory when trying to master information. This chapter will teach you how to use a holistic approach that involves processing information with all five senses, thus pointing the way to academic success. Being a student means

Where Are You Now?

We have prepared 10 Milestone questions, which are intended to cause you to think about how you learn and process information. Please consider each statement carefully and answer it as honestly as possible.

Answer each statement by checking "Y" for Yes, "N" for No, or "S" for Sometimes.

1.	I understand how the brain processes information.	Y	N	S
2.	I know my preferred learning style.	Y	N	S
3.	I use a variety of senses when studying and learning.	Y	N	S
4.	I enjoy learning.	Y	N	S
5.	I know how a visual learner processes information.	Y	N	S
6.	I know how a kinesthetic learner processes information.	Y	N	S
7.	I know the characteristics of a global thinker.	Y	N	S
8.	I know how an auditory learner processes information.	Y	N	S
9.	I use mnemonic devices.	Y	N	S
10.	I know how to store information in long-term memory.	Y	N	S

How did you do with the self-analysis? Are you familiar with any of the terms presented? Do you understand that there are different ways people learn? If you are unfamiliar with any or all of the terms used, do not despair. This chapter is intended to teach you about learning styles and the various ways people learn.

accepting responsibility for learning the information presented to you. In a nutshell, when you understand how material is processed by your brain and how to use your preferred learning style, you can overcome academic barriers.

Studying is not necessarily natural or easy for everyone. It is, however, a learned skill that you can become proficient in if you are aware of your own individual learning style. ■

INFORMATION PROCESSING THEORY

Learning and processing information are primarily functions of the brain. The human brain is divided into two halves, called the *left* and *right hemispheres*, and they deal with information in different ways. The human brain functions best when both sides work together.

The left hemisphere is the part of the brain that does the thinking and reasoning. It exhibits most of the characteristics associated with *analytical thinking*. The right hemisphere controls mostly feelings and actions. It gives us most of the characteristics associated with *global thinking*. The two styles of thinking are of equal importance, each balancing the other and contributing to learning and information processing.

The traditional school setting is designed to meet the needs of students who think analytically (that is, those likely to find reading, writing, and math easy to learn). However, there are many students who fail to learn in school or who experience difficulty understanding new information. Many of these students are global thinkers and need to use this strength to master the analytical skills. When students use analytical and global thinking together (using both halves of the brain), learning becomes easier. As a student, it may be useful for you to figure out what type of thinker you are—analytical or global—and how to use both types of thinking at the same time.

You have strengths associated with both types of processing. However, everyone has a dominant style. Completing the Information Processing Inventory (see Exercise 5.1) will help you to identify the style of thinking that is dominant for you. Complete the inventory before going on.

Most individuals spend about 70 percent of their time completing and participating in analytical activities and only about 30 percent of their time in global activities. By learning how to develop both styles of processing or thinking, you can significantly improve your ability to learn.

Because everyone has a preference for one style of thinking, the key to successful learning is to use both styles of thinking at the same time. For example, if you are unorganized and always forgetting assignments, then writing down assignments will be very helpful to you as a student. In addition, when taking notes, you might find it helpful to use colored pens and pencils. The color is helpful because it stimulates global processing while you are completing the analytical skill of taking notes. When learning vocabulary, you might use index cards.

After you discover how you learn best, you can apply that knowledge to each class. You may even be able to help your instructors teach you more effectively.
Source: SHUTTERSTOCK

Exercise 5.1 Information Processing Inventory

Directions: First, read through all of the following statements. Then, place a checkmark (✔) or an X next to each statement under column "A" Traits and column "B" Traits that applies to you. Keep in mind that there are no right or wrong answers.

"A" TRAITS

_____ I am good at remembering faces.

_____ I remember how to perform a task better when someone shows me how to do it.

_____ I like expressing my feelings.

_____ I enjoy doing many things at once.

_____ I can sense how someone feels.

_____ I can create funny things to say or do.

_____ I like having fun when I am doing things.

_____ I like studying in groups.

_____ I am easily distracted.

_____ I am disorganized.

_____ I enjoy art, music, and/or dance.

_____ I prefer essay tests.

_____ I like meeting new people.

_____ I make decisions with my heart.

_____ I like to answer questions by guessing.

_____ I don't pay attention to details.

_____ I learn best by seeing or doing things.

_____ I have difficulty following directions.

_____ I use my hands when I talk.

_____ I lose track of time.

"B" TRAITS

_____ I am good at remembering names.

_____ I remember information best when I can read about it.

_____ I do not like expressing how I feel.

_____ I like to work on one thing at a time.

_____ I usually cannot tell how someone is feeling.

_____ I find it difficult to create funny things to say or do.

_____ I like to be serious when doing things.

_____ I prefer to study alone.

_____ I am not easily distracted.

_____ I am organized.

_____ I enjoy reading, math, and/or science.

_____ I prefer multiple-choice tests.

_____ I am uncomfortable meeting new people.

_____ I make decisions with my head.

_____ I like to think through questions before answering them.

_____ I pay attention to details.

_____ I learn best by hearing about things.

_____ I can follow directions.

_____ I rarely use my hands when I talk.

_____ I can keep track of time.

Now, count the number of checks you made for "A" and "B" traits, and record the totals:

Total "A" Traits = _____

Total "B" Traits = _____

"A" traits are associated with *global thinking*.

"B" traits are associated with *analytical thinking*.

MATH —the four letter word!

As we discuss later in the chapter, using mnemonics can be quite helpful when you are learning new concepts. That is the case with math, as well. In this section, you will find several mnemonic devices to help you learn key mathematical concepts. Commit them to memory, and you will no doubt remember operations, functions, and the like related to math.

Exercise:

Take each statement listed below, and write the acronym or acrostic on an index card. On the back of the card, write the concept the acronym or acrostic is intended to help you remember. In doing so, you will be making flashcards, which can be helpful in understanding and comprehending one concept at a time. Have a friend or relative quiz you using the flashcards. You will be amazed at how well this technique works!

1. Some Old Hippy, Caught Another Hippy, Trippin Over Apples
   Used in math to remember the equations for Sine, Cosine and Tangent, O stands for opposite, A stands for adjacent, and H stands for hypotenuse. Therefore, Sine = Opposite/Hypotenuse; Cosine = Adjacent/Hypotenuse. Tangent = Opposite/Adjacent.

2. Please Excuse My Dear Aunt Sally
   This mnemonic helps in remembering the order of operations in math: Parentheses, Exponents, Multiplication, Division, Addition, Subtraction.

3. I Valentine X-mas Love Candy During Math
   This mnemonic identifies roman numerals 1 to 1,000 in order:

   I = 1

   V = 5

   X = 10

   L = 50

   C = 100

   D = 500

   M = 1,000

4. King Henry Died Monday Drinking Chocolate Milk
   Used to remember the metric units of measurement:

Kilometer	Decimeter
Hectometer	Centimeter
Decameter	Millimeter
Meter	

5. May I have a large container of coffee?
   To remember the first eight digits of pi—3.1415926—count the number of letters in each word of the phrase:

   May(3) I (1) have(4) a(1) large(5) container(9) of(2) coffee(6)

Flashing through the cards is a global activity that helps the analytical processing needed to develop vocabulary.

When you learn to use both styles of thinking at the same time, retaining and understanding information will become much easier. Albert Einstein and Pablo Picasso, along with many other scientists and artists, saw the value of using both styles of thinking. These individuals had well-developed analytical and global thinking skills.

Characteristics of Analytical and Global Thinkers

Analytical Thinkers	Global Thinkers
Concerned with details	Concerned with the "big picture"
Organized	Disorganized
Predictable	Spontaneous
Auditory	Visual and kinesthetic
Consecutive	Random
Aware of time	Unaware of time
Math (algebra)	Geometry (shapes, etc.)
Reading, spelling, writing	Music, art, drama, dance
Practical	Creative
Logical	Instinctive
Focused	Easily distracted

The following sections describe strategies and techniques for activating analytical and global processing. Some of these strategies and techniques are personal preferences, but others have been shown to actually increase your ability to learn more efficiently.

ANALYTICAL PROCESSING OR THINKING. When learning, analytical thinkers prefer these conditions: bright light, a quiet study environment, working on one activity at a time, and studying alone.

GLOBAL PROCESSING OR THINKING. When learning, global thinkers prefer these conditions: short breaks, low lighting, eating/drinking while learning, music or sound in the background, informal learning environment, working on many activities at a time, and studying in groups.

Brainteaser

This activity does not measure your intelligence, your fluency with words, or your mathematical ability. It will, however, give you some indication of your mental flexibility and creativity. To achieve success, you will be required to apply both styles of thinking. Few people can solve more than half of the items, so do not get discouraged if you have trouble.

This exercise focuses on mental agility and your ability to recognize visual clues for solving problems. Translate each item, and write what it means on the line provided.

Examples:

	4 W on a C	Four Wheels on a Car
	13 O C	Thirteen Original Colonies
1.	SW and the 7 D	
2.	I H a D by M L K	
3.	2 Ps in a P	
4.	HDD (T M R U T C)	
5.	3 S to a T	
6.	100 P in a D	
7.	T No P L H	
8.	4 Q in a G	
9.	I a S W A A	
10.	50 S in T U	

 # LEARNING PREFERENCE THEORY

Many of you have undoubtedly wondered how information gets into your brain. The stimuli coming into your brain through your five senses travel along several common avenues or pathways. When you are learning or processing information, you are in fact using one or more of your five basic senses (sight, touch, sound, smell, or taste) to gather information for your brain to process. Successful learning of new information occurs when you use as many of your senses as you can to transmit new material to your brain.

Everyone has a preferred learning style or dominant sense that he or she uses to learn information—especially information that seems difficult. Most students use a combination of senses to help guarantee that their brains will understand the material. If you are learning a new song, for instance, your sense of *hearing* is challenged more than your other senses. Your sight may also play a part in the learning process, if you feel as though you can see the musical notes. In addition, by using a musical instrument to play the song, you are using *touch* to learn it. These examples show that you can use a combination of senses to experience a new song.

Another illustration of how you might combine your senses in learning involves studying a new type of flower. First, you may examine it closely. Next, you may smell its scent. You may also be able to taste the flower, if it is edible, and finally, you may even observe how it feels. Once again, you would be using several of your senses (sight, smell, taste, and touch) to identify the new flower. If you receive information through as many senses as possible, you will be more likely to understand a new concept.

Using the five senses, explain how you would teach each of the following items to someone who has never been exposed to it before. Be creative and have fun!

SOCIAL MEDIA . . .

Making Connections!

Learning style plays a key role in your success as a student. Some students must hear, see, or feel a concept before they fully grasp it. With the advent of YouTube and other social media outlets, if you stumble on a concept that you do not quite grasp in writing, you should use one of the many available search engines to explore the topic.

"Googling" has become an acceptable word in our language, because so many people use the Google search engine to research subjects. Go to www .google.com to enter a topic into the search engine. If videos are available on a particular subject, download them so you use your senses of sight and hearing.

Additionally, when a report is due in class, use some of the other social media sites to build your own presentation, instead of using just note cards. Integrate videos into your PowerPoint presentation to address more than just one learning style. Some of the social media that are available to you include Slide-Share, Flickr, iTunes, and Blog Talk Radio. Check out the variety of ways that using social media can help you master course material.

Lesson 1. *A vocabulary word: beautiful*

Sight _____

_____

Smell _____

_____

Taste _____

_____

Touch _____

_____

Hearing _____

_____

Lesson 2. *A math problem: 2 + 2 = 4*

Sight _____

_____

Smell _____

_____

Taste _____

_____

Touch _____

_____

Hearing _____

_____

Lesson 3. *To spell a word: success*

Sight _____

_____

Smell _____

_____

Taste _____

_____

Touch _____

_____

Hearing _____

_____

Lesson 4. *An object: a lemon*

Sight _____

_____

Smell _____

_____

Taste _____

_____

Touch _____

_____

Hearing _____

_____

After completing the activity, answer the following questions:

Were you able to use all of the senses for each lesson? Why or why not?

_____

_____

Which senses were harder to use? Why do you think they were harder to use?

_____

_____

Which senses do you feel most students use when they are learning new information? Why?

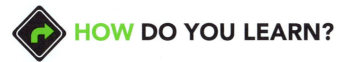

HOW DO YOU LEARN?

As you have discovered, effective learning involves using a range of senses. We all learn differently, and some students must use specific senses to learn. Students generally use one or more of the following senses when learning a new skill:

- *Visual:* sense of sight
- *Auditory:* sense of sound
- *Kinesthetic:* sense of touch

Everyone has a preferred style that he or she uses regularly to achieve academic success. Which style do you think you use most often? Circle your preferred style:

Visual   Auditory   Kinesthetic

It is important that you know your preferred style and how to use the other styles to reach your academic potential. Knowing about other learning styles can also help when material seems difficult to learn. The inventory in Exercise 5.2 will help you identify your preferred learning style.

It is important to note that there are *no* right or wrong answers. We are all different, and we all learn differently. One style is not more important or better than the others, and you may see a little of yourself in all of the styles. This inventory identifies the style you prefer when learning new material. The following sections describe the three types of learners and strategies for using each style.

Visual Learners

Visual learners process information through their sense of sight. They need to see something to understand and remember it. This learning style is the most common.

The following activities help to develop visual strengths: read or study the written word, pictures, or charts; take notes (especially using colored pens); draw pictures or diagrams; and visualize information in your mind.

Visual learners, who learn primarily through their sense of sight, may be challenged in college, where a lot of material is presented through lectures and discussions.
Source: ANNIE FULLER/PEARSON

Exercise 5.2 Learning Preference Inventory

Before completing this activity, read each statement in each category. For each category, put a checkmark (✔) or an X over the appropriate number for each statement. Keep in mind that there are no right or wrong answers.

1 = Least like me   **2** = Sometimes like me   **3** = Most like me

"A" LEARNING PREFERENCE

① ② ③   In my spare time, I enjoy watching TV or reading a magazine.

① ② ③   When putting something together, I need to look at a diagram.

① ② ③   I like teachers who write on the board and use visual aids.

① ② ③   I need to see things to remember them.

① ② ③   When I solve math application problems, I draw pictures.

① ② ③   I need a map to find my way around.

① ② ③   I can tell how someone feels by the expression on his or her face.

① ② ③   At a meeting, I prefer to watch people.

"B" LEARNING PREFERENCE

① ② ③   In my spare time, I enjoy listening to music or talking on the phone.

① ② ③   When putting something together, I need someone to explain how to do it.

① ② ③   I like teachers who lecture on the subject of the course.

① ② ③   I need to hear things to remember them.

① ② ③   When I solve math application problems, I need to talk them out.

① ② ③   When getting directions, I need to hear them.

① ② ③   I can tell how people feel by the sounds of their voices.

① ② ③   At a meeting, I prefer to listen and talk to people.

"C" LEARNING PREFERENCE

① ② ③   In my spare time, I enjoy physical activities (running, playing ball, etc.).

① ② ③   When putting something together, I need someone to show me how to do it.

① ② ③   I like teachers who provide classroom activities and encourage student involvement.

① ② ③   I need to write things down to remember them.

① ② ③   When I solve application problems (in math), I prefer to have someone show me what to do.

① ② ③   When getting directions, I need to write them down to remember them.

① ② ③   At a meeting, I prefer to take part in the conversation or activities.

Total points for "A" Learning Preference = _____

Total points for "B" Learning Preference = _____

Total points for "C" Learning Preference = _____

"A" learning preference is visual, involving the sense of sight.

"B" learning preference is auditory, involving the sense of sound.

"C" learning preference is kinesthetic, involving the sense of touch.

Auditory Learners

Auditory learners process information through their sense of hearing. They need to hear something to learn and remember it. Approximately 80 percent of the material presented in college is taught this way. Therefore, it is extremely important that you develop this learning style to experience academic success.

The following activities help to develop auditory skills: stop talking and listen, focus on what the teacher is saying, make audiotapes of class lectures and discussions, talk to yourself or others about the information, and study in a group.

Kinesthetic Learners

Kinesthetic learners process information best through their sense of touch. Students who learn in this way must physically experience the information to understand and remember it.

The following activities help to develop the kinesthetic sense: act out the information (role-play); use your hands; make models, charts, diagrams, and so on; take notes; add movement when studying, such as walking, tapping a finger, or rocking in a chair; chew gum; and study in a group.

Learning new information can sometimes be difficult, but it can sometimes be easy. Regardless of its difficulty level, to successfully master new material, students should involve as many of their senses as possible.

 # USING MNEMONIC DEVICES

People forget about 98 percent of what they learn. This is an alarming statistic, especially when you consider the enormous amount of time and effort that many people put into studying. Understanding human memory and applying memory techniques can help increase the chances that you will be able to recall the information you have studied when the time comes to take an exam.

According to psychologists, there are three types of human memory:

1. Sensory memory
2. Working memory
3. Long-term memory

Sensory memory stores information gathered from your five senses. This memory is usually temporary, unless it is important to you. *Working memory* is the information gathered from your senses that you feel is important. You can only store a limited amount of information in your working memory, however. If you want to ensure that you will remember this information, you must store it in your long-term memory. *Long-term memory* stores information permanently. How you organize and remember information is extremely important.

HELP!
I Need A Job!

Cabot Corporation is a global performance materials company, headquartered in Boston, Massachusetts. The primary products made are rubber and specialty-grade carbon blacks, inkjet colorants, fumed metal oxides, aerogel, tantalum and related products, and cesium formate drilling fluids, among others. Cabot operates 39 manufacturing facilities in the United States and 19 other countries. During its more than 125-year history, Cabot has earned a reputation for producing high-quality materials with an unwavering respect for sustainability and safety.

A Response from Cabot Human Resources

1. WHAT DO YOU LOOK FOR IN AN EMPLOYEE?

"We are a values-based company. We look for people who share our values of integrity, respect, responsibility, and excellence. Further, we're a midsize company. We are big enough to operate on a global scale but small enough that we all get the opportunity to work with each other. Because of this dimension, we highly value people who are team players and engaging communicators. If you are interviewing with us, you need to show us that you're passionate about our business and that you're committed to making a difference. We also want well-rounded individuals. The people who are successful here have a solid educational foundation, coupled with a good mix of relevant professional experiences and extracurricular activities. Finally, we look for people who demonstrate the ability and desire to continuously learn. Our business is complex, and the world is constantly changing. The best people understand that the need for learning never stops."

What can you do to be the prospect Cabot is looking for in an employee?

_____

_____

_____

_____

2. WHY WOULD YOU HIRE ME?

"You have the necessary skill set for the job, and you have demonstrated the potential to contribute in future assignments of greater responsibility. Your personality and career ambition are evident throughout the hiring and selection process, and we are convinced you are eager to apply your educational and professional experiences to our business. You have a strong work ethic, collaborate well with others, and come prepared with superior recommendations and performance reviews."

What can you do to make Cabot Corporation want to hire you?

_____

_____

_____

3. HOW CAN I GAIN A COMPETITIVE EDGE?

"Come to the office dressed appropriately to make a positive impression. Arrive early enough for an interview to be able to begin on time in a calm, professional manner. It is best to bring enough copies of your résumé for each interviewer, just in case, and be prepared to complete an application on site, including reference contact information. Research our company completely. Make the interview process as interactive as possible by having a deep level of knowledge. You can elaborate on specific experiences you've had and proactively relate those experiences to the available position. Always remain positive and maintain eye contact. Keep the interview personable. Know each interviewer's role, and use his or her name during the interview. Follow up promptly with a thank-you note. If you demonstrate the ability to learn quickly and demonstrate the appropriate skill sets, then you will gain a competitive advantage compared to other applicants."

What can you do to gain the competitive edge for a Cabot job?

_____

_____

_____

4. WHAT ROLE WOULD MY EDUCATION PLAY IN GETTING A JOB AT CABOT?

"Your education is extremely important and establishes a foundation for your skills and knowledge. Achieving your degree is a personal statement regarding your desire, ambition, and commitment to pursue excellence. Remember that academic grades alone will not automatically make you an effective employee. You must also come prepared to deliver results, and you must always continue learning."

How can you demonstrate that your education is relevant and competitive?

_____

_____

5. WHAT VALUE CAN I BRING TO YOUR COMPANY?

"New employees usually bring new ideas and creative approaches. At the same time, finding the right balance of offering new ways of doing things and also adapting to the company's current processes is very important. You can add value by accepting ownership and being accountable for delivering results. Be ready to 'hit the ground running.' Bring your enthusiasm and energy, and your career will be fulfilling and rewarding!"

How can you convince Cabot that you would be a valuable employee?

_____

_____

> Our ability to retrieve information from our memory is a function of how well it was learned in the first place.
>
> —Josh R. Gerow

In many ways, your brain is like a room with file cabinets along the walls. On the floor in the middle of the room is a huge pile of papers. Each sheet of paper contains a separate and distinct piece of information. This pile of papers is your working memory. As the pile gets larger and larger, pieces of information get covered up and forgotten. The only way to move this pile of working memory into long-term memory (where it will not be forgotten) is to organize it and to place it into one of the file cabinets along the wall. You can, for example, put equations into a folder in the "Math" file cabinet. (This folder may hold equations that solve certain types of math problems.) You can also put the definition of a word into a folder in the "Language" file cabinet.

One way to organize this information is to use *mnemonic devices*, or memory tricks. Mnemonic devices help you to store information in your long-term memory by associating that information with information you already know (that is, by putting it into a folder).

There are five basic types of mnemonic devices:

1. *Jingles/Rhymes*. You can create jingles and rhymes to remember information.

    Example: In fourteen hundred ninety-two, Columbus sailed the ocean blue.

2. *Associations*. Create associations by putting together words, ideas, and symbols to remember information.

    Examples: Lightbulb = an idea
    Apple = Macintosh

3. *Sentences*. Create a sentence (called an *acrostic*) using the first letter in each word from a list of information that you want to remember.

    Example: To remember the order of operations in math, use "Please excuse my dear Aunt Sally." This stands for Parentheses, Exponents, Multiply, Divide, Add, and Subtract.

4. *Words*. Create a word to represent the information you need to remember.

    Example: To remember the colors in the spectrum, use the name Roy G. Biv (which stands for Red, Orange, Yellow, Green, Blue, Indigo, and Violet).

5. *Visualization*. Create a picture in your mind of what you want to remember.

    Example: Italy looks like a boot on a map.

Create a mnemonic for each of the following concepts:

1. *Parts of speech (nouns, pronouns, verbs, adverbs, adjectives, prepositions, conjunctions, and interjections)*

   _____

   _____

   _____

2. *The five Great Lakes (Michigan, Erie, Superior, Huron, Ontario)*

   _____

   _____

   _____

3. *The first five presidents of the United States (Washington, Adams, Jefferson, Madison, and Monroe)*

   _____

   _____

   _____

4. *The seven continents (North America, South America, Europe, Asia, Africa, Antarctica, and Australia)*

   _____

   _____

   _____

5. *The eight planets (Mercury, Venus, Earth, Mars, Jupiter, Saturn, Uranus, and Neptune)*

   _____

   _____

   _____

Milestones

Now That You Are Here . . .

Now that you have completed reading this chapter, take a few moments to complete the Milestones checklist.

Answer each statement by checking "Y" for Yes, "N" for No, or "S" for Sometimes.

1. I understand how the brain processes information.	Y	N	S
2. I know my preferred learning style.	Y	N	S
3. I use a variety of senses when studying and learning.	Y	N	S
4. I enjoy learning.	Y	N	S
5. I know how a visual learner processes information.	Y	N	S
6. I know how a kinesthetic learner processes information.	Y	N	S
7. I know the characteristics of a global thinker.	Y	N	S
8. I know how an auditory learner processes information.	Y	N	S
9. I use mnemonic devices.	Y	N	S
10. I know how to store information in long-term memory.	Y	N	S

How did you do with the questions this time? Do you understand more about how the brain works and how learning is affected by individual preferences? What changes might you make in the way you approach studying, now that you are aware of how you learn? Certainly, much can be gained by focusing on your individual learning preferences and how they affect the way you approach academic material.

TIPS FOR SUCCESS

To become an effective learner, you need to . . .

- Become actively involved when studying, reading, and taking notes.
- Get organized! Develop a note-taking system, record assignments, and keep an organized notebook.
- Ensure study environment is quiet and free of distractions.
- Use colored pens and pencils when taking notes and studying.

- If you are a kinesthetic learner, create movement when studying.
- Use mnemonics to store and retrieve information.
- Get involved! Use both analytical and global thinking and as many senses as possible when learning.

APPLYING WHAT YOU KNOW

This chapter was designed to teach you about learning styles and the various ways people learn. Applying the strategies suggested in this chapter will allow you to take charge of your learning, since you are ultimately responsible for your academic success.

Now that you have finished reading this chapter on information processing and learning styles, refer to the Case Study about Gwen at the beginning of this book. Based on Gwen's situation, answer the following questions:

1. How would you explain to Gwen the differences between global and analytical thinking?

    _____

    _____

2. Assuming Gwen is a global thinker, what would you suggest she do to improve her grades in ENG 101?

    _____

    _____

3. Assuming Gwen is a visual and kinesthetic learner, what strategies would you suggest she implement to improve her grades in MAT 101?

    _____

    _____

GETTING THERE ON TIME

Once you have mastered techniques related to learning styles, you will realize that you can save a great deal of time studying. For example, consider how the use of mnemonic devices will help you. If you become proficient in the use of these devices, you will be able to recall facts more readily and more easily. Doing so will allow you to spend more time studying theory and logic as it relates to your particular subject.

JOURNAL

The purpose of this journal exercise is to give you a chance to think about what you have learned from this chapter about goal setting and motivation. Consider what you have learned by completing the various exercises, and comment on your newly found knowledge. List the steps you are going to take to implement these new goal-setting and motivational skills.

As a result of reading this chapter and in preparing for my journey, I plan to . . .

chapter 6

COMMUNICATIONS

SCANNING THE RADIO

Freshman year! Day one! First class! The History of Western Civilization! Instructor, Ms. Wilkerson!

"Your life will never be the same after you leave here," were her first words. She meant it. Ms. Wilkerson had been an award-winning basketball coach for almost 20 years and had retired to teach college history. She was tough in class, tough in the hallway, tough in her office, tough in the parking lot, tough while giving notes, tough when reviewing for a test, and even tougher when test day arrived. She was really, really tough, man!

Usually, on the first day of classes, the instructor would go over the syllabus, talk about the class, and let the students go. "Don't expect to leave here one second before my time is up," she said. "You paid for history, and that is exactly what you are going to get." She reviewed the syllabus, spoke briefly about the class, and began to lecture on Mesopotamian civilization. The entire class scrambled for notebooks and pens. Most of us would have written on anything so as not to miss a word of what she was saying. For the next 37 minutes, we listened and she talked. Our hands were aching from the speed at which we had to take notes as she lectured, wrote on the board, and used the overhead projector.

Shortly before our 50-minute period was over, she closed her book and said the words that I remember verbatim 18 years later:

"You'd better get ready. Do not come to this class unprepared. Bring your notebook, textbook, five pencils or two pens with you daily. I shall not stop this class for you to sharpen or borrow an instrument.

"You will come to this class ready to listen to me. You will not talk to your friends during my class. If you stick with me, listen to me carefully, and take your notes, you'll learn more about history than you ever dreamed possible. If you come to me unprepared, you will not know if you are in Egypt, Mesopotamia, or pure hell! Class dismissed!"

With horror and fear running through our bodies, my friend and I left the class bewildered and exhausted. We had never seen anything like it before. She was a tornado . . . a 65-year-old tornado! ■

> It is the province of knowledge to speak, and it is the privilege of wisdom to listen.
> — Oliver Wendell Holmes

You will possibly run into a Ms. Wilkerson from time to time. You may have already encountered her or professors like her who speak so rapidly that you have to have a sixth sense just to keep up. The nation's college campuses are full of Ms. Wilkersons. She was a fantastic teacher, but she moved through the centuries at the speed of sound. The students had to learn how to listen as quickly as she spoke and realized that they either had to keep up with her or withdraw from the class.

Objectives

THIS CHAPTER is intended to help you develop your listening skills. In becoming a more active listener, you will be able to take better notes in class, participate more, and retain more information. After reading this chapter and completing the exercises, you will be able to do the following:

- Distinguish between *listening* and *hearing*.
- Explain the listening process of receiving, focusing, interpreting, and responding.
- Define *effective listening*.
- Recognize and eliminate the obstacles to effective listening.

- Identify active and passive listening characteristics.
- Use the four-step process for getting others to listen to you.
- Understand and use the "roadways" to effective listening.
- Understand the fundamentals of written communication.

Where Are You Now?

The Milestones checklist includes statements to help you assess where you are as a listener at this moment. Take your time, and evaluate each question carefully.

Answer each statement by checking "Y" for Yes, "N" for No, or "S" for Sometimes.

	Y	N	S
1. I know how to listen with my whole body.	Y	N	S
2. I enjoy listening.	Y	N	S
3. I know how to listen for cues.	Y	N	S
4. I ask questions when listening.	Y	N	S
5. I know how to listen in different settings.	Y	N	S
6. I can identify the steps in the listening process.	Y	N	S
7. I usually keep listening when I do not agree with someone.	Y	N	S
8. I usually keep listening even if I do not like the speaker.	Y	N	S
9. I know the difference between *active listening* and *passive listening.*	Y	N	S
10. I know how to get others to listen to me.	Y	N	S

If most of your answers were "No" or "Sometimes," do not despair. This chapter is included to help you increase your listening skills and become a more active listener.

How do you feel about the importance of listening skills to your success as a student? A key step in becoming a good student is knowing how to listen and evaluate the information you hear. ■

TO BE A CAPTAIN, YOU FIRST HAVE TO BE A SAILOR

Many connections and relationships have to be made to survive in this world. You have already figured out many of them, or you would not be in college. As the heading of this section states, to be a captain, you have to know how to be a sailor. You may even have read the quote by poet Ralph Waldo Emerson: "The only way to have a good friend is to be one." The same connection can be made between listening and note taking. If you do

HELP!
I Need A Job

GMM Insurance is an independent insurance agency that was started in December 2005. Co-owners Scott Middleton and Marilyn Gray seek to serve the community and to make a difference in the lives of their customers and employees. GMM Insurance prides itself on looking at each customer individually and then helping him or her identify needs in the following areas: personal insurance (home, auto, boat, umbrella, rental, and other items owned by the insured); commercial (business insurance, including general liability, property, automobile, professsional, directors and officers liability, and specialized liability pertaining to businesses); and life (term and universal), long-term care, annuities, and health.

The quotations that follow present comments about what GMM insurance looks for in an employee.

1. WHAT DO YOU LOOK FOR IN AN EMPLOYEE?

"At GMM Insurance, we look for people who care about other people. This caring must be combined with commitment to the job and also independence to complete a task without constant supervision. We look for team players who are also responsible and independent people."

What can you do to be the prospective employee GMM is looking for?

_____

_____

_____

2. WHY WOULD YOU HIRE ME?

"We would hire you because you had an interview that showed that you had the same values as GMM Insurance: energy, independence, team players, and dedication. We look for someone who wants to make a difference in the lives of people and who truly enjoys being with people. It is very important that you are a good student and have proven yourself independent in learning. We would also look for you to tell us why we should hire you and convince us that we at GMM need you."

What can you do to make GMM want to hire you?

_____

_____

_____

3. HOW CAN I GAIN A COMPETITIVE EDGE?

"You can gain a competitive edge by beginning communication with us, either by e-mail or telephone, and by beginning to build a relationship prior to the interview. It is also important that you do your homework by researching what we do and the insurance industry. You would need to sell yourself from the minute you walk in the door by dressing in an appropriate business suit, shaking hands, and looking at us when being interviewed. It is also very important that you are engaged in the conversation and not just answering questions. We are looking for someone who thinks quickly on their feet and is articulate in a variety of situations whether it is a formal interview or lunch. Preparation is the key."

What can you do to gain the competitive edge for a GMM job?

_____

_____

_____

4. WHAT ROLE WOULD MY EDUCATION PLAY IN BEING ABLE TO GET A JOB WITH YOU?

"Education is very important in the insurance industry. It is a career where you will be continually learning and then learning some more. We look for someone who has excelled in school, because this is an indication of the desire to succeed. Are you a good worker who gets good grades, has a variety of extracurricular activities, and also finds time to improve yourself? Your education shows us much about you and your future."

How can you demonstrate that your education is relevant and competitive?

_____

_____

_____

5. WHAT VALUE CAN I BRING TO YOUR COMPANY?

"You bring yourself to our company. We want to see energy and enthusiasm combined with the desire to help people and work as a team. We want you to always be looking to learn and to come to us with new ideas. We look for you to be courageous and not afraid to get to work and make a difference."

How can you convince GMM that you would be a valuable employee?

_____

_____

_____

Listening is a skill critical to success in school, in work, and in life.
Source: ANNIE FULLER/PEARSON

not have the necessary listening skills, you will not likely be able to take useful notes in class.

Listening is necessary for establishing relationships, growing, surviving, gaining knowledge, enjoying entertainment, and even being healthy. It is one of the most important and widely used tools humans possess.

How much time per day do you think you spend in listening situations? Research suggests that we spend almost 70 percent of our waking time communicating (Adler, Rosenfeld, & Towne, 1989). Fifty-three percent of that time is spent in listening situations. Effective listening skills can mean the difference between success or failure, A's or F's, successful relationships or strained ones.

For students, listening is a skill that is critical to success. Much of the information you will receive over the next two to four years will be provided to you in lecture format. Cultivating and improving your active listening skills will assist you in understanding lectures, taking accurate notes, participating in class discussions, and communicating with your peers.

THE DIFFERENCES BETWEEN LISTENING AND HEARING

We usually do not think much about listening until a misunderstanding occurs or something goes wrong. You have probably been in a situation in which someone misunderstood you or you misunderstood someone. These misunderstandings often occur, because we tend to view listening as an automatic response. But in fact, listening is a *learned, voluntary* activity, just like driving a car, painting a picture, or playing the piano.

Hearing is not learned. It is automatic and involuntary. As a matter of fact, if you are within the range of the sound that is made, you will probably hear it. That does not mean, however, that you will listen to it. Just because you heard the sound does not guarantee that you know what the sound was or where it came from. To listen actively, you have to make a conscious effort to focus on the sound and determine what it was.

Listening is a four-step process. It can be remembered by using the mnemonic **ROAR:**

R Receiving the information
O Organizing the sounds heard and focusing on them
A Assigning meaning
R Reacting

This process is discussed in more detail in the following sections.

Receiving

Receiving simply involves being within the range of the sound that was made. It may have been a baby crying, a dish breaking, or a human voice speaking. Receiving a sound does not necessarily mean that you are listening, however.

Take a moment and determine what sounds you are receiving at this exact moment. List them.

_____

_____

_____

Organizing and Focusing

We organize and focus when we choose to listen actively to the sound and pay attention to its origin, direction, and intention. Our minds begin to organize the information we hear. You just did this in the previous exercise.

Spend the next few moments talking with a partner in class. Put your pen down, and listen carefully and actively. Do not take notes on the conversation. Spend at least four to five minutes talking to your partner. Ask your partner about his or her goals, dreams, plans, major, and life's work.

Paraphrase what your partner said to you.

_____

_____

_____

To become an active listener, make an effort to do the following when **receiving** information:

1. Tune out distractions and focus on the conversation at hand.
2. Avoid interrupting the speaker.
3. Pay close attention to nonverbal communication, such as gestures, facial expressions, and movements.
4. Focus not on what will be said next but on what is being said at the moment.
5. Listen for what is **not** said.

To become an active listener, do these things when **organizing and focusing** on information:

1. Sit up straight or stand near the person speaking, so that you involve your entire body.
2. Make eye contact. Listen with your eyes and ears.
3. Try to create a visual picture of what is being said.

If you were actively listening, you were able to write about your partner's goals, major, dreams, and careers. How did you do? Were you actively listening?

Assignment

Assignment occurs when we mentally assign a name or meaning to what we have been hearing. We may have to pay special attention to some sounds to assign them the correct names or meanings. Have you ever been sitting in your room and heard a crash? You might have needed to hear it again before

To become an active listener, try to do the following when **assigning meaning to information**:

1. Relate the information to something you already know.
2. Ask questions to ensure you understand everything.
3. Identify the main idea(s) of what is being said.
4. Try to summarize the information into small "files" in your memory.
5. Repeat the information to yourself. (Repeat it aloud, if appropriate.)

To become an active listener, do the following when **reacting** to information:

1. Leave your emotions behind. Do not prejudge.
2. Avoid overreacting.
3. Avoid jumping to conclusions.
4. Ask yourself, "How can this information help me?"

being able to identify the sound as dishes falling, books dropping, or static on the radio.

In this step of the listening process, your brain is trying to establish a relationship between what you just heard and what you have heard before. It is trying to associate one piece of information with another. When the assignment has been made, you will be able to identify the new sound by remembering the old sound.

When you are listening in class and taking notes, you will find information that is similar to or related to information you have previously heard. If you hear about Einstein in history, you will probably make the connection to science. Active listening allows us to make associations, thus assisting us in creating learning patterns for long-term memory. Simply hearing the information will not allow you to make these relationships, however.

Listen carefully to the sounds made by your professor. He or she will ask you to close your eyes and listen actively. Try to identify the sounds without asking him or her to repeat them.

Sound 1 _____

Sound 2 _____

Sound 3 _____

Reacting

The reacting stage is nothing more than responding to the sound that was heard. If we hear a crash, we may jump. If we hear a voice, we may turn to face the person speaking.

Our reaction can also be a barrier to active listening. Have you ever "tuned out" or ignored someone because he or she was boring or because you did not agree with his or her point of view? These are also reactions to sounds. Having no reaction at all is highly unusual.

 **PRACTICAL DEFINITIONS OF LISTENING**

Perhaps the drawing of the Chinese verb "to listen" is the most comprehensive and practical definition of *listening*. To speakers of Mandarin Chinese, listening involves many parts of the body: the ears, the eyes, the mind, and the heart.

Do you make it a habit to listen with more than your ears? The Chinese view listening as a whole-body experience. People in Western cultures may have have lost the ability to involve the whole body in the listening process, favoring the ears and sometimes not even using them to their fullest extent.

In the dictionary, *listening* is defined as involving hearing. Although that meaning is commonly accepted, it does not offer a great deal of concreteness or direction for active listening. Listening must be personalized and internalized.

To understand listening as a whole-body experience, we will define it on three levels:

- Listening with a purpose
- Listening objectively
- Listening constructively

Listening with a Purpose

Listening with a purpose requires being able to recognize the different types of listening situations in which we might be involved, such as class, worship, entertainment, and relationships. We do not listen the same way in every situation.

When we go to a concert, for instance, we turn on our "concert ears," because we are listening for the sake of pleasure. When you go to class, you are listening to gain a deeper understanding of the materials presented. Have you ever listened to a friend who needed advice? If so, you were listening with different "ears" than you would in a classroom or in an entertainment setting.

Each situation demands that you know which type of listening will be required. This is called *listening with a purpose*.

List some different listening situations in which you will be involved this semester.

1. _____

2. _____

How do they differ?

1. _____

2. _____

Listening Objectively

To listen objectively means that to listen with an open mind. Few gifts you give yourself will be greater than knowing how to listen without bias or prejudice.

Many times, we tend to shut out or ignore information that we do not agree with or that appears obscure or irrelevant. Listening objectively requires us to listen with an open mind and then make a decision about the value of the information. Too often, we do the reverse. We make a judgment and then try to listen. Have you ever done that?

List two situations in which you might be involved this semester that will require you to listen with an open mind.

1. _____

2. _____

Why will you have to listen objectively in each situation?

1. _____

2. _____

Listening Constructively

To listen constructively means to listen with this attitude: "How can this information be helpful to my life or my education?" This approach to listening involves evaluating the information being given and determining if it has meaning in our lives. Does this sound easy?

Actually, listening constructively is more difficult than it sounds, because, once again, we tend to shut out information we do not see as immediately helpful or useful. To be constructive listeners, we need to know how to listen and to store information for later situations.

John was a student who disliked math intensely. He could never understand why, as a history major, he had to learn algebra. So, he would automatically tune out the math professor when she presented information he did not see as necessary.

From time to time, we have all probably felt this way about some information or another. However, when we tune out information because we cannot see or refuse to see its relationship to our lives, we are not listening constructively.

When was the last time you tuned out for some reason? Explain the situation and the reason for tuning out.

_____

_____

_____

Looking back, could you have benefited from the information or the source of the information, had you not tuned out? Why or why not?

_____

_____

_____

M**A**TH —the four letter word!

The following quotation reveals that without language and mathematics, we are incapable of communicating anything of value to others. The source of the quotation goes on to point out that those students who are deficient in expressing themselves in either language or mathematics are crippled:

"Language and mathematics are the mother tongues of our rational selves"—that is, of the human race—and no student should be permitted to be speechless in either tongue, whatever value he sets upon his special gifts, and however sure he may be at sixteen or eighteen that he knows the uses to which his mind will eventually be put. This would be like amputating his left hand because he did not seem to be ambidextrous. The languages of art and science are of twin importance. It is crippling to be illiterate in either, and the natural curriculum does not choose between them. They are two ways in which the student will have to express himself; they are two ways in which the truth gets known. —Mark Van Doren

What does Mark Van Doren seem to be saying in this quote?

_____

_____

Like a written language, the language of math is symbolic. Students perceive the beauty of mathematics through an understanding of its symbols, in much the same way they understand the beauty of a written language.

The interpretation of symbols plays a prominent role in mathematics. Often, students think the goal of mathematics is to find an answer to a problem. Indeed, calculating the answer is important, but knowing and expressing what the answer means is more important. Communicating through language and mathematics is vital to the transmission of knowledge to peers and future generations.

Since mathematical concepts are used to explain events in our everyday lives, it is important that you understand math concepts, definitions, and applications to communicate effectively. The underlined words in the following sentences communicate mathematical concepts. Please read each sentence and use the space provided to explain what the sentence means.

1. John's happiness is in <u>direct proportion</u> to Sue's misery.

_____

_____

2. The movie seemed to last for <u>infinity</u>.

_____

_____

3. The number of cases of influenza is growing <u>exponentially</u>.

_____

_____

4. The <u>perimeter</u> of Tonya's property is 372 feet.

_____

_____

(continued)

5. The <u>probability</u> that it will rain today is 80 percent.

_____

_____

6. A <u>fraction</u> of your salary will go to taxes.

_____

_____

7. The two roads run <u>parallel</u> to each other.

_____

_____

8. My teacher's explanations often go off on a <u>tangent</u>.

_____

_____

Answers

1. **John's happiness is in <u>direct proportion</u> to Sue's misery.** The happier John becomes, the more miserable Sue becomes.

2. **The movie seemed to last for <u>infinity</u>.** The movie lasted too long.

3. **The number of cases of influenza is growing <u>exponentially</u>.** The number of cases of influenza is increasing rapidly.

4. **The <u>perimeter</u> of Tonya's property is 372 feet.** The distance around Tonya's property is 372 feet.

5. **The <u>probability</u> that it will rain today is 80 percent.** There is an 80 percent chance that it will rain, or a 20 percent chance that it will not rain.

6. **A <u>fraction</u> of your salary will go to taxes.** A portion of what you earn will be withheld to pay taxes.

7. **The two roads run <u>parallel</u> to each other.** The roads run side by side and never cross each other.

8. **My teacher's explanations often go off on a <u>tangent</u>.** The teacher often gets off the topic.

OBSTACLES TO LISTENING

Several major obstacles can interfere with your becoming an effective listener. To start building active listening skills, you first have to remove some of these barriers.

Obstacle 1: Prejudging

Prejudging is one of the biggest obstacles to active listening. *Prejudging* means automatically shutting out what is being said for any of several reasons. You may prejudge because of the content being communicated, or you may prejudge because of the person communicating. Prejudging can also stem from environment, culture, social status, or attitude.

Willistine enrolled in a religion class at her college entitled "Faith, Doubt, and Reason." Shortly after the class began, the instructor began asking questions and making statements that challenged what Willistine had believed all of her life. The instructor was trying to get the students to explore thoughts beyond what they held at that moment. After two weeks in the class, Willistine decided to drop it, because she did not want to hear the instructor's comments. Willistine was prejudging. She shut out what the instructor was saying, because it went against what she believed.

It is almost impossible to prejudge and then actively listen. The best approach is to listen with an open mind and then make judgments.

DO YOU PREJUDGE THE INFORMATION OR THE SOURCE? Answer each of the following questions "Yes" or "No."

Yes No   1. I tune out when something is boring.

Yes No   2. I tune out when I do not agree with the information.

Yes No   3. I argue mentally with the speaker about information.

Yes No   4. I do not listen to people I dislike.

Yes No   5. I make decisions about the information before I understand all of its implications or consequences.

If you answered "Yes" to two or more questions, you might be inclined to prejudge.

Tips for Overcoming Prejudging

1. Listen for information that may be valuable to you as a student. Some material may not be pleasant to hear, but it may be useful to you later.

2. Listen to the message, not the messenger. If you do not like the speaker, try to go beyond personality and listen to what is being said, not to the person saying it. This is a double-edged sword: You may dislike the speaker so much that you do not listen objectively to what is being said. Or you may accept the information or answer just because you **do** like the person.

3. Try to remove cultural, racial, gender, social, and environmental barriers. Just because a person is different from you or holds another point of view does not make him or her wrong. Conversely, just because someone is like you and you have the same point of view, he or she is not necessarily right. Sometimes, we have to cross cultural and environmental barriers to learn new material and see with greater clarity.

Obstacle 2: Talking

No one, not even the best listener in the world, can listen well and talk at the same time.

To become effective listeners, we must learn the power of silence. Silence gives us the opportunity to do several things: think, listen, and consider. Silence also allows us to listen. The near impossibility of trying to listen and talk at once illustrates the importance of silence. Silence allows us to consider and reflect on what others are saying.

ARE YOU A TALKER RATHER THAN A LISTENER? Answer each of the following questions "Yes" or "No."

Yes No   1. I often interrupt the speaker so I can say what I want to say.

Yes No   2. I am thinking of my next statement while others are talking.

Yes No   3. My mind wanders when others talk.

Yes No   4. I answer my own questions when I listen to someone talk.

Yes No   5. I answer questions that are asked of other people.

If you answered "Yes" to two or more questions, you may not fully appreciate the importance of silence.

Tips for Overcoming the Urge to Talk Too Much

1. Force yourself to be silent at parties, family gatherings, and friendly get-togethers. Do not necessarily be antisocial, but force yourself to be silent for at least 10 minutes. You may be surprised at what you hear. You may also be surprised at how hard it is to do this! Test yourself.

2. Ask someone a question, and then allow the person to answer the question. Many times, we ask a question and either answer it ourselves or cheat the other person out of a response. Force yourself to wait until the person has finished his or her response. By asking questions and waiting for answers, we force ourselves to listen.

Obstacle 3: Bringing Your Emotions to the Table

Another barrier to active listening is to bring your emotions to the listening situation. Your worries, problems, fears, and anger can prevent you from listening to your greatest advantage.

Have you ever sat in a lecture and, before you knew what was happening, found your thoughts a million miles away, because you were angry or worried about something? If so, you have experienced this obstacle: bringing your emotions to the table.

DO YOU BRING YOUR EMOTIONS TO THE LISTENING SITUATION?

Answer each of the following questions "Yes" or "No."

Yes No   1. I get angry before I hear the whole story.

Yes No   2. I look for underlying or hidden messages in information I hear.

Yes No   3. Sometimes, I take on a negative frame of mind while I am listening.

Yes No   4. I base my opinions on what others say or do.

Yes No   5. I readily accept as correct information from people I like or respect.

If you answered "Yes" to two or more questions, you tend to bring your emotions into the listening situation.

Tips for Controlling Emotions That Interfere with Listening

1. Know how you feel about the topic or the speaker before you begin the listening experience.

2. Focus on the message, and determine how you can use the information.

3. Try to create a positive image about the message you are about to hear.

Active and Passive Listening Characteristics

Active Listeners	Passive Listeners
Lean forward and sit up straight	Slouch and lean back
Make eye contact with the speaker	Look away from the speaker
Listen for what is not said	Hear scattered information
Are patient	Get frustrated easily
Leave their emotions outside	Get angry at the speaker
Avoid jumping to conclusions	Make immediate assumptions
Ask questions	Urge the speaker to finish quickly
Focus on the topic	Daydream
Have an open mind	Prejudge
Do not argue mentally	Create mental arguments
Empathize	Criticize
Tune out distractions	Get distracted easily
React to ideas	React prematurely to the person speaking

Listening is hard work. It is a voluntary, learned skill that few people ever truly master. Active listeners seek to improve their skills by constantly involving themselves in the communication process.

HOW DO I GET OTHERS TO LISTEN TO ME?

As a college student, employee, leader, spouse, or caregiver, you will have situations in which you want people to listen to your views and opinions. You can use several "roadways" to get other people to listen to you.

- **Repetition.** Make an effort to state your main ideas or points more than once during the conversation. People need to hear things as many as 14 times to store them in long-term memory. Repetition helps.

- **Movement.** When you are speaking, move your body in subtle ways, such as making gestures and facial expressions. If you are standing in front of a group of people, you might move from one side of the room to the other.

- **Energy.** When you are trying to get others to listen to you, be energetic and lively with your voice. It is hard to listen to someone who speaks in the same tone all of the time. Be enthusiastic about what you are saying, and people will listen to you more readily.

- **Creativity.** Make sure you have something substantive to say and that you say it in a way that is creative, fresh, and new. When you speak, make sure you are contributing something to the conversation.

LISTENING FOR KEY WORDS, PHRASES, AND HINTS

Learning how to listen for key words, phrases, and hints can help you become an active listener and a more effective note taker. For example, when the English professor says, "There are 10 basic elements to writing poetry," you should jot down the number "10" under the heading "Poetry" and make a list of items 1 through 10, leaving space for taking the actual notes. If the professor completes the lecture and you have notes about only 6 elements to writing poetry, you know you missed some information. At that point, you should ask questions.

Here are some key phrases and words that may help you become an active listener:

on the other hand	as stated earlier	in contrast
another way	the main issue is	characteristically

The Top-10 Reasons for Actively Listening

Once you have learned how to listen actively, you will enjoy several key benefits that will help you as a student, employee, and citizen:

1. You will be exposed to more information and knowledge about the world, your peers, and yourself.

2. You will be able to help others, because you will have listened to their problems and fears. You will have a greater sense of empathy.

3. You will be able to avoid more problems at school or work than people who do not listen.

4. You will be able to participate in life more fully, because you will have a more keen sense of what is going on in the world around you.

5. You will have more friends and healthier relationships, because people are drawn to those they can talk to and whose sincerity they can sense.

6. You will be able to ask more questions and gain deeper understanding of subjects that interest you or ideas you wish to explore.

7. You will be a more effective leader. People follow those they feel genuinely listen to their ideas and give them a chance.

8. You will be able to understand more about different cultures from around the world.

9. You will be able to make more logical decisions about difficult issues in your life and studies.

10. You will feel better about yourself, because you will know in your heart and mind that you put the best effort possible into every situation.

in addition	for example	moreover
most importantly	to illustrate	such as
specifically	because	due to
once again	in comparison	finally
therefore	nevertheless	above all
as a result		

Knowing how to pick up on these kinds of *transition words* will help you filter out information that is less important, thus listening more carefully to what is most important. You should listen carefully when the professor does any of the following: writes something on the board, uses an overhead, draws on a flipchart, uses computer-aided graphics, speaks in a louder tone or changes vocal patterns, or uses gestures more than usual.

TEST YOUR LISTENING SKILLS

This section provides a series of activities that will test your active listening skills. You will be assisted by your professor. The activities test a variety of listening situations and require you to use several types of listening skills.

Exercise 6.1   Circles and Lines

Respond to the directions given by your professor using the diagram below.

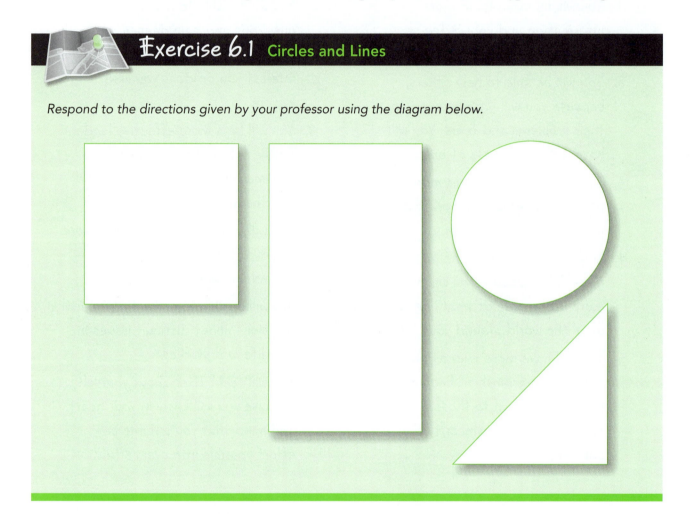

WRITTEN COMMUNICATION

In addition to all of the aspects of listening just discussed, an equally important aspect of communication is writing.

Good writing skills are essential for success as a student. Much of what you will be expected to do in college involves writing. Therefore, it is important that you develop the key writing skills today that will serve you well in the years to come. Learning the difference between citing references and plagiarizing, about the various research styles used in scholarly work, about conducting research, and about editing your written work are the concepts covered in this section.

Exercise 6.2 Cabbie

Close your book, listen to the professor's story, and then follow the professor's directions.

1. A thief approached a cab driver at a traffic light.
2. The thief demanded money.
3. The thief was a man.
4. The cab driver's window was down all the way when the thief approached the cab.
5. The cab driver gave the thief the money.
6. Someone sped away with the money.
7. The money was on the dash of the cab.
8. The amount of money was never mentioned.
9. The story mentions only two people: the cab driver and the thief.
10. The following statements are true: Someone demanded the money; the money was snatched up; and a person sped away.

Exercise 6.3 The Accident

Listen to the scenario read by your professor. Follow the professor's directions after hearing the scenario.

LISTENER	ADDITIONS	DELETIONS
1.		
2.		
3.		
4.		
5.		

Exercise 6.4 Visual Listening

Listen to your peers, and draw the design they verbally create for you.

Exercise 6.5 Whispers

Write down what the person next to you whispers in your ear.

Exercise 6.6 I Can Name That Tune

Answer the questions asked by the professor after listening.

1. _____

2. _____

3. _____

4. _____

5. _____

What Is Plagiarism?

Plagiarism involves using another person's ideas or work without getting permission or without providing credit. It is stealing in the sense of taking something that is not yours. Often, students who plagiarize do so unknowingly.

You can avoid plagiarizing by citing where a particular point came from that you include in your writing. This is called a *reference,* and it can be noted in your writing in a number of ways. Providing references also gives credibility to the ideas you have developed and can often help you prove a point in your writing.

One simple way to provide a reference is to tell the reader where you found the information—specifically, by mentioning the title of the book, article, or website. There are also other ways to reference information that you include in your written work. You will often see some of these methods when you read a college textbook.

Select a textbook that you are using this semester. Where are the references provided? Are most of them provided within the text? In a list at the conclusion of each chapter or article? At the end of the book?

_____

_____

Whatever the case, the author has taken care to give credit to the people who originally presented the ideas. When writing, always keep in mind this simple idea: Give credit where credit is due.

Some students think that if they have properly referenced a paper, they do not have to add any original thoughts or ideas. Professors like to see what *you* think about the material based on what information you have gathered. A good rule of thumb is that your paper should be at least two-thirds original thoughts supported by one-third facts that are properly referenced.

SOCIAL MEDIA . . .

Making Connections!

With the evolution of social media, students have a wonderful opportunity to learn (often in real time) through the spoken word, not just the written word. With social media sites so readily available, students can pause, rewind, play back, and save for future references a variety of sources. YouTube is a popular vehicle for viewing relevant visual lectures and discussions. With the help of Skype, students can meet virtually without having to travel to a central site and are able to work collaboratively on projects and assignments.

Just as with any other approach to learning, students using social media should know (1) what key words (or concepts) they are listening for and then (2) configure the Web tools that will enable them to be alerted when those key phrases are used. For example, if a student is attempting to locate the latest research on *infant mortality*, he or she might use a tool such as Google Alert or some other flagging service and set up "infant mortality" as a key phrase. A student might also create an information "fire hose" by using Yahoo and some key words by accessing this URL: http://pipes.yahoo.com/pipes/pipe.info?_id=aa 96c7b899cedb84a5d6bd64ba2d1543.

(If this URL does not work, use your favorite search engine and research this concept.)

Once a student has established a filter, any relevant and current communication on infant mortality will be sent directly to him or her.

This is but one example of how to use the vast array of social media tools to enhance communication and learning.

Search your college's catalog or handbook to find out the school's policy on plagiarism. Summarize the policy.

_____

_____

Review your syllabi for this semester. How many of your professors included information about plagiarism? And what are the consequences for plagiarizing?

_____

Writing Styles

Various professional organizations, such as the American Psychological Association, have developed *styles* of writing that help ensure research articles will be consistent in appearance. Some organizations have books called *style manuals* that outline their guidelines. Elements of style include whether paragraphs are indented, how the references are provided (both within the text and at the end of the text), and how information is organized and formatted.

Before beginning *any* written assignment, make sure you are aware of which style your professor prefers. Then, go promptly to the Internet or your campus library and find that particular style manual. Specific elements of style change periodically, so make sure you have the most current manual.

Examine the syllabi for your other courses this semester.

Do any of them require written papers?

If so, what style or styles are required?

If one of your syllabi does not indicate which style the professor requires, you should ask. It is better to be safe than sorry!

Conducting Research

You have been given an assignment in your psychology class to write a research paper. Where do you start?

The first task is to determine your research topic. Is the topic preassigned, or can you select your own? If you select your own topic, is it necessary to have the instructor approve the topic?

Once you have answered these basic questions, you are ready to complete the research phase of your assignment. Research can be exciting and fun, or it can be pure drudgery. If at all possible, find a topic in which you are interested. Then after you have selected an exciting topic, it is time to get to work finding all that you can about that topic.

The library is one of your greatest resources here. *Use the library, and get to know the reference librarian.* The reference librarian's job is to point you in the direction of as many difference resources as possible. The Internet is another fabulous resource for conducting research. Use as many search engines as you can to find out what is available about your topic. Remember, though, to always give proper credit to each resource you use by providing a reference. Spending time reading about the topic you will write about is invaluable research time.

Editing Your Work

Each year, more and more faculty complain that students do not adequately edit their written work. It seems that many students believe that with today's technology, a paper that *looks* professionally typed and presented must be a good paper.

Nothing could be farther from the truth. There is no substitute for editing—not spell check, not grammar check, and not word processing! *You must spend adequate time editing your work before turning it in.*

If nothing else, find a student to share your work with, and ask him or her to help you edit. Sometimes, when you spend so much time writing something, you lose sight of the "big picture" and overlook the mistakes (both in writing and in logic) that may make your paper a disaster. Do not be embarrassed to ask someone else to help you edit. In this case, the old cliché is true: "Two heads are better than one."

Now That You Are Here . . .

We have covered a few of the elements of effective writing. Nothing can replace good writing. You should develop your writing skills just as you would your listening, public speaking, and study skills. All are essential if you are to continue your journey to be a successful student. Answer the Milestones questions again, and see how you have improved.

Answer each statement by checking "Y" for Yes, "N" for No, or "S" for Sometimes.

1. I know how to listen with my whole body.	Y	N	S
2. I enjoy listening.	Y	N	S
3. I know how to listen for cues.	Y	N	S
4. I ask questions when listening.	Y	N	S
5. I know how to listen in different settings.	Y	N	S
6. I can identify the steps in the listening process.	Y	N	S
7. I usually keep listening when I do not agree with someone.	Y	N	S
8. I usually keep listening even if I do not like the speaker.	Y	N	S
9. I know the difference between *active listening* and *passive listening*.	Y	N	S
10. I know how to get others to listen to me.	Y	N	S

You should have more "Yes" answers now than you did before you read this chapter. If not, go back over the chapter exercises and review the Tips for Success that follow. Doing these things should help you turn all your "No" and "Sometimes" answers into "Yes" answers.

TIPS FOR SUCCESS
In order to become an effective communicator, you need to . . .

- Make the decision to listen. Listening is voluntary; you must choose to listen.
- Approach listening with an open mind.
- Leave your emotions at the door.
- Focus on the material at hand. How can it help you?
- Listen for key words and phrases.
- Listen for how something is said.
- Listen for what is not said.
- Stop talking.
- Eliminate as many distractions as possible.

- Listen for major ideas and details.
- Take notes. That will make you actively involved in listening.
- Paraphrase the speaker's words in your notes.
- Relate the information to something you already know.
- Encourage the speaker with your body language and facial expressions.
- Do not give up too soon. Listen to the whole story.
- Avoid jumping to conclusions.

APPLYING WHAT YOU KNOW

Now that you have completed this chapter, refer to the Case Study about Gwen at the beginning of this book. Based on Gwen's situation, answer the following questions:

1. One possible reason Gwen failed in her earlier academic pursuits is that she might not have known how to be an effective listener. How does listening affect your academic success? Describe the link between the two.

    _____

    _____

    _____

2. Active and passive listening were explained in the chapter. What situations in your own life can you identify that would be categorized as passive listening?

    _____

    _____

    _____

GETTING THERE ON TIME

This particular section focuses on listening as it relates to time management. When was the last time you missed some important information because you were not listening actively? When you completed Exercises 6.1 through 6.6, how well did you do?

Your time is affected by how well you listen. Below, list some time wasters that are the result of poor listening. (*Example:* You have received verbal directions and are driving to a destination. You did not listen carefully, though, so you are late getting there.)

_____

_____

_____

Because your time is so valuable, it is important to master the art of listening. It is costly to have to repeat an activity because you did not listen carefully at the beginning when directions or guidelines were given. By becoming a better listener, you can become a better time manager.

JOURNAL

The purpose of this journal exercise is to give you a chance to think about what you have learned from this chapter about communications. Consider what you have learned and comment on your newly found knowledge. List the steps you are now going to take to implement these new communication skills.

As a result of this chapter and in preparing for my journey, I plan to

_____

_____

_____

_____

_____

_____

_____

_____

_____

_____

_____

_____

_____

_____

_____

_____

_____

_____

_____

_____

_____

_____

_____

_____

chapter 7

THE PROCESS OF NOTE TAKING

CHARTING YOUR JOURNEY

William loved to play pool. It was his passion, his hobby, his job, and his first love. Few things ever got in the way of William's pool game. On more than one occasion, he cut class to go to the pool hall with his buddies. "I'll just get the notes from Wanda," he said. "She's always there."

When class met on Monday morning, William asked Wanda for her notes. She explained to him that her handwriting was poor and that she took notes in her own shorthand. "Oh, that's alright," William said. "I'll be able to get what I need from them." Wanda agreed to make a copy of her notes for William and bring them to him on Wednesday.

Wanda kept her promise and brought a copy of her notes. William put them into his backpack just before class began. The notes stayed there until the night before the midterm exam. William never took them out to look at them or to ask Wanda any questions. When he finally unfolded the notes and smoothed out the wrinkled pages, he was shocked at what he found:

> Psy started as a sci. disc. from Phi and Physio. Wihelm Wundt/GERM and Will James/US=fndrs. in lt. 19th cent. APA est. by Stanley Hall in US.
>
> 5 mjr Pers in PSY=   Biopsy. Per   Cog. Per.
>   Psychodyn. Per   Beh. Per.
>   Humanistic. Per
>
> Psy wk in 2 mjr. areas   1. Acad.   2. Practicing

The pen is the tongue of the mind.
—Miguel de Cervantes

William was in big trouble. He could not understand Wanda's shorthand and had not bothered to ask her to translate her notes. To make matters worse, William had lost his book a few weeks earlier. After trying to make sense of Wanda's notes, he gave up and went to the pool hall to relax and have fun before the test. William failed his midterm. ■

Objectives

THIS CHAPTER will help you to develop a system of note taking that works for you. After reading this chapter and completing the exercises, you will be able to do the following:

- Identify key phrases and words for effective note taking.
- Understand why note taking is an essential skill for successful students.
- Use the L-STAR system.
- Develop and use a personalized shorthand note-taking system.

- Use the outline technique.
- Use the mapping (or webbing) system.
- Use the Cornell system.
- Put into practice effective note-taking strategies.

We have all missed a few classes from time to time, haven't we? There are very few students who have not missed a class for one reason or another.

Even so, there are two important reasons for attending almost every class meeting:

1. Being there will give you the opportunity to take your own notes.
2. Even if you choose to use another person's notes because they are better than your own, being in class will give you a better chance of understanding and deciphering those notes upon later review.

William seems to have several problems, including setting priorities. But one of his biggest problems as a student is that he does not go to class to

Milestones

Where Are You Now?

The following 10 Milestones questions are intended to make you think about your ability to take effective notes. Take a moment to answer each statement carefully.

Answer each statement by checking "Y" for Yes, "N" for No, or "S" for Sometimes.

	Y	N	S
1. I am an excellent note taker.	Y	N	S
2. I am a good listener.	Y	N	S
3. I have a personal note-taking system.	Y	N	S
4. I use abbreviations when taking notes.	Y	N	S
5. I use symbols when taking notes.	Y	N	S
6. I read each assignment before class.	Y	N	S
7. I ask questions in class.	Y	N	S
8. I know how to listen for clues.	Y	N	S
9. I recopy my notes after each class.	Y	N	S
10. I reread my notes before each class.	Y	N	S

How many of your answers were either "No" or "Sometimes"? If you want to change more of your "No" answers to "Yes" answers, reading this chapter will help you to achieve that goal.

Also consider this: Taking notes effectively is one of the most important academic skills you can develop. It is also one of the easiest skills to learn. Effective note taking will help you record all of the important information presented by your instructors. In addition, it will provide you with information that will become your foundation for later review. Think of note taking as a tool that will help you achieve academic success.

take his own notes or to listen to the professor's presentation. His other problem is that he did not bother to review the notes with Wanda to make sure he understood them. ■

WHY TAKE NOTES?

You might ask, "Is note taking really important?" Actually, knowing how to take useful, accurate notes can dramatically improve your life as a student.

To ensure that you record the appropriate information, you will need to check your emotions at the class door, refrain from prejudging, and resist the

SOCIAL MEDIA . . .

Making Connections!

You can take advantage of social media in many ways to make connections with your classmates and to apply the note-taking strategies explained in this chapter. For example, you and your classmates could create a *wiki*: a simple set of Web pages that you and others can edit together. Starting your wiki at Wikispaces is fast, free, and easy. (Search the Internet for instructions about creating a free wiki.) After you have created your wiki, you can post your lecture notes from class, which can be edited by others. Often, it is hard to capture everything your instructor shares during a class. Using a wiki can be an easy and fun way for you and your classmates to update the information as a group.

Follow these steps for one of the classes you are taking:

1. *Form a study group.*

2. *Create a wiki using one of the many free websites on the Internet.*

3. *Begin posting lecture notes from the class, and ask everyone in your study group to begin editing to create detailed notes.*

4. *Consider asking your instructor to join your wiki. Instructors can be valuable resources in assisting with editing class lecture notes.*

---

urge to be distracted. You will *not* be an effective listener or note taker, for example, if you come to class upset by a conversation with your significant other, if your mind is closed to a new or different idea, or if you are talking or texting during a lecture. If you are an effective listener and note taker, you have two of the most valuable skills any student will ever need.

Taking notes is important for several reasons:

1. You become an active part of the listening process.
2. Your notes serve as a record of the course content.
3. You have written information to review when studying.
4. You have a visual aid for studying the material.

As mentioned in the last chapter, listening is a learned skill. So is note taking. Simply writing down information does not constitute good note taking. To become an effective note taker, you can learn several note-taking systems and helpful clues.

This chapter will discuss, review, and analyze these note-taking systems and provide helpful clues to assist you in determining what works best for you. Just because your friend uses the outlining method of note taking does not make that method right for you. If you are a visual learner, you should consider the mapping system. The use of a note-taking system is personal and individualized. You will discover the best style for you as you move through this section of the chapter.

DO I NEED TO WRITE THAT DOWN?

College professors hear this question daily: "Do I need to write that down?" If it were up to them, most professors would have students write down the majority of what they say in class (although professors realize that taking down everything is nearly impossible).

With that in mind, students who are effective listeners and note takers have figured out how to listen actively and distinguish the most important material. They know how to listen for key words and phrases. Here are some of the most important key phrases professors use:

in addition	as a result of	above all
because	finally	in contrast
due to	most importantly	to illustrate
the main issues are	you'll see this again	specifically
such as	nevertheless	characteristics
another way to	for example	in comparison
on the other hand	therefore	as stated earlier

Generally, when a professor uses one of these phrases, you can be assured that he or she is making a major point and that you should listen carefully and write it down. In addition, if material is presented on an overhead or a chalkboard, or by using electronic media technology, it is important and you should be ready to take accurate notes.

PREPARING TO TAKE NOTES

To become an effective note taker, you must be prepared. An artist must have materials such as a brush, palette, canvas, and paints to create a painting. Likewise, a student must have certain materials and make detailed preparations for note taking.

You should prepare in the following ways:

- *Attend class.* Telling students to go to class may sound obvious, but you will be surprised at how many college students feel they do not have to go to class. "Oh, I'll just get the notes from Wanda," they say, like William did in the story at the beginning of this chapter. The primary problem with getting the notes from Wanda is that they are *Wanda's notes.* You may be able to copy her words, but you will likely miss the meaning behind them. And if Wanda has developed her own note-taking style, you may not be able to decipher much of her notes. She may have written something like this:

G/Oke lvd in C/SC for 1yr ely 20c.

Can you decode Wanda's notes? It would be difficult, if not impossible, to know that these notes translate to mean this:

Georgia O'Keeffe lived in Columbia, South Carolina, for one year in the early part of the twentieth century.

To become an effective note taker, going to class is crucial. There is no substitute for it.

■ *Come to class prepared.* Do you read your assignments nightly? College professors are amazed at the number of students who come to class and *then* realize they should have read the homework materials. Reading your text, handouts, and workbooks or listening to media is one of the most effective ways to become a better note taker. It is always easier to listen and take notes when you have at least been exposed to the material being covered. Few student tasks are more difficult than trying to take notes on material you have never confronted before. Preparing to take notes involves doing your homework and coming to class ready to listen.

Coming to class prepared also means having along the proper materials to take notes. That includes your textbook or lab manual, at least two pens, enough sharpened pencils to make it through the lecture, a notebook, and a highlighter. Some students also bring some kind of recorder. If you choose to use a recorder, always get permission from the instructor before recording. Also, do not rely solely on the recordings and not take notes. Relying on recordings is inadequate because recordings—like lectures—must be converted to notes for the best retention of the material to occur.

■ *Bring your text to class.* Many students feel it is unnecessary to bring the textbook to class if they have read the homework. You will find that many professors will refer repeatedly to the text while lecturing. Always bring your text to class with you. Having it will assist you with note taking, especially if the professor asks you to highlight, underline, or refer to the text in class. Following along in the text during the professor's lecture may also help you organize your notes.

Come to class prepared. It is easier to take notes when you have a preliminary understanding of the material.
Source: ISTOCKPHOTO

■ *Ask questions and participate in class.* One of the most critical actions a student can perform in class is to ask questions and otherwise actively participate in the class discussion. If you do not understand a concept or theory, you *must* ask a question. Not asking and leaving class bewildered is foolish. Many professors use students' questions as a way of teaching and reviewing materials. Your questioning and participation will definitely help you, but it could also help others who do not understand. Asking questions moves you from a *passive* learner to an *active* learner.

NOW WE'RE READY TO BEGIN
THE BUILDING PROCESS

At this point, you have been exposed to several thoughts about the nature and importance of note taking:

1. You have to cultivate and build your active listening skills.
2. You must overcome the obstacles to effective listening, such as prejudging, talking while someone else is speaking, and bringing emotions to the table.
3. You have to be familiar with key phrases used by professors.
4. You must understand the importance of note taking.
5. You need to prepare yourself to take effective notes.
6. You must realize that scanning, reading, and using your texts help you understand the materials being discussed.

THE L-STAR SYSTEM

One of the most effective ways to take notes begins with learning the L-STAR system. L-STAR stands for these tasks:

Listening

Setting It Down

Translating

Analyzing

Remembering

Following this five-step process will allow you to compile complete, accurate, and visually oriented notes for future reference. By using this system, you will greatly improve your ability to take accurate notes, participate in class, help other students, study more effectively, and perform well on your exams and quizzes.

Listening

One of the best ways to become an effective note taker is to become an active listener. Developing both skills will be easier if you sit near the front of the room, so you can hear the professor and see the board and/or overheads. Also try to sit where you can see the professor's facial expressions and mouth. If you see that the professor's face has become animated or expressive, you can be sure the information is important. Write it down! If you sit in the back of the room, you may not be able to hear the professor or see his or her expressions.

Setting It Down

The actual writing of notes can be difficult. Some professors are very organized in their delivery of information, but others are not. Your listening skills,

MATH —the four-letter word!

Yes, you do need to take notes in your math class! It is critical! You cannot just copy the problem the teacher is presenting in your notes and think you will understand it when you want to practice it later. Solving mathematical problems is a sequential process. Knowing the basic steps to solve a problem is important!

For example, suppose your instructor asks you to find the zero of the following linear function by graphing it in your graphing calculator: $f(x) = \frac{2}{5}x - 10$.

You would use the following calculator steps:

1. Enter the function into Y_1.
2. Enter "0" into Y_2.
3. Zoom 6 to view the graph in a standard window.

4. Adjust the window, if needed, until you can see the function/graph crossing the x-axis.
5. 2nd; calc/trace; select #5: intersection; then move the cursor to where the graph crosses the x-axis.
6. Hit "Enter," "Enter," "Enter" to view the intersection $X = 25$ when $Y = 0$.

Imagine trying to do a similar problem while doing your homework later that day without having these notes/steps. It is not enough just to watch and listen to your instructor explain how to graph a linear function to identify its 0. You must also capture the steps to solving the problem. So, yes, the note-taking process is even necessary in your math class!

Practice creating notes/steps to solve the following math problems.

1. Find the mean of the following test grades: 95, 87, 69, 72, 84.

2. Solve the following polynomial using the quadratic formula: $x^2 + 4x = 5$.

3. Evaluate the function $f(x) = 3x + 2$ for $x = 2$.

Answers

1. The steps will vary from student to student. The mean of the five test grades is 81.4.
2. The steps will vary from student to student. The solutions are $x = 1$ and $x = 5$.
3. The steps will vary from student to student. Since $f(x) = 3x + 2$, then $f(2) = 3x + 2 = 8$.

once again, will play an important role in determining what needs to be written down. In most cases, you will not have time to write down the information word for word. You will have to be more selective about the information you choose to set down.

One of the best ways to keep up with the information being presented is to develop a shorthand system of your own. Many of the symbols note takers use are universal, but you may use some symbols, pictures, and markings that are uniquely your own. You can even incorporate the abbreviations you use when texting! Some of the most common note-taking symbols include the following:

w/	with	w/o	without	etc	and so on
=	equals	≠	does not equal	e.g.	for example
<	less than	>	greater than	vs	against
%	percentage	#	number	esp	especially
@	at	$	money	"	quote
&	and	^	increase	?	question
+	plus or addition	–	subtract	...	and so on
*	important				

Using these symbols and abbreviations can save you valuable time when taking notes. You may even wish to memorize them, because you will use them frequently. As you become more adept at note taking, you will quickly learn how to abbreviate words, phrases, and names.

Using the symbols listed and your own shorthand system, practice note taking by reducing the following statements. Be sure not to reduce them to the extent that you will not be able to understand them at a later date.

1. *It is important to remember that a greater percentage of money invested does not necessarily equal greater profits.*

   Reduce: _____

   _____

2. *She was quoted as saying, "Money equals success." Without exception, the audience disagreed with her logic.*

   Reduce: _____

   _____

3. *He found a greater number of books at the new store than he thought possible. For example, there were over 1,000 dictionaries available—a far greater number than at any other store.*

   Reduce: _____

   _____

4. *The increase in scholarship money has allowed a greater number of students to attend college.*

   Reduce: _____

   _____

Translating

One of the most valuable things that you can do as a student is to translate your notes immediately after each class. This can save you hours of work later, when you begin to prepare for exams. Many students feel this step is not important and do not do it. *Don't make the same mistake.* Many times, students take notes so quickly they make errors or use abbreviations they may not remember later.

After each class, go to the library or some quiet place and review your notes. It may not be possible to do this immediately after class, but before the day ends, rewrite and translate your classroom notes. Doing so gives you the opportunity to put the notes in your own words *and* to incorporate notes you have written in your textbooks into your classroom notes. It also gives you the chance to correct spellings, reword key phrases, spell out abbreviations, and prepare questions for the next class.

This sounds like a lot of work, doesn't it? Well, it is, but if you try this technique for one week, you will likely see a vast improvement in your understanding of the material and your grades.

Translating your notes helps you to make connections among previously discussed material, your own personal experiences and readings, and new material. Translating aids in recalling and applying new information. Few things are more difficult than trying to reconstruct your notes the night before a test—especially when you likely recorded the notes several weeks ago. Translating your notes daily will prove its value many times over when exam time comes.

Analyzing

Analyzing occurs when you are translating your notes from class. When you analyze your notes, you are asking yourself two basic questions:

1. What does this mean?
2. Why is it important?

If you can answer these two questions about your material, you have almost mastered the information. It is true that some instructors want you to "spit" back the exact same information you were given. Most professors, however, will ask you for a more detailed understanding and an application of the material. When you are translating your notes, begin to answer these two basic questions using your notes, textbook, supplemental materials, and information gathered from outside research.

Again, this is not simple or easy. Regardless, it is important to test yourself to see if you understand the information. Consider that many lectures are built on past lectures. So, if you do not understand what was

When you are translating your notes, ask yourself, "What does this mean, and why is it important?"
Source: SHUTTERSTOCK

discussed in class on September 17, you will not likely understand what is discussed on September 19. Analyzing your notes while translating them will give you a more complete understanding of the material.

Remembering

Once you have listened to the lecture, recorded notes, and translated/analyzed the material, it is time to commit the material to memory. Some of the best ways to remember information are to create a visual picture, to read the notes out loud, to use mnemonic devices, and to find a study partner.

PUTTING IT ALL TOGETHER: NOTE-TAKING TECHNIQUES

There are as many systems or methods of note taking as there are people who take notes. Some people write too small; others too large. Some write too much; others not enough. Some write down what is really important, while others miss key points. This section is provided to help you use the L-STAR system as a formalized note-taking technique. The L-STAR system can be used with any of the techniques discussed in the following sections.

Before we examine the three most commonly used note-taking systems, we need to review a few principles about basic note taking:

- Date your notes and use headings to break them into sections.
- Keep notes from different classes separate by using a divider or separate notebooks.
- Take notes on 8½" × 11" paper that is three-hole punched. (Students who take notes on computer should try to organize and store their notes as if they were a part of a paper note-taking system.)
- Copy information that is displayed using electronic presentation technologies.
- File your notes in a three-ring binder.
- Review and rewrite your notes the same day you take them.
- Try not to doodle while taking notes.
- Develop your own shorthand system.
- Clip related handouts to appropriate notes.

The following sections will review the three most common note-taking systems:

1. The outline technique
2. The Cornell system (also called the T-system)
3. The mapping system

The Outline Technique

Although the outline technique is one of the most commonly used note-taking systems, it is also one of the most misused systems. Outlining your notes in class can be difficult, especially if your professor fails to follow an outline while lecturing.

When using the outline system, it is best to get down all the information from the lecture and then *combine* the lecture notes and text notes to create an outline after class. Most professors would advise against using the outline system of note taking in class. You may be able to use a modified outline system in class, but the most important thing to remember is not to get bogged down in a system. It is much more important that you concentrate on getting the key ideas down on paper. You will always be able to go back after class and arrange your notes accordingly.

If you are going to use a modified or informal outline system while taking class notes, consider grouping information under headings. It is easier to remember information that is logically grouped, rather than scattered throughout the pages. For instance, if you are in an economics class and listening to a lecture on taxes, you might organize your notes using these headings: "Local Taxes," "State Taxes," and "Federal Taxes."

After you rewrite your notes to add class lecture information and materials from the text, your pages may look something like the page shown in Figure 7.1.

Figure 7.1 Sample Outline-Style Notes

Study Skills   Oct. 18
                                                       Wednesday

Topic: Listening
I. The Process of Listening (ROAR)
    A. R= Receiving
        1. W /in range of sound
        2. Hearing the information
    B. O= Organizing & focusing
        1. Choose to listen actively
        2. Observe the origin, direction & intent
    C. A= Assignment
        1. You assign a meaning
        2. You may have to hear it more than once
    D. R= Reacting
        1. Our response to what we heard
        2. Reaction can be anything
II. Definitions of Listening (POC)
    A. P= Listening w/ a purpose
    B. O= Listening w/ objectivity
    C. C= Listening constructively

The Cornell System

The Cornell system was developed by Dr. Walter Pauk of Cornell University. It is sometimes called the *split-page* or *T-system* of notetaking. The basic principle underlying this system is to split the page into three sections. Different information is then recorded in each section. Section A is used for questions about information found in section B. Section B is used for the actual notes from class, and section C is used for summary comments. Your blank note page should look like the page shown in Figure 7.2.

When taking notes in section B, you should choose a technique that is comfortable and beneficial to you. You might use mapping (discussed next) or outlining in this section of a Cornell page. A page of notes using an outline with the Cornell method will look like the one in Figure 7.3.

In a fast-paced lecture, using the Cornell system can be difficult. Completing sections A and C requires quite a bit of reflection about the actual notes in section B.

The Mapping System

If you are a visual learner, you should read this section carefully. The mapping system of note taking creates a picture of your information. Having pictures to refer to may make the recall of information easier for those who

Figure 7.2   Sample Note Page Using the Cornell System

Section B
(Notes)

Section A
Questions

Section C
Comments

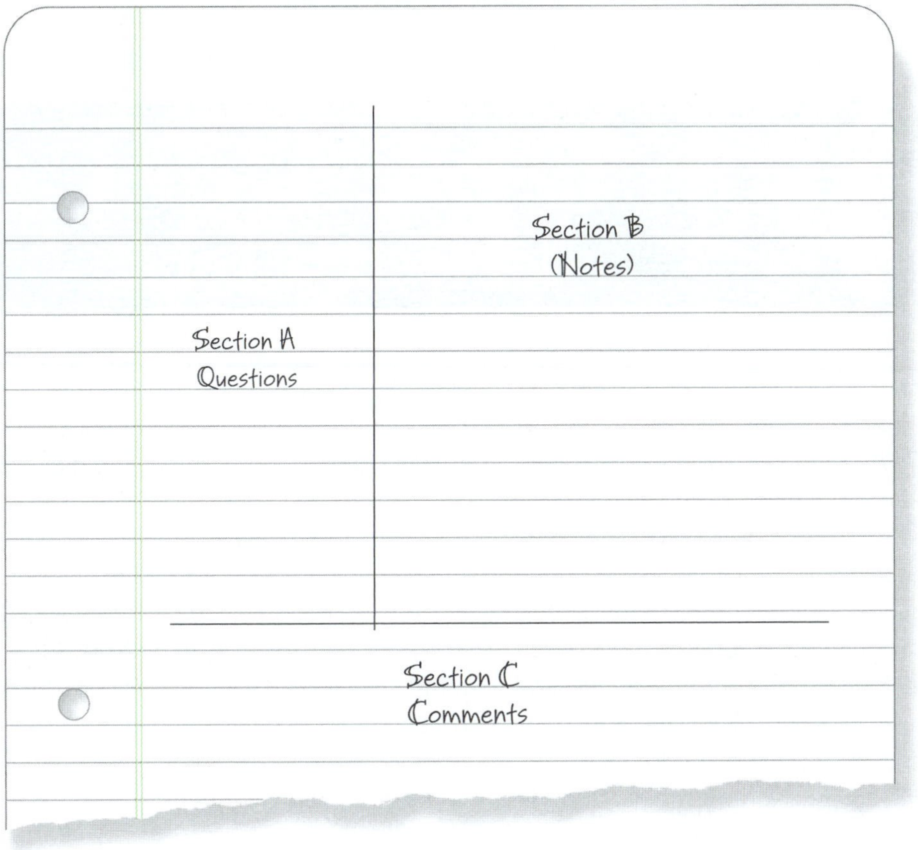

Figure 7.3   Sample of Using an Outline in the Cornell System

Study Skills 101   Oct. 20
                                                          Friday
Topic: Listening

	*The Listening Process or (ROAR)
	A = Receiving
What is the	1. Within range of sound
listening process?	2. Hearing the information
(ROAR)	B = Organizing & focusing
	1. Choose to listen actively
	2. Observe origin
Definition	*Listening Defined
of listening	A. Listening w/ a purpose
(POC)	B. Listening w/ objectivity
	C. Listening constructively
Obstacles	*What interferes w/ listening
(PTE)	A. Prejudging
	B. Talking
	C. Emotions

The listening process involves Receiving, Organizing, Assigning & Reacting—Talking, Prejudging & Emotions are obstacles.

HELP!
I Need a Job

What Is the Tennessee Valley Authority (TVA)?

A federally owned corporation, the Tennessee Valley Authority (TVA) was created when President Franklin D. Roosevelt signed it into law in May 1933. It was created to assist a region of the country particularly affected by the Great Depression. It was the TVA's mandate to provide navigation, flood control, electricity generation, fertilizer manufacturing, and economic development to the area in and around the Tennessee River Valley. The TVA serves most of Tennessee and parts of Alabama, Mississippi, Kentucky, Georgia, North Carolina, and Virginia. Initially, it was not only the goal of the TVA to be a service provider to this region but also to be a catalyst to modernize quickly the region's economy and society.

John Kammeyer is the Vice President of Coal Combustion Products (CCP), Projects and Engineering at TVA. He is also responsible for establishing and implementing the TVA fossil fleetwide program to remediate all CCP storage facilities. This $1.5 to $2.0 billion program remediates and closes all ash and gypsum wet-handling facilities (prioritized by risk); converts handling systems to dry; and constructs new dry storage landfills. Kammeyer is responsible for all aspects of the engineering, construction, and project management for this effort. He is also responsible for all engineering activities associated with the remediation of the Kingston Ash Recovery Project and closure of the failed dredge cell.

Kammeyer is a registered professional engineer with 30 years of engineering and leadership expe-rience in the utility industry. He has a bachelor of science degree from the Ohio State University and served six years in the US Navy's nuclear power pro-gram. Kammeyer successfully completed the Watts Bar Senior Reactor Operator Certification program.

The quotations that follow present Kammeyer's com-ments about what he looks for in a TVA employee.

1. WHAT DO YOU LOOK FOR IN AN EMPLOYEE?

"Attributes that I'm looking for are a willingness to work, a desire to succeed, and a sense of personal accountability. How does a prospective employee demonstrate that in an interview? Open and direct communications and, of course, a quality résumé are two ways. . . . What has a prospective employee done to get themselves educated and prepared for work? Things that count include a person's work record (part time or summer). Any experience that says a prospective employee has chosen a situation that caused growth in a working environment is valuable. The other piece is grades. Has a prospective employee worked hard to learn and demonstrated a desire to be the best?"

What can you do to be the prospect Kammeyer is looking for?

_____

_____

_____

_____

2. WHY WOULD YOU HIRE ME?

"Most careers, including engineering, require an ability to work in a team environment with good com-munication skills. You can have the best ideas and solutions in the world, but if you can't sell your ideas (both orally and written) you won't succeed. . . . So you have to demonstrate those attributes with your written résumé and with your communications skills during the interview. You have to sell yourself. . . . You have to believe in yourself and demonstrate a strong desire for the job you are seeking. That may sound pretty basic, . . . but I interview a lot of young college graduates that just come across as indif-ferent, as if they are doing you a favor by taking a position with your company."

What can you do to make Kammeyer want to hire you?

_____

_____

_____

_____

3. HOW CAN I GAIN A COMPETITIVE EDGE?

"Get a degree and work hard so your grades reflect your work ethic. Get work experience as best you can to set yourself apart from the crowd. Do your homework on the company you are interviewing with. . . .

Understand their business so you know how you would fit in. Be prepared to answer questions about why you want to work for that company and about what you want to accomplish in your work life. Be clear about your short-term and long-term goals. . . . Nothing is worse in an interview than a lack of direction. If you can't articulate personal goals, why would anyone want to hire you and entrust their company's goals to you?"

What can you do to gain the competitive edge for a TVA job?

_____

_____

_____

4. WHAT ROLE WOULD MY EDUCATION PLAY IN BEING ABLE TO GET A JOB WITH THE TVA?

"A college degree is necessary to get into the game. Prospective employees can't even get their foot in the door for an interview unless they possess the education requirements. A college degree is a minimum requirement for work in the electric generation field for engineering, project management, or construction management."

How can you demonstrate that your education is relevant and competitive?

_____

_____

_____

5. WHAT VALUE CAN I BRING TO YOUR COMPANY?

"Every company is looking for problem solvers, . . . and the world is full of problem finders. So set yourself up as serious about wanting the job you are interviewing for, know how you would fit in, have specific goals, and express a desire to take on challenges. If you can demonstrate a willingness to work, an urge to learn new things, a strong desire to make a contribution, and a need to be part of something bigger than yourself, . . . you'll get the job."

How can you convince Kammeyer that you would be a valuable TVA employee?

_____

_____

_____

What would you include in your résumé that will address Kammeyer's comments about prospective employees?

_____

_____

_____

How could you use your cover letter to demonstrate your strengths relative to the job description?

_____

_____

_____

learn best by visualization. The mapping system is just that: It creates a map or web of the information, which allows you to see the relationships among facts, names, dates, and places.

Like outlining, mapping can be difficult during an actual lecture. For instance, if a lecture is not well organized, your mapping may appear a bit disjointed. It is often best to jot down notes about information during the lecture and then map the information when translating your notes after class. Your mapping of information might look something like the page shown in Figure 7.4. Mapping using the Cornell system might resemble the page shown in Figure 7.5.

Choosing a Note-Taking System

The most important thing to remember about choosing a note-taking system is that it *must* work for you. Do not use a certain system because your friends use it or because you feel you have to. Experiment with each system to determine which one you feel works best for you. A combination might even work best.

Always remember to keep your notes organized, dated, and neat. Notes that cannot be read are no good to you or anyone else. An example of a note-taking system that is inappropriate for anyone is shown in Figure 7.6.

Figure 7.4 **Sample Note Page Using the Mapping System**

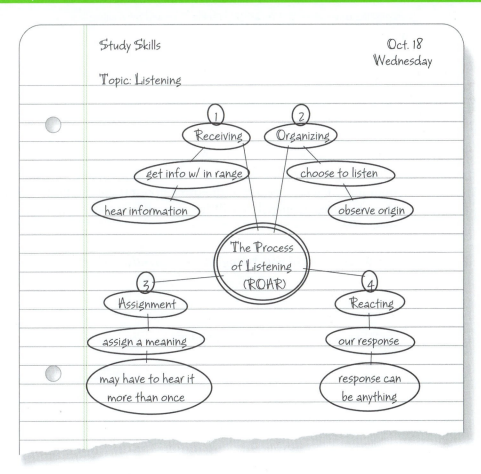

Figure 7.5   Sample of Using Mapping in the Cornell System

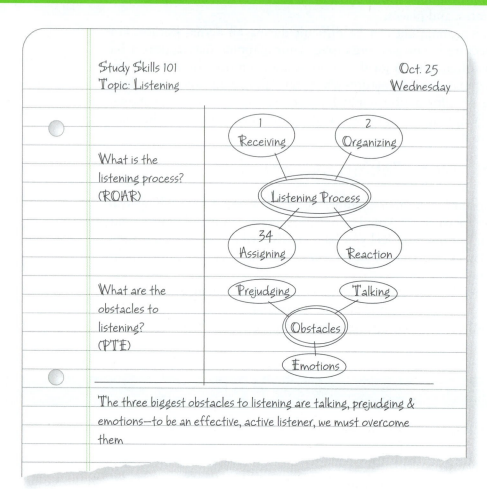

Study Skills 101
Topic: Listening

Oct. 25
Wednesday

What is the
listening process?
(ROAR)

Receiving — 1
Organizing — 2
Listening Process
Assigning — 34
Reaction

What are the
obstacles to
listening?
(PTE)

Prejudging
Talking
Obstacles
Emotions

The three biggest obstacles to listening are talking, prejudging &
emotions—to be an effective, active listener, we must overcome
them

To evaluate your current note-taking system, ask yourself the following questions. Then, use each of the three note-taking methods during your next three lectures. Doing that will be a good way to determine which system is most effective for you.

1. *What system of note taking do you currently use?*

2. *Does it work well? Why or why not?*

Figure 7.6 Doodles, Not Notes

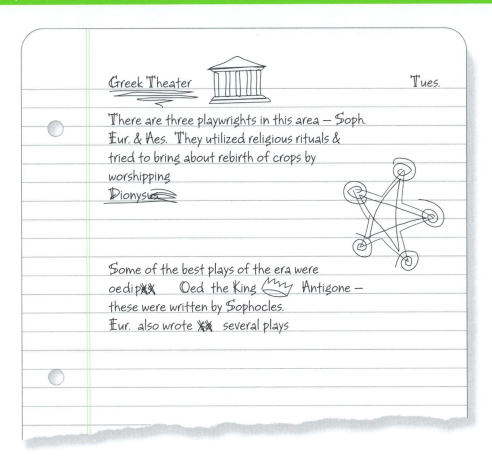

3. What advantages do you see in using the outline technique?

_____

_____

_____

4. What advantages do you see in using the Cornell system?

_____

_____

_____

5. What advantages do you see in using the mapping system?

_____

_____

_____

Use the spaces provided to practice the three note-taking methods during lectures of your choosing.

The Outline Technique

_____

_____

_____

_____

_____

_____

_____

_____

_____

The Cornell System

_____

_____

_____

_____

_____

_____

_____

_____

_____

_____

_____

The Mapping System

_____

_____

_____

_____

_____

_____

_____

_____

Milestones

Now That You Are Here . . .

Take a moment to complete the Milestones checklist again.

Answer each statement by checking "Y" for Yes, "N" for No, or "S" for Sometimes.

	Y	N	S
1. I am an excellent note taker.	Y	N	S
2. I am a good listener.	Y	N	S
3. I have a personal note-taking system.	Y	N	S
4. I use abbreviations when taking notes.	Y	N	S
5. I use symbols when taking notes.	Y	N	S
6. I read each assignment before class.	Y	N	S
7. I ask questions in class.	Y	N	S
8. I know how to listen for clues.	Y	N	S
9. I recopy my notes after each class.	Y	N	S
10. I reread my notes before each class.	Y	N	S

Hopefully, you have turned some of your "No" and "Sometimes" answers to "Yes" answers as a result of reading this chapter. Have you effectively used the Cornell and mapping systems of note taking? Which system works best for you? How does taking notes effectively assist you in your studying? Do you take advantage of using a note-taking partner? Why or why not?

All of these questions relate to your ability to use new techniques to tackle study tasks. *None* of these techniques will be successful if you do not try it. Take time to get acquainted with each method. You will find that your overall note-taking ability will improve and directly affect the grades you earn.

TIPS FOR SUCCESS

To become an effective note taker you need to . . .

- Attend class.
- Be prepared for every class by doing homework assignments.
- Sit where you can see and hear the professor.
- Recopy your notes after each class.
- If information is displayed using electronic media technologies, write it down.
- Use loose-leaf paper and a three-ring binder.
- Keep your notes for each course separate.
- Use good, straight posture when in class.
- Develop your listening abilities, and tune out chatter.
- Ask questions.
- Use abbreviations and write special notes to yourself.
- Keep your notes neat and clear. Do not doodle on your notes.
- Ask questions and participate in class.

APPLYING WHAT YOU KNOW

Developing the art of taking notes can be challenging, but with practice, you can become an effective and efficient note taker. Hopefully, reading this chapter gave you the opportunity to improve your note-taking skills.

Now that you have finished this chapter on the process of note taking, refer to the Case Study about Gwen at the beginning of this book. Based on Gwen's situation, answer the following questions:

1. Which note-taking technique would you suggest that Gwen implement? Why?

_____

_____

_____

_____

_____

2. How would you explain to Gwen how to use the L-STAR method in her MUS 105 class?

_____

_____

_____

_____

_____

3. How would you convince Gwen that taking notes would help her to improve her grades in all her classes?

_____

_____

_____

_____

_____

GETTING THERE ON TIME

Once again, it is important to realize the impact that time management has on the study skill of note taking. Not using a system of note taking can directly affect the amount of time you need to spend preparing for an exam.

How much time do you usually spend with your notes before a test? If you have been an effective note taker throughout the course, you can spend less time studying them immediately before the test. Filing your notes in a three-ring binder is another time-saving technique.

Is the time you spend taking notes and reviewing them well spent? Why or why not?

_____

_____

_____

_____

_____

_____

How does not having any notes affect the time you spend preparing for an exam?

_____

_____

_____

_____

_____

_____

Effective note taking is a combination of listening, recording, and efficiently using a valuable resource: time.

JOURNAL

The purpose of this journal exercise is to give you a chance to think about all that you have learned from this chapter about note taking. Consider what you have learned and comment on your newly found knowledge. List the steps you are now going to take to try to become a more effective and efficient note taker.

As a result of reading this chapter and in preparing for my journey, I plan to . . .

chapter 8

LEARNING HOW TO STUDY

DRIVER TRAINING

How well Lisa remembers her first semester at college. Being on her own was great. Everything was going well, until her economics professor returned her first exam. Lisa remembers the exam having 25 multiple-choice questions and 3 discussion questions. Lisa also remembers the shock she received when the test was returned with a failing grade.

Lisa was devastated! She couldn't believe it! How could this have happened? She remembers hoping that maybe her professor had made a mistake, but he had not. She remembers feeling scared and doubting if she belonged in college at all.

Lisa also found a note on her exam from the professor that said to see him after class. She waited fearfully to speak to him. During their discussion, he shared with Lisa that he felt she

> The only man who is educated is the man who has learned how to learn; the man who has learned how to adapt and change; the man who has realized that no knowledge is secure, that only the process of seeking knowledge gives us a basis for security.
> —Carl Rogers

had not studied for the test. Lisa explained that she had indeed studied. She explained that she had reviewed her class notes for almost an hour before the exam. The professor felt that an hour was not enough. He offered to work with her during his office hours.

Lisa faithfully attended the study sessions, and she learned a variety of strategies to help her learn the material. At first, she was overwhelmed with the amount of study time, but as she became proficient in the new studying skills, the amount of time she had to spend decreased.

Even though Lisa only made a C in this class, she learned how to study. As a result, she was better prepared for the classes she took after economics. ■

Some students think homework and studying consist merely of writing or glancing at notes. That is a myth! Achieving success in school requires more. Unfortunately, many students are less than successful in school because they have never learned how to study.

In this chapter, you will "learn how to learn." When implementing the suggested techniques, be sure to keep an open mind. You will be encouraged to try new things that will make a difference. Learning the skills, however, will require commitment, dedication, and time. The more you use the study skills, the better you will get at using them. Eventually, you will be able to spend less time and get better grades. ■

Objectives

AFTER READING this chapter and completing the exercise, you will be able to do the following:

- Understand the importance of class attendance.
- Explain and use various organizational strategies.
- Use various textbook-reading skills.
- Apply techniques to learn vocabulary words.

- Describe how to study math.
- Understand the importance of critical thinking.
- Appreciate the importance of information literacy.

ATTENDING CLASS

Studying includes being organized and using a variety of study techniques. Before we begin discussing these skills, we must discuss the importance of attending class.

Some students fail to take attending class seriously. But in fact, attending class is crucial to effective studying and learning. Your instructor may guide you by providing course outlines, instructions, and suggestions. By making

Where Are You Now?

The Milestones checklist will help you assess where you are with your current study habits. Answer each question as truthfully and honestly as possible.

Answer each statement by checking "Y" for Yes, "N" for No, or "S" for Sometimes.

1. I am organized.	Y	N	S
2. I follow a study plan.	Y	N	S
3. I know how to study math.	Y	N	S
4. I schedule time to study.	Y	N	S
5. I know how to read a textbook.	Y	N	S
6. I always attend class.	Y	N	S
7. I know how to learn vocabulary.	Y	N	S
8. I know how to use the SQ3R study method.	Y	N	S
9. I highlight my notes and textbooks.	Y	N	S
10. I have an appropriate place to study.	Y	N	S

How did you do? Are your study habits as good as you think they should be? If not, do not despair. This chapter will help you develop study habits and skills that will serve you well for the rest of your academic life. After completing this chapter, you should have all of the necessary skills to make the most of your valuable study time.

every attempt to attend class, you are aiding in your success. If you are unable to attend class, you are still responsible for the material covered.

TECHNIQUES FOR SUCCESSFUL STUDYING

How Well Organized Are You?

Being organized is essential to studying well. You should develop a notebook system that allows you to store and retrieve class notes, handouts, and assignments. Organization also involves having an appropriate study environment, having accessible study supplies, planning time to study, and developing a study plan.

What Note-Taking System Do You Use?

It is difficult to study information presented in class if you fail to record it. Taking notes during class gives you valuable information to review or study prior to an exam. It is critical that you spend time reviewing various note-taking systems, as discussed in Chapter 7, and select a system that works best for you.

When Do You Study?

To study effectively, you must set aside a time specifically for studying. If you fail to schedule that time, you will most likely not have *enough* time to study.

How many hours do you spend studying each day? Each week? Unfortunately, the average college student spends five hours or less studying

SOCIAL MEDIA . . .
Making Connections!

As will be discussed in this chapter, developing effective study skills is essential to your success as a student. Although social media may sometimes distract you from your studies, using these media appropriately may give you an advantage in studying for your classes.

For example, Facebook is a website that offers users social networking services. It has hundreds of millions of users around the world. It allows each user to create a personal profile, add other users as friends, exchange messages, and receive automatic notifications when friends update their profiles. Additionally, users may join common-interest user groups related to workplace, school, college, or another characteristic.

The term *Facebook* comes from the colloquial name for an actual printed book often published by universities and given to students at the beginning of an academic year. The printed book was intended to help students get to know each other better. Facebook allows anyone who declares himself or herself to be at least 13 years old to become a registered user.

Founded by a group of Harvard computer science students, Facebook—unlike a static print publication—was designed to add an interactive component to helping students meet and get better acquainted. Facebook membership was initially limited to Harvard students but was expanded to include other Ivy League institutions, as well as Stanford University and other colleges in the Boston area. It gradually added support for students at various other universities before opening up to high school students and finally to anyone age 13 and over.

Facebook has indeed grown rapidly in recent years and now ranks as one of the most-visited websites in the world. Since most students of all ages have Facebook accounts, using this site can be an excellent way for formal and informal student groups to meet about and discuss issues related to education. In fact, Facebook is a powerful study tool to assist students in making the content and concept connections in their classes.

Follow these steps to create a social media connection for one of the classes you are taking:

1. Create a class Facebook account, and invite all of your classmates to join the page. Do not forget to include your instructor.

2. Throughout the semester, join classmates in posting notes from class, chatting about topics that were unclear, identifying times to meet to study and prepare for tests, and so on.

per week, according to reports. Since it is recommended that students spend two hours studying for every hour spent in class (this varies from student to student), we know students fail to dedicate the amount of time needed to be academically successful.

Organizing your time is critical to your success. In fact, you must schedule and plan your study time.

Where Do You Study?

Choosing the best study environment is another factor in how successful you will be when studying. What constitutes the appropriate study place is different for everyone. It must be a place where you are comfortable. Therefore, paying attention to the physical condition of the room is important. Proper lighting and temperature, for instance, should be considered. When the lights are low and the room is warm, you may have an urge to take a nap.

Some students need a certain level of noise in the background to concentrate, while others are disturbed by any noise at all. It is, therefore, okay to play soft music when studying. But choose a station or recording that is *not* your favorite. You will be less likely to be distracted from your studying. And by all means, turn off your phone, as it will distract you, as well. It will be too tempting to respond to a text or to check your Facebook account if your phone is making noise.

When you study at home, choose a room that is relatively quiet (except, perhaps, for the music) and free of distractions. The dining room or your bedroom might be good choices, provided that your bedroom has a desk. If you find that you cannot concentrate at home, you should choose another place for studying. A great choice is the college library or student study center.

Describe your study environment.

_____

_____

_____

Is your study environment appropriate? Why or why not?

_____

_____

_____

List other potential environments you could study in.

_____

_____

_____

Do You Have Necessary Study Supplies on Hand?

Once you have identified where you will do most of your studying, the next step is to be prepared to study. Each time you study, you should have all of your study supplies on hand. It is amazing how much time can be wasted due to poor preparation. To be well prepared, you should have everything you regularly use in a portable basket or box.

Your study supplies should include but not be limited to the following items:

Pencils/Pens	Computer disks (CDs)/USB flash drives
Pencil sharpener	Highlighters of different colors
Notebook paper	Folders
Stapler/Staples	Paper clips
Thesaurus	Dictionary
Colored index cards	Colored pencils
Graphing calculator	

Also, take advantage of today's smart phone technology. Several free applications, or apps, are available for download that are worth considering as study tools. Included among these apps are dictionaries, periodic and conversion tables, calendars, time-management tools, graphing calculators, and so on.

In addition, you may find today's tablet PCs and e-readers convenient and helpful. For example, you may choose to use the electronic version of your course textbook. Just remember that when studying via an e-reader or tablet PC, you should turn off your browser and social media sites, as the temptation to interact with friends on Facebook will be a distraction.

List additional study supplies you feel you need.

_____

_____

_____

_____

 ## A STUDY PLAN

Now that you have chosen a note-taking system, decided on a place to study, put all of your study supplies in a basket, and identified specific times for studying, you must create a study plan. Making a to-do list will help you organize your study time. And using this plan will enable you to get the most from your valuable time.

In making a plan, list the most difficult assignments to be completed first. If you save those assignments until the end, you will not be at your best when you do them. Also, by waiting until the end to complete difficult tasks, your level of frustration will increase, and you may decide not to complete the tasks at all. If you do not complete everything on your list, transfer the unfinished work to your study plan for the next day.

Based on the courses you are taking this semester, create a study plan using the following to-do list.

To-Do List

1. _____

2. _____

3. _____

4. _____

5. _____

➤ EFFECTIVE STUDYING

Effective studying involves being organized and actually studying. The first step, not surprisingly, is to be *organized*. The tips mentioned at the beginning of this chapter describe ways to achieve that. The second step is to *study*. Studying is what you do to learn a new skill and to reinforce prior knowledge.

This section covers seven skills that are key to effective studying:

1. Learning vocabulary
2. Reading and using textbooks
3. The SQ3R method
4. Reviewing class and textbook notes
5. Studying math
6. Critical thinking
7. Information literacy

Learning Vocabulary

You must understand the meanings of words to effectively communicate with those around you. How well you speak, write, read, and understand words will likely influence how successful you will be in school.

Students with weak vocabularies are at a distinct disadvantage. They have trouble understanding their college textbooks and their instructors' class lectures. It is, therefore, important that you make a commitment to build your vocabulary.

Perhaps one of the best strategies to improve vocabulary and reading comprehension is (to put it simply) *to read*. When you read, it is crucial that you not skip over words that are unfamiliar to you. Skipping over difficult words affects your ability to understand what you have read. Instead, use *context clues* and *word analysis* to define the unfamiliar words.

CONTEXT CLUES. The sentence or paragraph that a word appears in is known as the *context* of the word. In reading a section of text, looking at nearby words and phrases can be helpful in figuring out the meaning of an unfamiliar word.

> Learning is not a task or a problem; it is a way to be in the world. Man learns as he pursues goals and projects that have meaning for him.
>
> —Sidney Journard

For instance, what does the word *capricious* mean? By itself, the word may be difficult to define, but in the context of the following sentence, its meaning should seem clearer: "Her capricious or impulsive nature caused her to make many mistakes." In this context, the word *capricious* means "impulsive." The sentence itself provides the meaning of the word.

Context clues usually give you at least a vague meaning of a word and allow you to continue reading without stopping to look up the word in the dictionary. Look for three basic types of context clues as you read:

■ One type of context clue is a *definition of the word*. The sentence may actually define the unfamiliar word. Here is an example of this kind of sentence: "The apartment was so spacious and beautiful that it could be called *palatial*."

■ Another clue to look for is *opposition*. In this case, the context may explain what the word does *not* mean, as in this example: "She was not *egocentric*, because she was always concerned with other people."

■ The third context clue to look for is an example of what the word means. In this sentence, the context gives you a synonym for the word used: "*Horticulture*, or gardening, has become a popular way to reduce stress."

You may find that using context clues helps you understand what you are reading and limits the interruptions created by having to look up words in the dictionary. The dictionary is a valuable resource, however, and you should use it when you cannot determine the meaning of a word. It is also a good idea to write unfamiliar words and their definitions on index cards or to take a notebook and create your own "dictionary" of newly learned words.

Practice using context clues to define the italicized word in each sentence.

1. Many *kinesthetic* learners find that they must move during the learning process.

   Kinesthetic means _____

   _____

2. It's amazing that John is always *immaculately* dressed, yet his car is often dirty.

   Immaculate means _____

   _____

3. I was *mortified* and embarrassed when my voice cracked during my speech.

   Mortified means _____

   _____

4. Lisa *procrastinates* instead of getting her work done on time.

   Procrastinates means _____

   _____

5. You can save money by buying *generic* brands of food.

   Generic means _____

   _____

6. The South's warm and sunny climate is very comfortable or *hospitable* to many northerners.

   Hospitable means _____

   _____

WORD ANALYSIS. Another technique you can use to decode an unfamiliar word is word analysis. *Word analysis* involves examining parts of a word to determine its meaning.

Many words are made up of a root, or base, word, as well as a prefix that comes before the root word and/or a suffix that comes after the root word. An example is the word *disconnection:*

The root of this word is *connect.*
The prefix of this word is *dis-.*
The suffix of this word is *-tion.*

Becoming familiar with common prefixes and suffixes can help when you come across an unfamiliar word.

Here are some common prefixes:

Prefix	Meaning	Example
un-	not	unusual
in-	not	incomplete
pre-	before	preread
post-	after	posttest
re-	again	restart

And here are some common suffixes:

Suffix	Meaning	Example
-ness	full of	usefulness
-less	lack of	useless
-ful	full of	hopeful
-able	full of	knowledgeable
-ward	in the direction of	backward

Reading and Using Textbooks

Every textbook has a variety of features designed to guide you through the material you are reading. To use your textbooks successfully, you must become familiar with all these features.

Every time you get a new textbook, you should spend 20 to 30 minutes becoming familiar with its special features, such as the table of contents or glossary. See Figure 8.1 for a sample of a table of contents.

List the features most commonly found in a textbook.

_____

_____

_____

Figure 8.1   Sample Table of Contents

Your list might include the following: table of contents, chapter headings and subheadings, key vocabulary words, section questions, chapter introductions and summaries, study questions, glossary, index, appendix, and preface.

Using one of your textbooks, list some of the features and their purposes.

1. *Feature* _____

    Purpose _____

    _____

2. *Feature* _____

    Purpose _____

    _____

3. *Feature* _____

    Purpose _____

    _____

4. *Feature* _____

    Purpose _____

    _____

5. *Feature* _____

    Purpose _____

    _____

The SQ3R Method

After you have previewed your textbook, reviewed the table of contents, and identified chapter features, it is time to begin reading and learning the information. Some students find reading the chapters in a textbook difficult. One of the best ways to read, learn, and study a chapter is to use the SQ3R method. The acronym SQ3R stands for these steps:

Survey
Question
Read
Recite
Review

STEP 1: SURVEY. The first step of the SQ3R method involves surveying, or prereading, the chapter. You begin surveying by reading the title and introduction of the chapter. This gives you an overview of the material. As you survey the chapter, read the headings, subheadings, and key vocabulary (usually in bold print), and look at any graphs, tables, and photographs. Finally, read the chapter summary, if there is one, and the review or discussion questions.

After surveying the chapter, you should be familiar with the information it contains. Reading, learning, and studying the chapter becomes easier when you first take 15 to 20 minutes to survey its content.

Directions: Using the sample chapter in Figure 8.2 from *Understanding Plays*, by Millie Barranger (1994), practice using the SQ3R method. Answer the questions that follow on pages 178–179.

Figure 8.2 Sample Chapter for Practicing SQ3R

Understanding Plays

The manuscript, the words on the page, was what you started with and what you have left. The production is of great importance, has given the play the life it will know, but it is gone, in the end, and the pages are the only wall against which to throw the future or measure the past.

—Lillian Hellman[1]

DRAMA AND PERFORMANCE

We are bombarded daily with television, videos, newsprint, films, and dramatic events. Terrorists threaten the lives of airline passengers, battles are fought in faraway places, nations negotiate peace treaties, nuclear accidents threaten lives, and a famous boxer divorces his glamorous actress-wife. All are subjects for novels, films, miniseries, and plays. The larger subject is human experience (real or imagined), but the means of representing experience in artistic forms differ with the artist and with the medium. A play, or the dramatic text, is one of the theatre's principal media. It is at once a text to be read and a script to be performed.

Plays are read daily by individuals as diverse as stage directors, designers, actors, technicians, teachers, students, critics, scholars, and the general public. In contrast to novels and poetry, a play is often the most difficult type of prose or poetry to read because it is written not only to be read, but also to be performed by actors before audiences. Like a screenplay, a play is also given life by actors although the medium and technology are significantly different. Kevin Kline acts Shakespeare's Hamlet or Derek Jacobi performs Richard II on a stage before audiences for the time of the performance. In contrast, their film performances in *The Big Chill* and *I, Claudius*, respectively, are contained, unchanging, on videotape for all time.

Reading plays is a unique challenge. As readers, we must visualize all of the elements the playwright has placed on the page to convey a story to us: its characters in action and conflict, its happening in time and space, and, at the end, the completed meaning of all that has happened.

Plays have been formally analyzed since the days of classical Greece. Aristotle's *Poetics* (c. 330 B.C.) is our first record of a critical assessment of plays presented in the ancient Greek festivals. Since Aristotle, there have been many approaches to "understanding" plays. For our purposes, we will approach the analysis of plays from the viewpoint and techniques of the playwright who creates the dramatic text. As Lillian Hellman said, the words on the page are the playwright's measure, after all is said and done, of the future and the past: "The manuscript, the words on the page, was what you started with and what you have left."[2]

Although we call the playwright's words on the printed page "drama," we also use the words "drama" and "dramatic" to describe many events ranging from riots to parades, from sports events to political speeches. That these current events are "real" rather than "fiction" is the essential distinction between life's "dramas" and dramatic "texts." Martin Esslin wrote that "a dramatic text, unperformed, is literature."[3] Like a novel or poem, drama, as written words, is considered a literary text. The chief ingredient that distinguishes drama from other types of literature is, precisely, its potential for being performed or enacted. The very origin of the word "drama" implies its potential for becoming a performable script. We use the words "text" or "script" to describe this written form that becomes the basis for theatrical performance.

Drama comes from the Greek *dran*, meaning "to do" or "to act." Since the word is rooted in "doing" or "enacting," we have come to understand drama as a special way of imitating human behavior and human events. Drama is like narrative in that it tells a story; but unlike narrative, or story telling, it requires enactment before an audience. The story's events must be represented in drama, not merely told or narrated as in epic poetry. The word *"theatre"* has its roots in the Greek word, *theatron*, meaning "a place for seeing," or that special place where actors and audiences come together to experience a performance of the playwright's raw materials—the drama. The dramatic text is not wholly realized until the theatre's artists complete for audiences what the playwright began. As Hamlet, Kenneth Branaugh must breathe life into Shakespeare's character for the text to come alive in the imagined world of Elsinore Castle.

All dramatic texts are constructs. They have in common the fact that they set forth events taking place in an imagined or fictional world, whether it be ancient Thebes or contemporary Manhattan. The dramatic text is the playwright's blueprint for setting forth physical and psychological experience—to give shape and meaning to the world as the playwright sees and understands it. Over the centuries, these blueprints have related a variety of stories not as narrations, but as imitations of imaginary actions. Sophocles wrote

Exercise 8.1 Continued.

Figure 8.2 Continued.

of a king confronted by a plague-ridden kingdom (*Oedipus the King*), Sam Shepard depicted American midwesterners confronting their lost connections with the land and with one another (*Buried Child*), and Samuel Beckett presented worlds in which human beings "wait out" lifetimes (*Footfalls*).

Drama, then, is a special written way of imitating human experience. It is both a literary and a performance text. The fictional character, Hamlet, is played by the living actor Kevin Kline. It is our purpose here to learn to *read* plays, to understand the how and why of the dramatic text, without ignoring the fact that the playwright's words have the potential to be performed in the theatre. We must learn to analyze the pattern of words and conventions that have the potential for "becoming" living words and actions. The playwright provides us with dialogue—words arranged in a meaningful sequence—intended to be spoken aloud and enacted by actors before audiences. Often the playwright includes descriptions of scenes, characters, and activities in stage directions and dialogue. However, the actor remains the playwright's essential intermediary in that complex relationship between the drama and the performance.

DRAMATURGY

In its original Greek meaning, a *dramaturg* was simply a playwright. The word "dramaturgy" defines the playwright's craft. It involves the elements, conventions, and techniques the playwright uses to delineate general and particular truths about the human condition. Those elements involve plot, action, character, meaning, language, spectacle, space, and time. We must develop skills for understanding a writer's dramaturgical skills, which deal with plot, character, language, and so forth, so that we can read plays from all periods of theatrical, cultural, and social history. Styles, conventions, language, and techniques differ among playwrights depending on the physical theatre, the writing conventions of the historical period, and the society or universe mirrored in the writer's work. Also applicable are the ever-changing cultural, social, and technological conditions under which plays have been written, produced, and performed in western society for 2500 years.

DRAMATIC SPACE

Drama is unique among the arts in that it imitates reality through representation rather than narration. The playwright creates a fictional universe with human beings, familiar objects, and recognizable environments. Beckett's characters' feet hurt; August Wilson's hero idolizes his baseball bat; Shepard's Dodge lives out his last days on a frayed green sofa surrounded by pills and whiskey bottles. Like Beckett, Wilson, and Shepard, playwrights use "real" human beings in particular spaces and times to create the illusion of fictional worlds in which recognizable events take place in time and space. We distinguish between the *performance space* (the stage) and the *dramatic space* (the playwright's fictional locale). Dramatic space—or the play's environment—is usually described in dialogue or in stage directions found in modern texts. What is exhibited in the performance space is an interpretation, or staging, of the play's physical requirements set forth in those directions.

Dramatic space has essentially two characteristics. First, it is a "fictional" space—the characters' environment—described by playwrights in dialogue and stage directions. The fictional space may be the palace of Thebes (*Oedipus the King*), an eighteenth-century drawing room (*The School for Scandal*), or the neglected living room of a modern midwestern family (*Buried Child*). The fictional space may encompass simultaneously more than one space, such as palaces and battlefields or apartments and streets. Shakespeare's plays require locations that are miles apart, but the characters must appear in those locales within seconds. Hamlet moves from battlements, to chambers, to graveyards. Dramatic space is magical in its ability to present several locales simultaneously. Bertolt Brecht's Galileo travels many miles and journeys to many cities in his pursuit of truth and reason.

Second, dramatic space always assumes the presence of a stage and an audience and a relationship between the two. As we read plays, we are aware that they are written to be performed. While the stage where a play is produced may be almost any type—proscenium, arena, thrust, environmental—the characters may or may not be aware of the audience. In modern realistic plays, the characters are not aware that an audience is present. The pretense, or stage convention, is that a "fourth wall" exists through which the actors-as-characters cannot see, although audiences can. No character in Henrik Ibsen's *Hedda Gabler* ever acknowledges the audience. In other plays, characters directly address the audience, establishing an invisible flow of space between actor and audience. Sheridan's *The School for Scandal* has many asides where characters speak directly to the audience to comment briefly on some situation. As readers, we need to be sensitive to the "look" of the characters' environment and to the intended relationship of the dramatic space to the audience.

Exercise 8.1 Continued.

Figure 8.2 Continued.

DRAMATIC TIME

Dramatic time is a phenomenon of the text. Jan Kott wrote that "theatre is a place where time is always present."[4] Once begun, the time of a performance is one-directional. It follows a linear path for the two or more hours of its duration. Dramatic time, in contrast to performance time, is free of such constraints.

Within the fictional world of the play, time can be expanded or compressed. Unlike the film editor's manipulation of images in films, the playwright does not have the advantage of editing and splicing film to carry us forward or backward in time. Rather, dramatic time can be accelerated by using gaps of days, months, and even years; or, it can be slowed down by using soliloquies and flashbacks. Whereas real or performance time moves in one direction (present to future) and the past can never be recaptured, dramatic time can violate the relentless forward motion of performance time measured by the clock. For example, events may be shown out of their chronological sequence, or they may be foreshortened so they occur more swiftly than they would in nature. Shakespeare's battles, requiring only a few minutes of swordplay on stage, would ordinarily require days or even months in real time. In Samuel Beckett's plays, characters experience the relentless passage of time because there are no major events or crises. An unchanging sameness characterizes their lives. In Samuel Beckett's *Waiting for Godot*, Vladimir and Estragon wait for Godot's arrival which is always postponed by the messenger's announcement that "Mr. Godot told me to tell you he won't come this evening but surely tomorrow." In Beckett's plays the experience of dramatic time is cyclical—day becomes night and night becomes day—while his characters wait out their uneventful lives in patterns that are repetitive and are experienced as "waiting." In his plays, nothing happens in the traditional sense, but time erodes lives in a relentless journey toward death.

Time and space in the fictional universe of drama are highly malleable and unlike the actual time we experience in our daily lives. Consideration of dramatic time and space has always played a large part in the different theories and rules of drama. In his *Poetics*, Aristotle briefly suggested that the amount of time it takes the actors to tell the story should ideally be concurrent with the actual time it takes to perform the play. This attention to a *unity of time*, as it was later called, is still found in modern realistic plays. However, in the many words written about drama over the centuries, the most attention has been given to the playwright's meanings and messages.

DRAMA'S MEANINGS AND MESSAGES

The reader's greatest temptation is to concentrate on the general meaning of the literary work—the novel, poem, or play—overlooking the fact that meaning is generated as the work is experienced. A play's complete meaning does not emerge in the early pages of a text or in the first moments of a performance, but quite often the seeds of the message can be found there. Shepard's statement about the decay of American family values is evident in the first moments of *Buried Child*.

In creating the dramatic text, the playwright connects the reader (and audiences) with a common humanity through the progression of the play's events. Great plays confront us with life's verities, conveying the hope, courage, despair, compassion, violence, love, hate, exploitation, and generosity experienced by all humankind. They show us the possibilities of losing our families and property through accidents, catastrophes of war, or tyranny. Plays show us ways of fulfilling ourselves in relationships or confronting despair and death. August Wilson's characters struggle to show love and affection to one another. The most enduring plays explore what it means to be human beings in special circumstances. These circumstances may be unfamiliar, like the prince dispossessed of his rightful heritage through murder, marriage, and calumny (*Hamlet*); or bizarre, like the family that has literally buried its family skeleton in the back yard (*Buried Child*); or familiar, like the ambitions of a mother for her children (*The Glass Menagerie*).

Drama's most enduring achievements, like the representative plays contained in this book, serve as reflections of ourselves, or what potentially could be ourselves in different times and circumstances. Drama's best moments lead us to discoveries and reflections about our personalities, circumstances, desires, anxieties, hopes, and dreams. Playwrights also move beyond personal concerns to discuss social and political issues that are of a certain time, yet transcend specific historical periods. Playwrights stimulate social awareness and put us in touch with our thoughts and feelings about issues. The aim of great playwrights is to expand our consciousness on old and new social and personal issues, and to endow us with *new perspectives* on our humanity and the human condition.

Plays are written as a process of unfolding and discovery. To read plays successfully is to understand essentially "how" the playwright generates meaning. Scene follows scene in meaningful patterns; dialogue communicates feelings and ideas; characters display motives and emotions; locales give

Exercise 8.1 Continued.

Figure 8.2 Continued.

social and economic contexts. "What" a play means involves the completed action, that is, all that has gone before in organized, meaningful segments that, when taken in their totality, express the writer's vision or conviction about the world. As readers, we share that unfolding—those discoveries—with audiences. We also learn to experience the developing actions, events, and relationships which, in turn, produce a coherent statement about individuals, societies, and the universe. We learn to follow the playwright's ways and means of organizing the dramatic material into a coherent whole and to discover the writer's methods for developing the psychological and physical currents of human endeavor that result in visible (and meaningful) behavior.

The same process is at work in our personal experiences. In our daily lives, we are not instantly aware that some actions have repercussions far beyond our expectations. As we begin a trip, we cannot know the full extent of our experiences. With time, we come to understand the meaning of our experiences, feelings, and actions, as well as the motives and actions of others. In some instances, meanings are elusive—sometimes impossible to pin down. The same is true in understanding the how and the why of the dramatic text. When Tom Wingfield brings the "gentleman caller" to dine with his sister Laura in Tennessee Williams' *The Glass Menagerie*, he is not aware, nor are we as readers and audiences, of the psychological damage he is imposing on Laura's fragile emotional life.

All art condenses, clarifies, and orders the chaos, disorder, and inconsequential happenings of life. The poet William Wordsworth gives shape to girlhood innocence in his "Lucy Gray" poems. Tennessee Williams organizes Tom Wingfield's memo-

ries of his chaotic and unhappy life in his mother's home. However, great plays confront life's complexities in such a way that they cannot be reduced to a single meaning. Since there is usually no author's voice in drama, as there is in the novel where the writer can speak directly to the reader, we are left with layers of possible meaning based on the play's events. We can usually agree that Hamlet was given the task of avenging his father's murder, that he hesitated and ultimately achieved his objective at the cost of his life. What remains open to interpretation is the ultimate meaning or significance of the play—"what it was all about." For that reason, we can read and see *Hamlet* any number of times and continue to discover new meanings in this complex text. We want to learn to identify *how* playwrights order, clarify, and distill their imitations of real life in the dramatic text and what higher meanings emerge from these efforts.

Sam Shepard's Pulitzer-Prize-winning *Buried Child* (1978) is an interesting contemporary play with which to begin our process of understanding plays. Along with a post-Vietnam wave of American writers that includes David Mamet, Marsha Norman, Lanford Wilson, August Wilson, and many others, Shepard takes us into the inner workings of modern American family life which are both commonplace and bizarre. He writes about characters searching out their family histories in an effort to explain who they are and how they came to be that way. Similar to *Oedipus the King* and *Hamlet*, the central action of *Buried Child* is the individual's quest for roots and identity. Shepard's means of organizing and unfolding a family's history provide our initial introduction to play analysis. Let us begin this journey into the process of understanding plays with *Buried Child*.

Exercise 8.1 Continued.

Survey the chapter.

1. What is the title of the chapter? _____

2. How many major headings are found in the chapter? _____

3. Does the chapter include any graphs, tables, or photographs? _____

4. Is there a *chapter summary?* _____

Form **Questions** from the chapter headings.

Choose three headings, and turn them into questions for review.

1._____

_____

_____

2._____

_____

_____

3._____

_____

_____

Read the chapter, highlighting key phrases and making notes in the margin that answer the questions you developed.

1. *What is the answer to question 1?*

_____

_____

_____

_____

2. *What is the answer to question 2?*

_____

_____

_____

_____

3. *What is the answer to question 3?*

_____

_____

_____

_____

Exercise 8.1 Continued.

Recite the answers to the questions you asked earlier without referring to your notes. Jot down your responses.

_____

_____

_____

_____

_____

_____

Review the entire chapter.

1. *Where were plays first analyzed?*

_____

_____

_____

_____

_____

_____

2. *What is dramatic space?*

_____

_____

_____

_____

_____

_____

3. *What is dramatic time?*

_____

_____

_____

_____

_____

_____

4. *What is a dramaturg?*

_____

_____

_____

_____

_____

Help!
I Need a Job

Curtis Boyd owns and operates seven fitness centers, called Fitness World Gyms, in South Carolina and Tennessee. Boyd started this family-based business in 1991. In his words, "We offer 24/7 access in all locations." Two of the locations are located inside manufacturing plants owned by A. O. Smith, a company that makes water heaters. These locations also provide 24/7 access to employees. The concept underlying Fitness World Gyms is to offer a great product at an affordable price that allows members to train on their own time schedule. Again quoting Boyd, "We also offer group fitness classes at no additional charge. We offer a family atmosphere where there is no pressure. We are a Christian-based company that gives thanks to God for His many blessings."

The quotations that follow present Boyd's comments about what he looks for in an employee.

1. WHAT DO YOU LOOK FOR IN AN EMPLOYEE?

"When hiring a new employee, I look for a dependable and honest person with a strong desire to succeed. I seek out those willing to learn. Character is something that is difficult to teach, but it is a necessary requirement. Employees should be capable of solely handling all issues and concerns of members or potential members. We place a great deal of trust in our employees, so honesty is a must. We stress that employees should feel ownership in the gym. This sense of ownership makes the goal of improving all of our gyms a shared goal."

What can you do to be the prospect Boyd is looking for in an employee?

_____

_____

2. WHY WOULD YOU HIRE ME?

"Your appearance is very important. We run a family-oriented gym, with God being first. We trust the person behind the counter, not only with the money but also as a good representative of our company and facility."

What can you do to make Boyd want to hire you?

_____

_____

3. HOW CAN I GAIN A COMPETITIVE EDGE?

"Good references help influence our decision to hire. It is a strong reference when a former employer has good things to say about a prospective employee. Don't burn your bridges."

What can you do to gain the competitive edge for a job at Fitness World Gyms?

_____

_____

_____

4. WHAT ROLE WOULD MY EDUCATION PLAY IN BEING ABLE TO GET A JOB WITH YOU?

"Your education does play a role. When someone comes in with a degree, they have already shown that they can complete the task at hand and succeed. We will put time, effort, and money into training you, but we expect someone committed to working hard after the training period."

How can you demonstrate that your education is relative and competitive?

_____

_____

_____

5. WHAT VALUE CAN I BRING TO YOUR COMPANY?

"I have employees that I wouldn't trade for the world, but I have some that I would not be disappointed to see leave. A strong employee, who possesses the qualities mentioned above, brings high value to the business. It is good for an employee to have the mindset that no one owes you anything. You should believe that if you work hard and give it your best, your rewards will be adequate and plentiful. A good employee is a thankful employee. Jobs are hard to find, and when you get a good one, its best not to leave it until you can find another good one to replace it."

How can you convince Boyd that you would be a valuable employee at Fitness World Gyms?

_____

_____

_____

What would you include in your résumé that will address Boyd's comments about prospective employees?

_____

_____

_____

How could you use your cover letter to demonstrate your strengths relative to the job description?

_____

_____

_____

STEP 2: QUESTION. The second step of the SQ3R method is to form questions. Take each heading and subheading, and turn it into a question. Questions beginning with the words *why, what,* and *how* are the most effective. Creating questions establishes a purpose for reading and enables you to stay focused.

STEP 3: READ. The third step of SQ3R is to read with the purpose of answering the questions you have formed. Do not read passively! Become actively involved in what you are reading by highlighting key phrases and making notes in the margin that answer your questions. When you read actively, you are reading effectively.

STEP 4: RECITE. The next step in this method is to recite what you have learned. After you have read the entire chapter, go back and recite the answers to the questions. Reciting is important for remembering what you have read.

STEP 5: REVIEW. The final step in the SQ3R method is to review the entire chapter. This step is similar to surveying, which you did in step 1. Once again, go back and read the introduction, headings, subheadings, and vocabulary, along with the special notes you made in the margins or text, the summary questions, and the study questions. Make note of any questions you are unable to answer or information that is unclear, so you can ask your instructor for clarification.

The second step of the SQ3R method is to form questions from headings and subheadings. Looking for answers to these questions will help you stay focused as you read.
Source: FOTOLIA

Tips for Highlighting Textbooks

Highlighting textbooks or articles is a technique to use when you are reading, learning, and studying. Keep the following suggestions in mind when highlighting:

1. Highlight approximately one-third of a paragraph—that is, the main ideas and supporting details.

2. Label main ideas and supporting details using different-colored highlighters.

3. Make marginal notes using special notations such as "RR" for "reread,"
   "DEF" for "definition," "1, 2, 3" for steps or other enumeration, and "!!!" for "important."

4. Take notes on the highlighted material, and add them to your class notes.

5. Never rely on highlighting that someone else has done in your text.

The SQ3R method provides a thorough way to read, study, and learn new information. If you complete all of the steps, you will, in all likelihood, be thoroughly learning the material. You will be amazed at how easy it is to understand your textbooks when you use the SQ3R technique. The results will be far reaching. You will feel better prepared for class, lectures will be clearer, and most of all, your scores on tests will improve significantly.

Reviewing Class and Textbook Notes

Reviewing is another effective study strategy. Reviewing your class notes and textbook notes on a regular basis will help you become more successful as a student. You should even translate or recopy them on the same day you recorded them.

Each time you sit down to study, the first thing you should do is review what you studied last. This is an important critical-thinking skill that will help you see the "whole picture." Just as warming up prepares you for exercising, reviewing your notes prepares you for studying. If you study each assignment without first reviewing prior lessons, then you will have difficulty seeing the relationship between the various lessons and assignments.

One way to review class and textbook notes is to write a summary of what you have learned. This activity should be done on loose-leaf paper and added to the class notes in your binder. Writing a summary should take you only 15 to 20 minutes. Use the following questions to help guide you through your summary:

1. What four important facts have I learned in class and/or while reading my textbook?
2. What four connections can I make between today's class notes or reading assignments and my previous notes and assignments?

Writing a summary can make preparing for exams much easier. Summarizing is also an excellent way to remember what you are studying, because you are thoroughly learning the material. Thorough learning is the key to remembering information.

Using notes from a class you are currently taking, answer the following questions.

What four important facts have you learned in class and/or while reading your textbook?

1. _____

2. _____

3. _____

4. _____

What four connections can you make between today's class notes or reading assignments and your previous notes or assignments?

1. _____

2. _____

3. _____

4. _____

Studying Math

MATHEMATICS: IT DOESN'T HAVE TO BE A ROADBLOCK! Do you dislike numbers? Are you terrified of math? If so, you are not alone. Academic counselors report that students who seek academic counseling most often express anxiety related to their math courses.

Many students, in fact, try to avoid taking math at all costs. Some students go so far as to choose degrees that require little or no math. They will even put off taking math courses until the last possible semester. Does this sound familiar?

Have you made math a self-imposed "roadblock"? If you are avoiding math in your educational journey, you are not making the best decisions. If you want to study nursing, computers, or engineering but feel you will never do well because of the math required in these curriculums, then you are creating your own roadblock! And you need to remove it!

Unfortunately, your attitude toward and/or fear of math can keep you from learning important mathematical skills that can help you in all areas of life. So, an important first step in mastering math is to overcome your math anxiety. Let us begin by identifying what has caused your anxiety or fear.

List some reasons you dislike math or suffer from math anxiety.

_____

_____

_____

> You can choose to throw stones, to stumble on them, to climb over them, or to build with them.
> —William Arthur Ward

Your list might include having been embarrassed by a peer or teacher, experiencing conflict with a teacher, feeling family pressure, having a desire to be perfect, being subject to poor teaching methods, having a perceived lack of a "mathematical mind," or other self-stereotyping. Your reasons for fearing math may be legitimate, but it is important that you let go of your fears. Your negative thoughts are keeping you from reaching your math potential.

Some math instructors believe that students who fail to control their math anxiety have real difficulty in being successful in math. If your anxiety is extreme, then consider seeking counseling to help you learn how to deal with it.

WHAT IS MATH? AND WHY DO YOU NEED IT? Math is about solving problems. Today, we live in a world that increasingly requires math skills of all students seeking a college degree, diploma, or certificate. For example, it is a fact that today's jobs are less labor intensive and that workers are being replaced by a variety of electronic and mechanical technologies. Technology, in fact, performs many tasks more effectively and efficiently than human beings. However, it lacks the ability to control or fix itself.

The key to getting a well-paying job is to develop skills in using, controlling, or repairing technology. Being able to work with technology requires having strong technical, mathematical, reasoning, and communication skills.

Students often ask, "Why do I have to learn this? I am never going to have to graph a quadratic function when I am a nurse!" Although it is probably true that a doctor or patient will never ask a nurse to graph a quadratic function, he or she will expect a nurse to be able to solve problems that require critical-thinking skills. Math helps students to develop their critical-thinking, or reasoning, skills. As a nurse, you must be able make logical and sequential decisions in solving problems. These are the same skills that employers—and not just those in the medical field—are going to require of you! These are, in fact, the skills you will expect to be mastered by those people solving *your* medical problems.

To be successful in math, you must become a problem solver. What often happens when an instructor decides to discuss solving word problems is that students let out heavy sighs, roll their eyes, and ask "Why do we have to do word problems?"

You should understand that this is the primary purpose of a math class: to apply mathematical knowledge to real-world applications. Finding the rate at which a disease will spread, calculating the appropriate slope of a handicap ramp, or using Newton's law of cooling to predict when a murder was committed are all examples of using math to solve real-world problems.

Hopefully, you are not one of those students who approach a math test by saying "I will master all the calculations so I don't have to worry about the word problems." Is that you?

When solving a word problem, you must read the problem, assess the information to identify what is relevant and irrelevant, decide on a strategy to solve the problem, use the appropriate steps to solve it, and interpret your results. (What does your answer mean?) To accomplish this, you must develop a math "toolbox." Your toolbox will include all the things you have learned over the years to assist you in solving problems, such as simplifying fractions, solving equations, making predictions, and so on. You will use these skills to decide on the strategy that will best allow you to solve the equation in a step-by-step process. In completing this process, you will pay attention to any details that will help you accomplish your goal. Math is a way of thinking. It is a skill you can develop.

Believe it or not, the skills a plumber applies to solving a problem with a water leak are similar to the skills a math student applies to solving a word problem. In fact, when you call a plumber, you are calling a problem solver. A plumber arrives in his or her truck (or toolbox) to fix your leaking faucet. Before arriving at your house, the plumber has not seen the leak. So upon arriving, he or she has to assess the problem before deciding about what tools are needed to fix the problem. After examining your situation, the plumber will most likely have to go back to the truck (or toolbox) to get the appropriate tool to stop your leak.

Another problem solver with similarities to a math student is an auto mechanic. When your car is not running properly, you take it to a mechanic. Using his or her repair shop (or toolbox), along with knowledge and tools, the mechanic assesses your car, decides what is wrong, and repairs your car.

Math students do the same thing when solving math problems. They must assess the problem, search their toolboxes for the right technique, and use a step-by-step approach to solve the problem. You, too, can learn to follow this process in solving your own math problems.

Medical doctors are also problem solvers that use skills similar to those of math students. Perhaps you are not feeling well and schedule an appointment with your doctor. He or she will ask you about your symptoms and run a few tests. The doctor will then review the tests and rule out what *is not* wrong with you to determine what *is* wrong with you. The doctor's toolbox is primarily his or her knowledge of medicine (obtained over years of studying), which is supported by the state-of-the-art technology found in most hospitals.

When you are in a math class, your instructor will provide you with the knowledge needed to do your homework and take your tests. You will have to do your part, however, and master the material and technology associated with it. You will, for instance, need to know how to use a graphing calculator or computer spreadsheet program. Only then will you be able to effectively solve math problems. It will not be easy. It will take a lot of work and commitment to succeed.

To be an effective problem solver, your basic skills must be intact! If you have not mastered basic math skills, you will struggle to solve problems. If it has been a long time since your last math class or if your skills have deteriorated, it will be necessary for you to refresh your knowledge of basic math fundamentals. The skills taught in courses such as arithmetic, pre-algebra, algebra I, and algebra II are the skills you will need in your toolbox to successfully complete a college math course.

We all use math everyday—whether we realize it or not. Think about the last few days. Did you pay for gas? Did you tip a server? Did you pay your bills? Did you balance your checkbook? Did you calculate your test average in a class? Did you help your child with their homework?

List the ways you have used math in the last few days.

_____

_____

_____

_____

As you can see from the previous activity, using math helps you solve a variety of problems. Math will be one of the courses you are required to take in college, and it will be used in the other classes you take. Solving drug calculations in nursing, maximizing profits or minimizing costs in economics, balancing equations in chemistry, and analyzing statistics in psychology are a few examples of using math in other classes.

What degree, diploma, or certificate are you earning?

_____

What math courses are required to earn your degree, diploma, or certificate?

_____

What classes have you taken that required you to use math?

_____

_____

_____

If math is a roadblock for you, it should be apparent that removing this obstacle is crucial to your success—not only in your math class but also in the other classes you take. Being successful in math is instrumental to your achieving your academic goal of earning a degree, diploma, or certificate.

HOW TO LEARN MATH The most important thing you need to realize about math is that it is not a course for someone merely interested in being a spectator. In math, you cannot just attend class, listen to the instructor, and take home a good grade!

Math requires you to get involved. It is almost impossible to listen to a math lecture and think you will magically understand how to factor a polynomial, find the zero of a function, or apply trigonometric knowledge to identifying the length of a side of a right triangle.

MATH —the four-letter word!

How you study math is different from how you might study history—a class where you may be successful by listening, taking a few notes, and reviewing those notes before a test. Math requires a great deal more effort. You should not only listen and take notes during class, but you should also practice the math concepts outside class.

Learning and studying math requires a great deal of time, patience, and determination. In fact, you need to be committed to daily drill and review. Math concepts build on each other. If you do not establish a good foundation of math knowledge, then you will struggle with later concepts. For example, it is very important to learn and understand the concept of the least common multiple (LCM), since finding the LCM of two unlike denominators will allow you to add and subtract fractions.

Several practical suggestions for studying math are provided in the following list. If you want to experience success with math, you must be willing to implement as many of these suggestions as possible:

- Purchase the student solutions manual that is sold with your math textbook.
- Learn relaxation techniques to control math anxiety.
- Read the directions carefully.
- Ask yourself if your answer makes sense.
- Redo problems to reinforce understanding and to check them.
- Use a scientific/graphing calculator, if permitted.
- Ask your instructor about math teaching aids available on your campus, such as videos, tutoring services, calculator workshops, and the like.
- Hire a tutor.
- Create a math study group.
- Copy all examples the instructor puts on the board.
- Above all, practice, practice, practice! Probably the most important suggestion for studying math is to complete all homework problems after each class. After completing your homework, identify any problems you are unable to solve or understand completely. Then make a visit to your instructor's office for extra help.

Your approach to studying math begins with your attitude toward it. If you have a defeatist attitude and think math is too difficult, then you are going to fail. It is that simple! You need to check your attitude at the door, dump all your excuses, remove all your roadblocks, and embark on your journey toward math success. Here are some guidelines for starting on that journey:

- *Identify the state of your math skills.* Take a placement test, which is always available and often required on a college campus. Caution! You should be prepared for the results of the test. If you have not been working on fractions, equations, and logarithms, then your score will most likely reflect these deficiencies in your knowledge. Taking a placement test will let you know where you should begin. You need to accept the results and remember not to let your pride or ego get in the way. In fact, the test may reveal that you need remediation! You may even need to begin with arithmetic and build your skills through college algebra. This may mean that you will need to take three or even five classes before you can take the one class you need to graduate. That is okay! News like this is tough for many students to accept, but if some time has passed since you last thought about math, then do not expect your skills to be there.

- *Select the best math teacher.* Do your math homework before you even begin a math class. If several different faculty members teach the math class you need, then find out about each one. The best way to determine which teacher meets your needs is to talk to other students or to your academic advisor.

- *Do a reality check.* Get used to the notion that taking a math class will require *a lot* of study time outside of class. Remember that math is not a spectator sport. People who decide to run a marathon do not just walk outside and run 26 miles. They have to work toward being able to accomplish their goal. In fact, they may have to begin by walking just 1 mile and training for weeks or months to be able to run 26 miles. If you work hard, then you can go the distance against any roadblocks you may encounter in your pursuit of math knowledge.

- *Identify resources.* Most college campuses offer free resources to assist you with your math courses. Does your college, for example, have a math tutoring center? Many students identify tutoring centers as vital to their finding help and to being able to pass math classes. Your textbook will also have resources that can help you—from online tutoring options to math videos.

Math concepts build on each other. If you do not understand something, get help from a fellow student, your instructor, or a tutor to avoid struggling with later concepts.
Source: SHUTTERSTOCK

- *Get to know your instructor.* Be willing to ask for help. It will let your instructor know you are serious and care about the course!
- *Do your homework.* Practice! Practice! Practice!

Critical Thinking

Have you ever been a spectator at a trial? Maybe you have been a member of a jury or observed in a courtroom to learn more about the judicial system. What is amazing is that while watching a trial, you can see critical thinking at its best. Lawyers are able to piece together information that is seemingly unrelated and weave a story that the jury decides is either credible or not credible. Critical thinking is a skill that can be developed, but it definitely takes practice.

Have you ever wondered why you have to take a public speaking course when your major is nursing? By looking at all of the requirements for a particular major, you can begin to see how the different parts fit together to enable you to be better educated and more successful. Yes, oral skills are important in nursing and in any other occupation requiring communication with other people. To be able to recognize and understand the connections between courses in your curriculum is to critically analyze and to begin the process of critical thinking.

To think critically means to think with a purpose—with an end in mind. Critical thinking is more than just logical thinking. It requires you to remove all emotional biases from your thought process and to focus on what is real. Critical thinking also requires you to question, analyze, and solve problems. It forces you to think on a higher level.

Why is critical thinking an important skill to develop in college? More often than not, employers state that an employee who is able to anticipate situations and then act proactively, instead of reactively, is the most valuable employee in the organization.

Thinking critically requires using emotional restraint when listening. Consider these topics, which typically are fairly controversial:

- Should modern science be allowed to clone humans?
- Should airline pilots be allowed to carry guns?
- Should certain illegal drugs be legalized?

When you considered each question, did you immediately form an opinion? Did an old argument or a bias surface? Did you allow your prejudices and emotions to cloud your thinking? If you immediately answered "yes" or "no" to any of these questions, then you probably allowed your emotions to color your thinking. You should try to focus on thinking with a more open mind.

Often, when we read or hear news reports, we are bombarded with information that can be biased or slanted. For this reason, it is important to get news from a variety of sources, so you can form an objective opinion. Realizing there is a difference between *beliefs* and *facts* is the first step in higher-order thinking.

Critical thinking is vitally important in manufacturing, technology, and health-related professions. Most likely, your instructors will force you to

> A great many people think they are thinking, when they are merely rearranging their prejudices.
> —William James

think objectively about situations by presenting real-life scenarios, problems, or case studies for you to review. When you sift through information without emotion, unearth facts, and then analyze all the information, you have engaged in critical thinking.

Although critical thinking is not an easy skill to develop, it is of vital importance to your success in college. If you are interested in developing your critical-thinking skills, consider taking a course in philosophy or logic.

Information Literacy

Information literacy is a relatively new term for a set of skills and competencies that good students and successful citizens have possessed since humankind began collecting, storing, and transmitting information. A few decades ago, skills in information literacy were termed *library skills*. In recent decades, however, information literacy has expanded to include not only library skills but also those computer and Internet skills that make searching for information easier and quicker.

It can truly be said that information literacy skills are vital to everyone living and working in the twenty-first century. To be information literate, a person must realize the need for information and be able to locate, evaluate, and use the information appropriately. In fact, people who are information literate possess the skills to be lifelong learners.

Most college instructors make the assumption their students are information literate. They believe students can determine facts from opinions and know how to gather reliable information about any subject. It is through this process of gathering information about a subject that much learning takes place.

Information literacy includes accessing information effectively, evaluating it critically, and using it accurately and creatively. Students need, however, to be cautioned that using information inappropriately (claiming another person's words or ideas as their own) is called *plagiarism* and is a serious academic offense. Although the Internet has greatly increased students' access to information, it has also made it easier for instructors to detect plagiarism.

In recent decades, technology has made a tremendous impact on society. One of the areas of greatest impact has been on information literacy. Information has never been more accessible than it is now. In fact, with smart phones and personal digital assistants (PDAs), information is literally available at our fingertips. Since technology plays such a prominent role in information literacy, it is imperative that students embrace it.

Skills such as navigating the Internet, sending and receiving e-mail, and conducting online searches have become essential for finding and using information. Using social media to connect with classmates, participating in discussion boards, blogging, and Twittering are additional skills that today's students need to master to gather information and communicate it to others.

The information literacy skills mentioned at the beginning of the previous paragraph have as their foundation basic computer skills (e.g., downloading, compressing, troubleshooting, saving, and filing), and these skills need to be mastered. In addition, the mastery of basic computer applications (e.g., word-processing software, spreadsheet software, presentation software, and web browsers) is fundamental to developing information literacy. The good news is that as technology changes (and it does rapidly), the computer and information skills you develop as a student can be transferred from one software application or technological device to another. Embrace it now, and you can have the skill for life!

Students seeking to maximize their information literacy should also be familiar with their college's website and its student Web portal. Students should also become proficient at using their college's Web-based learning management systems (LMSs). These Web applications make it easier for colleges to communicate information to students and for students to interact with their college.

What is your college's Web address?

_____

What learning management systems (LMSs) does your college use? (Perhaps Desire2Learn, Blackboard, WebCT, MyMathLab, etc.)

_____

_____

How many of your classes this semester use a LMS?

_____

_____

Select one of your courses, and search the Internet for websites that may assist you when studying for this course. Make a list of the helpful websites.

_____

_____

_____

_____

_____

_____

_____

_____

_____

Milestones

Now That You Are Here . . .

Now that you have completed the chapter, complete the Milestones checklist again.

Answer each statement by checking "Y" for Yes, "N" for No, or "S" for Sometimes.

1.	I am organized.	Y	N	S
2.	I follow a study plan.	Y	N	S
3.	I know how to study math.	Y	N	S
4.	I schedule time to study.	Y	N	S
5.	I know how to read a textbook.	Y	N	S
6.	I always attend class.	Y	N	S
7.	I know how to learn vocabulary.	Y	N	S
8.	I know how to use the SQ3R study method.	Y	N	S
9.	I highlight my notes and textbooks.	Y	N	S
10.	I have an appropriate place to study.	Y	N	S

How did you do? Do you feel more comfortable about basic study skills? Do you feel that reading this chapter has had a positive impact on how you perceive yourself as a student? Do you feel more self-assured and confident about your study skills at this point?

TIPS FOR SUCCESS

To be effective and efficient when studying, you need to . . .

- Get **organized**.
- Create and use a **notebook** system (a three-ring binder).
- Identify an appropriate study **environment** and study **time**.
- Create and use a study **plan**.
- Use the **SQ3R** studying method.
- Thoroughly **learn** material.
- Use **mnemonic** devices.

- **Summarize** class and textbook notes.
- Use **context clues** and **word analysis** to define unfamiliar words.
- Use the **tips** recommended to study math effectively.
- Use **index cards** for vocabulary, formulas, concepts, and so on.
- Above all, study over a **period of time** rather than "cramming" at the last minute.

APPLYING WHAT YOU KNOW

Learning how to learn is the single most important skill you need to master as a student. Knowing how to get organized and applying the strategies presented in this chapter will enable you to overcome even the most difficult academic subjects. There are no quick fixes or substitutions for studying. Achieving academic success requires organization and time.

Now that you have finished this chapter on learning how to study, refer to the Case Study about Gwen at the beginning of this book. Based on Gwen's situation, answer the following questions:

1. How would you help Gwen to identify her best study environment?

2. How would you explain to Gwen how to apply the SQ3R method to her PSY 201 class?

3. What recommendations would you make to Gwen to help her improve her grades in her MAT 101 class?

GETTING THERE ON TIME

Having effective study skills can greatly enhance your time-management skills. For instance, consider how much time you will save if you routinely use a study plan. After looking at your schedule, how much time *do* you allocate for studying? Is is adequate? Why is it important to schedule study time?

If you had problems answering any of these questions, go back over this chapter and review some of the tips provided. Efficient time management and effective study skills go hand in hand.

JOURNAL

The purpose of this journal exercise is to give you a chance to think about all that you have learned from this chapter on learning how to study. Think about what you have learned, and comment on your newly found knowledge. List the steps you are going to take to become more effective and efficient when studying.

As a result of reading this chapter and in preparing for my journey, I plan to

_____

_____

_____

_____

_____

_____

_____

_____

_____

_____

_____

_____

_____

_____

_____

_____

_____

_____

_____

_____

_____

_____

chapter 9

TEST-TAKING STRATEGIES

GETTING YOUR LICENSE

Ann, a 35-year-old single mother of three, decided to go back to school to make a better life for herself and her children. She wanted a better job, but she did not have the necessary skills to get one.

Ann had worked as an administrative assistant in a small law office for 10 years, and she enjoyed working in the legal profession. This work experience led her to apply for admission to the paralegal program at the local community college. She enrolled as a night student and decided to take just one course her first semester. Her advisor encouraged her to take PSY 201, a general requirement for her degree.

The semester seemed to be going fine until Ann's instructor announced the date of the first test. Ann was terrified of taking tests! She had never been very good at it. She knew, however, that if she did not overcome her fear, she would never be able to earn her degree and reach her goal.

Determined to do well, Ann began studying three weeks before the exam. She rewrote all of her notes on large index cards, and she divided the cards into six different groups. She carried the cards with her everywhere she went. She studied and studied and studied.

On the day of the exam, Ann felt confident she could pass. She completed the first part of the exam without much trouble. But when she attempted to answer an essay question, a wave of anxiety swept over her. She later remembered feeling very hot, realizing that her hands were sweating, and having a sense of being overwhelmed. Ann's mind had gone blank. She did not know how to write the essay. She did not even know where to begin. It was a timed test, and time was running out. Ann wanted to give up—to crawl into a corner and start crying.

Ann must have spent 15 minutes trying to get herself under control. Finally, she decided to write anything that came to mind. She would just do the best she could.

Ann was amazed at how easy the writing became after she took control of her anxiety. Because she had prepared for the exam and thoroughly learned the material, she was able to finish the test with confidence. At the next class meeting, she learned she had passed the exam.

Ann was so relieved and proud! Her hard work had paid off, and she knew she was going to make it. ■

It is natural for us to be nervous or anxious about taking tests, because we attach great importance to passing tests and to the grades we receive. You can improve your ability to succeed and decrease your test-taking anxiety by becoming testwise. Preparing for tests, knowing how to control your fears, and understanding types of tests will lessen your test anxiety.

This chapter will teach you how to take tests. It is important that you understand that the tips and techniques discussed should not take the place of studying for a test. The best way to be successful when taking a test is to learn the material thoroughly and to have a positive attitude. ■

> No one can make you feel inferior without your consent.
> —Eleanor Roosevelt

Objectives

AFTER READING this chapter, completing the exercises, participating in class, reading additional assignments issued by your instructor, and keeping an open mind, you will be able to do the following:

- Explain the purposes of tests.
- Describe how to control test anxiety.
- Use tips for reducing test anxiety.
- Apply general test-taking techniques.
- Use strategies for answering various types of test questions.

Milestones

Where Are You Now?

You have probably been taking tests your entire academic life, but how testwise are you? The 10 questions in this Milestones checklist are intended to make you think about the purposes of tests, test anxiety, and how to take various types of tests. Take a moment and respond to each statement.

Answer each statement by checking "Y" for Yes, "N" for No, or "S" for Sometimes.

1.	I am relaxed when taking a test.	Y	N	S
2.	I am always physically and mentally ready to take a test.	Y	N	S
3.	I look at tests as opportunities.	Y	N	S
4.	I read the entire test before answering any of the questions.	Y	N	S
5.	I know how to answer an essay question.	Y	N	S
6.	I know what qualifiers make a statement true or false.	Y	N	S
7.	I agree that you can never study enough for a test.	Y	N	S
8.	I always set aside time to study for tests.	Y	N	S
9.	I enjoy multiple-choice tests.	Y	N	S
10.	I enjoy fill-in-the-blank tests.	Y	N	S

Did you answer "Y" to most of the questions in this inventory? Do you feel good about your test-taking ability? If you do not feel confident, reading this chapter will help you become more self-assured. Pay close attention to the activities and exercises in this chapter, and after you complete them, you should feel more confident when taking a test or exam.

 ## WHY DO I HAVE TO TAKE A TEST?

Do you enjoy taking tests? Most students will answer "no!" They dread taking tests and believe teachers use tests to try to make their lives miserable.

Having this attitude can defeat you. You should view a test as an opportunity to show how much you know about a skill or subject. Each test should be viewed as a challenge that can help you learn and grow.

Tests are designed to measure how well you have mastered a skill or concept. In addition, taking a test is another opportunity for you to learn new information. Tests are a fact of life, and they are everywhere. The driver's test, the SAT, employee evaluations, and eye exams are all examples of types of tests. The list could be endless. Doing your best on a test might mean passing a course, earning a degree, or being promoted at work. Therefore, it is important that you accept test taking as a fact of life. If you prepare appropriately and have confidence, then your chance for experiencing success will be greatly enhanced.

List the reasons you believe instructors give tests.

1. _____
2. _____
3. _____
4. _____
5. _____

Your list may include the following reasons: to make my life miserable, to motivate me to learn and study, to show me what I do not know or understand, to show the teacher what needs to be taught again, to determine my grade in a course, and to learn information.

HELP!
I Need A Job

STINGRAY Boats Barry Godwin is the controller of Stingray Boats, located in Hartsville, SC. Founded in 1979 by Al Fink, Stingray has manufactured fiberglass pleasure boats for more than 30 years. Stingray markets its products throughout the United States, Canada, Europe, Australia, and the Middle East.

The quotations that follow present Godwin's comments about what he looks for in a Stingray employee.

1. WHAT DO YOU LOOK FOR IN AN EMPLOYEE?

"Ninety percent of our jobs are in manufacturing. These manufacturing jobs are for craftsmen. Whether it's a laminator, sewer, woodworker, assembler, or machinist, we look for people that can use their minds to fabricate parts with their hands."

What can you do to be the prospect Godwin is looking for in an employee?

_____
_____
_____
_____

2. WHY WOULD YOU HIRE ME?

"We hire motivated individuals that demonstrate the ability to utilize hand-eye coordination with a focus upon work quality."

What can you do to make Godwin want to hire you?

_____

_____

_____

_____

3. HOW CAN YOU GAIN A COMPETITIVE EDGE?

"Enrolling in classes that focus upon a trade, such as a machine tool technology, industrial electricity, auto-body repair, automotive technology, etc., gives applicants competitive skills."

What can you do to gain the competitive edge for a job at Stingray Boats ?

_____

_____

_____

_____

4. WHAT ROLE WOULD YOUR EDUCATION PLAY IN BEING ABLE TO GET A JOB WITH STINGRAY?

"Graduation from a school that emphasizes the development of technical skills demonstrates your ability to accomplish goals and develop skill sets we look for in applicants."

How can you demonstrate that your education is relative and competitive?

_____

_____

_____

_____

5. WHAT VALUE CAN YOU BRING TO THE COMPANY?

"A person starting a career today brings energy, ambition, and fresh skills to the workplace."

How can you convince Godwin that you would be a valuable employee for Stingray Boats?

_____

_____

_____

_____

What would you include in your résumé that will address Godwin's comments about prospective employees?

_____

_____

_____

How could you use your cover letter to demonstrate your strengths relative to the job description?

_____

_____

_____

CONTROLLING TEST ANXIETY

Okay, so test anxiety is a natural response. You may be nervous prior to taking a test, because you want to do well on it. Anxiety is created because you fear that you may not do as well as you had hoped.

Believe it or not, feeling some anxiety can actually increase your success in test taking, because you will be more aware, attuned, and alert. However, there are reasons other than the fear of failure that may make you anxious during a test.

List the reasons students become anxious during tests.

1. _____

2. _____

3. _____

4. _____

Perhaps your list includes such reasons as studying the wrong material, failing to study, not understanding the information, being afraid of becoming too nervous when taking a test, being unable to concentrate, experiencing distractions in the room, forgetting to bring materials needed during the test, failing to know the day of the test, and fearing being asked questions about information other than what was studied.

Which reasons in your list can be controlled?

1. _____

2. _____

3. _____

4. _____

Test anxiety can be frustrating, but you can overcome it if you allow yourself to relax. Test anxiety is dramatically reduced when you take control of the testing situation. By studying and thoroughly learning the material, using test-taking strategies, and entering the testing situation with confidence, you can gain the measure of control you need. As long as you give 100 percent (your very best), the outcome will be positive.

It is important to realize that we all have limitations and academic weaknesses. None of us is good at everything. Identify and focus on your strengths, and do not let your weaknesses hold you back.

When do you experience test anxiety?

_____

_____

_____

_____

> In this age, which believes that there is a shortcut to everything, the greatest lesson to be learned is that the most difficult way is, in the long run, the easiest.
> —Henry Miller

STRATEGIES FOR REDUCING TEST ANXIETY

- Thoroughly learn the material.
- Approach the test with a positive attitude.
- Chew gum or eat hard peppermint candy, as this helps relax some students.
- Take a break from the test by looking around or leaving the room, if permitted.
- Get a good night's sleep prior to the day of the test.
- Eat a healthy (high-protein) meal before the test.
- Arrive 20 minutes early.
- Take deep breaths if you find yourself becoming nervous.
- Enter the room with all the materials needed for the test.
- Reward yourself for a job well done!

Test anxiety is a fact of life for most students. Learning to cope with this anxiety is a step in the right direction. Understanding the different types of test questions and having strategies for dealing with each type can help you to reduce test anxiety.

 **PREPARING FOR TESTS**

Students prepare for tests in many different ways. The following sections provide examples of how three different students—the Dreamer, the Procrastinator, and the Planner—prepare for a test.

The Dreamer

The Dreamer is the student who fantasizes or dreams up excuses or scenarios that will keep him or her from having to take a test. The night before the exam, this student hopes for some type of national disaster, such as a snow-storm or flood, that will close school. Or this student hopes the instructor will be sick and class will be cancelled. Most students who are Dreamers will fail the test or just barely pass.

The Procrastinator

The Procrastinator is the student who puts off studying until the night before the test. This student will stay up all night cramming as much information as possible into his or her brain. Some Procrastinators will manage to make a C on the test, and a few of them—those who do their best work under pressure—will manage to do better than that.

The Planner

The Planner is the student who prepares for the exam. This student spends several days, even weeks, preparing. He or she reviews reading assignments, notes, and handouts. The Planner creates a mock test consisting of questions that might be asked. This student tends to be more confident and experiences less test anxiety than fellow test takers. The Planner has learned that there is no substitute for studying and preparing for a test. Planners are able to do their best on the exam and usually make the best grades.

Which type of test taker most closely matches your approach?

_____

Are you satisfied with the results of your approach to test taking? If not, what changes do you plan to make? Why?

_____

_____

_____

TEST-TAKING STRATEGIES

Instructors present information in a variety of ways, and how they ask questions on tests varies, too. When you spend time preparing for a test, your goal is to do well. You can accomplish this by understanding the different kinds of test questions and knowing the best ways to answer them.

Most students prefer certain types of test questions. For example, you may prefer multiple-choice questions over essay questions. Regardless of your preferences, you should be familiar with all kinds of questions and know how to answer them.

These are the most common kinds of test questions:

Matching questions

True/False questions

SOCIAL MEDIA . . .
Making Connections!

Being able to use the test-taking strategies discussed in this chapter will help you be more successful when taking tests. But keep in mind that nothing takes the place of studying for a test.

One of the best ways to study for a test is with a study group. Hopefully, you have established study groups for all of your classes. While there are many benefits to studying with a group, it also can be challenging—from determining an appropriate study location, to seeking transportation to and from the study session, to ensuring appropriate child care for your children, and so on.

One way to resolve these challenges is to take advantage of a free social media service known as Skype. Skype is a software application that allows making free video calls to others with a Skype connection and the appropriate computer hardware (microphone and webcam). In many cases, calls to landline and mobile phones (not on the Skype system) can also be made at a reduced rate.

Skype has grown in popularity because of its features of instant messaging and file transferring. Using a service like Skype allows you and your classmates to meet when you cannot get together in person. Using Skype, you can share study notes, discuss possible test questions, and quiz each other while preparing for an upcoming test. With Skype, you can hold study sessions at a time that works best for everyone and from the convenience of your home computer.

Follow the steps below for one of the classes you are taking:

1. Establish a study group.

2. Have each member in the group (if each member has a home computer) install Skype on his or her computer and create a Skype account. To do so, visit **Skype.com**. Each member will need a microphone and webcam.

3. Share Skype usernames with all members of your study group. Then select a time when everyone will be available to study for an upcoming test via Skype!

Multiple-choice questions

Short-answer questions

Essay questions

In addition to knowing about kinds of test questions, it is helpful to know general test-taking techniques and specific strategies for answering each kind of question. The information in this chapter will help you take tests and answer different kinds of questions. However, relying on the strategies alone will not help you. As previously mentioned (several times), the best approach to test taking is to thoroughly learn the material. Doing so reduces anxiety and builds confidence. Being prepared means increasing the odds of doing well on the test.

GENERAL TEST-TAKING TECHNIQUES

The following techniques apply to all tests, regardless of the types of questions they include:

1. Read and follow all directions.
2. Skim through the entire test before answering any of the questions. Skimming the questions allows you to get a feel for the test and will help you calm down.
3. Answer the easiest questions first.
4. Watch the time limits.
5. Read the questions carefully.
6. Answer every question, if there is no penalty for guessing.
7. Ask for clarification, if permitted.
8. Watch for words that may change the meaning of a question, such as *not*, *either/or*, and *always*. Underline or otherwise mark these words, since they indicate the way a question needs to be answered.
9. Answer the questions neatly.
10. Above all, *think positively!*

Using these techniques can increase your academic success. The following section offers explanations and simple examples of the various types of test questions.

When taking a test, skim through the entire test before answering any of the questions. Doing so will allow you to get a feel for the test and help you calm down.
Source: SHUTTERSTOCK

Strategies for Answering Matching Questions

Matching questions often test your understanding of people, places, things, dates, and vocabulary. The objective when answering a matching question is to match pieces of information in two columns. Here are strategies for answering matching questions:

1. Read through each column of items.
2. Match the easiest items first.
3. Lightly cross out or check off each item as it is matched.
4. Use the process of elimination to match difficult or unknown items.
5. Leave *no* questions blank, if there is no penalty for guessing.

Directions: *Match each term in column A with the appropriate characteristic in column B.*

A

1. Listening
2. Objective
3. Obstacle

B

a. Open minded
b. Hurdle
c. Attentive to sound

Strategies for Answering True/False Questions

In a true/false question, you indicate whether or not a statement is correct. To do so, make use of these strategies:

1. Read each statement carefully.
2. Pay attention to special words that may increase the likelihood the statement is true. Words such as *some, few, many,* and *often* are examples.
3. Pay attention to special words that may indicate the statement is false. Words such as *never, all, every,* and *only* are examples.
4. If any part of a statement is false, then the entire statement is false.
5. Answer every question, if there is no penalty for guessing.
6. When in doubt, choose "True."
7. Never try to fudge the answer by making the "T" look like it could be either a "T" or an "F."

Directions: *Write T for True or F for False.*

_____ 1. System-imposed time can always be controlled.

_____ 2. Everyone has the same amount of time.

_____ 3. Prioritizing is a technique that identifies what is most important.

Strategies for Answering Multiple-Choice Questions

Multiple-choice questions are commonly found on tests. In fact, most standardized tests use this format. When answering a multiple-choice item, you must answer a question or complete a statement by selecting the correct answer from two, three, or more possible choices. Use these strategies for answering multiple-choice questions:

1. Carefully read the question, and try to answer it in your mind before reading the answer choices.
2. Answers containing words such as *never, all, every, best, worst,* and *only* can usually be eliminated as choices.
3. Lightly cross out answers you feel or know are incorrect.
4. Read all the options before deciding on an answer.

MATH —the four-letter word!

As you know, math is used every day in a variety of ways. As a student, you have probably asked yourself the following question on numerous occasions: "What do I need to make on the final exam to pass this class?" Does this question sound familiar?

Calculating the grade you need to make on a final exam should not be difficult. Before you take any final exam, you should know what grade you need to achieve the overall course grade you desire: an A, B, or C. In some cases, a D is considered passing, as long as your overall GPA meets graduation requirements. (Please remember, though, that a course in which you earned a D usually will not transfer to another college!)

Here is an example of how to calculate the grade needed on a final exam:

Prior to taking a final exam, a student has a 76 average in the class. The final exam will count for 25 percent of the final grade. The student wants to make a B in the class, which will require an overall average of 80.

Since the 76 average represents 75 percent of the final grade, you would calculate the grade needed on the final exam as follows:

$$76(.75) + x(.25) = 80$$
$$57 + x(.25) = 80$$

$$x(.25) = 23$$
$$x = 23/.25$$
$$x = 92$$

This student needs to make a score of 92 percent or better on the final exam to earn a B in this class. Since the student's average was only a 76 going into the final exam, he or she will *really* need to prepare for the final to score 92 percent!

Now, let us change the scenario. A student has a 72 average, which counts as 75 percent of the grade, going into the final exam. This student also wants to make a B, which requires an 80 overall average. Since the final exam counts for 25 percent, is it possible for the student to get a B?

You would solve this problem as follows:

$$72(.75) + x(.25) = 80$$
$$54 + x(.25) = 80$$
$$x(.25) = 26$$
$$x = 26/.25$$
$$x = 104$$

This student needs to make a 104 percent on the final exam to get a B for the course. Clearly, it is impossible for this student to get a B!

Below are a couple of problems you can try:

1. A student has a 63 average in a class going into the final exam. The final exam counts for 20 percent of the final course grade. Can the student pass the class with a final average of 70 percent? *Note:* The 63 average counts for 80 percent of the student's grade.

2. A student wants to earn an A in history class. The student has an 88 average before the final exam. The final exam counts as 20 percent of the course grade, and the student must have an overall average of 90 to get an A. Can the student earn an A in this class?

3. You are taking an English class, and you have an 80 average before you take the final exam. The final exam counts as 15 percent of your grade. You would like to get a B in the class. To do that, you must have an overall average of 83. Can you earn a B?

Answers:

1. $63(.80) + x(.20) = 70$ $x = 19.6/.20$
   $50.4 + x(.20) = 70$ $x = 98$
   $x(.20) = 19.6$

Yes, this student can earn a passing grade, but the student will really have to work hard to get a 98 or better on the final exam. Hopefully, this example shows you how important it is to do well on your class assignments and tests leading up to a final exam. Do your best throughout the course so you have the highest possible average going into the final exam.

2. $88(.80) + x(.20) = 90$

$70.4 + x(.20) \quad = 90$

$x(.20) \qquad\quad = 19.6$

$x \qquad\qquad = 19.6/.20$

$x \qquad\qquad = 98$

Yes, this student will be able to get an A in history class. It appears the student has been working hard all semester, based on having an 88 average going into the final exam. As long as the student makes a 98 or better on the final exam, he or she will earn an A.

3. $80(.85) + x(.15) = 83$

$68 + x(.15) \quad\; = 83$

$x(.15) \qquad\quad = 15$

$x \qquad\qquad = 15/.15$

$x \qquad\qquad = 100$

It is possible for you to get a B in your English class, but you will have to get 100 percent on the final exam!

5. If the answers are dates or numbers, you can usually rule out the lowest and highest answers.

6. Answer each question, if there is no penalty for guessing.

Directions: Read each statement and circle the correct answer.

1. Which is not a step in the listening process?

    a. Receiving   c. Organizing

    b. Reacting   d. Accepting

2. Which behavior is not likely to increase self-esteem?

    a. Embracing the notion "I am responsible for my own life."

    b. Comparing yourself to others.

    c. Controlling your self-talk.

    d. Taking at least one positive risk a week.

3. Which strategy should not be used when answering a multiple-choice test question?

    a. Read the statement carefully.

    b. Lightly cross out incorrect answers.

    c. Read all options.

    d. Always choose answer "B."

Strategies for Answering Short-Answer Questions

Tests that include short-answer or fill-in-the-blank questions ask you to supply the needed information. These kinds of questions do not provide answer choices. To answer them, you must draw on the information you have stored in your long-term memory. Strategies for answering short-answer or fill-in-the-blank questions include the following:

1. Read each question carefully to make certain you understand how to answer it.
2. Provide answers that are short and to the point.
3. Never leave a blank, unless there is a penalty for guessing. Write in something, because getting a few points is better than none.
4. Look for answers or clues to the questions in the test itself.

Directions: Answer each question or statement by filling in the blank or writing a complete sentence.

1. *Name five of the seven strategies for answering true/false questions.*

   _____

   _____

   _____

2. *One of the best ways to prepare for test is to be a Planner. What does a Planner do?*

   _____

   _____

   _____

3. *Students who put off preparing for a test until the night before are known as*

   _____

Strategies for Answering Essay Questions

Answering an essay question gives you an opportunity to share what you know. Like a short-answer question, an essay question also requires that you supply the entire answer from memory.

Answering essay questions can be difficult if you lack certain skills. In particular, being able to write well and to think clearly are two skills you will need. Writing well includes the ability to choose the correct words, to punctuate correctly, and to organize your ideas. To do well answering an essay question, you also have to understand what the question is asking and to think clearly when preparing your answer. Many essay questions ask you to explain, to compare, to contrast, or to define an event or idea.

When you are asked *to explain* an event or idea, the instructor is asking you to give reasons an event took place or to offer a description of an idea. An instructor might ask you to explain the events leading up to a particular incident. In that case, you might list the events in chronological sequence (what happened first, next, and last).

EXAMPLE: *Explain* why you would rather travel on a small, two-lane highway than on a freeway.

> There are a number of reasons I would prefer to travel on a two-lane highway rather than a freeway. First, two-lane highways take you to places where freeways are unwelcome. Two-lane roads, for instance, can take you to small towns, through national forests, and to remote areas with beautiful scenery. Second, I prefer traveling on two-lane highways because of the terrible traffic on giant freeways. When traveling on two-lane roads, I don't feel like I'm constantly dodging other cars. Finally, on a two-lane road, I can take my time and enjoy the view. I can, for example, travel at my own pace and stop to look at something that captures my interest.

If an instructor asks you *to compare* one event or idea with another event or idea, he or she expects you to show how the two are alike. Similarly, if the instructor asks you *to contrast* two events or ideas, he or she expects you to show how they are different. An instructor will sometimes ask you *to compare* and *to contrast* at the same time. In this case, you simply tell how two events or ideas are alike and how they are different. (Writing one paragraph about similarities and another about differences is a good idea.)

EXAMPLE: *Compare and contrast* a freeway and a two-lane road (sometimes called a *country road*).

> Freeways and two-lane roads are alike in at least two ways. First, they are both pathways designed to take you to some other place. Second, they are alike in the materials used in their construction. Concrete and asphalt, for instance, are used to construct both freeways and two-lane roads.
>
> Although freeways and two-lane roads are similar in at least two ways, they are also different in several ways. Freeways take up much more space (because of the numerous lanes of traffic) than two-lane roads. And unlike two-lane roads, freeways don't run through picturesque small towns.

When you are asked *to define* a term, you are being asked to provide information about what something means. A definition should include placing the thing to be defined in a class of similar things and then telling how it is different from all of the other things in the class.

EXAMPLE: *Define* the term *freeway*.

> A freeway is a type of highway that has many lanes of traffic. The traffic is sometimes going in only one direction, but in most cases, there are numerous lanes of traffic going in two or more directions.

Note that in this definition, the freeway is put in a class (highways). The definition also tells how the freeway is different from other highways (many lanes of traffic).

Follow these strategies for answering essay questions:

1. When reading each question, pay particular attention to key words, such as *explain, compare and contrast,* and *define.* Make sure you are answering the question correctly.

2. Make a simple outline to organize your thoughts.

3. Be neat.

4. Use correct grammar, spelling, and punctuation.

5. Mention details, such as names, dates, and events.

6. Write a strong introduction and conclusion.
7. Do not write meaningless information just to fill the page. (Instructors cannot stand this!)

Directions: Explain why it is important to have a good education. In writing your response, use complete and coherent sentences.

_____

_____

_____

_____

_____

Milestones

Now That You Are Here . . .

Now that you have finished reading this chapter, complete the Milestones checklist again.
Answer each statement by checking "Y" for Yes, "N" for No, or "S" for Sometimes.

1.	I am relaxed when taking a test.	Y	N	S
2.	I am always physically and mentally ready to take a test.	Y	N	S
3.	I look at tests as opportunities.	Y	N	S
4.	I read the entire test before answering any of the questions.	Y	N	S
5.	I know how to answer an essay question.	Y	N	S
6.	I know what qualifiers make a statement true or false.	Y	N	S
7.	I agree that you can never study enough for a test.	Y	N	S
8.	I always set aside time to study for tests.	Y	N	S
9.	I enjoy multiple-choice tests.	Y	N	S
10.	I enjoy fill-in-the-blank tests.	Y	N	S

How did you do on this inventory after reading the chapter? Do you feel that your test-taking skills are as good as they should be? If not, go back over some of the tips and suggestions covered in this chapter. After all, being a successful student can often be demonstrated by being a successful test or exam taker. Take some time to master this skill now, because it will pay huge dividends in the future.

TIPS **FOR SUCCESS**

To become a successful test taker, you need to . . .

- Create a study schedule as soon as a test is scheduled.

- Ask your instructor what specific information will be tested.

- Find out how you will be tested—for example, if you will be asked essay or multiple-choice test questions.

- Write a list of questions you think might be asked on the test.

- Form a study group for reviewing the material several days before the test.

- Review your notes and reading assignments, and make a list of questions about topics that still do not make sense to you. Then ask the instructor for clarification.

- Above all, get a good night's sleep the night before the test, and eat a healthy meal before the test.

Effective test taking involves careful preparation. Create a study schedule, study individually and with a group, review the material, and get a good night's sleep before the test.
Source: ISTOCKPHOTO

APPLYING WHAT YOU KNOW

It is natural to be nervous or anxious when taking a test. But by learning test-taking skills and techniques, you can ease your anxiety and become an effective test taker. Providing those skills and techniques was the goal of this chapter.

Now that you have finished this chapter on test-taking strategies, refer back to the Case Study about Gwen at the beginning of this book. Based on Gwen's situation, answer the following questions:

1. How would you help Gwen learn how to control her test anxiety?

    _____

    _____

    _____

2. How would you explain to Gwen how to write effective essay responses on her MUS 105 final exam?

    _____

    _____

    _____

3. You have discovered that Gwen is a procrastinator when it comes to preparing for her tests. Explain how you would help Gwen implement a plan for studying for tests.

    _____

    _____

    _____

GETTING THERE ON TIME

Can you see any connection between time management and test taking? What is the best way to manage your time when the test is timed? What role does time management play when you are preparing for a test? Do you ever feel that you just do not have enough time to prepare for a test? If so, why? What can you do differently so that you will have enough time to adequately prepare for a test?

Luckily, time management is a learned skill. Test-taking skills are learned, too. In short, you can learn to be successful in school by using time-management tips discussed elsewhere in this book, and you can be a successful exam or test taker by following some of the guidelines provided in this chapter.

JOURNAL

The purpose of this journal exercise is to give you a chance to think about all that you have learned from this chapter on test-taking strategies. Think about what you have learned and comment on your newly found knowledge. List the steps that you are going to take to become a more effective and efficient test taker.

As a result of reading this chapter and in preparing for my journey, I plan to . . .

chapter 10

HEALTH AND WELLNESS: MIND, BODY, SPIRIT

EXTENDING YOUR WARRANTY

Jane is a 26-year-old student and the mother of two young children. She married right out of high school and had her first child at age 19. To help her husband make ends meet, Jane began working part time that same year. With the arrival of her second child, her part-time job evolved into a full-time job.

Jane's young husband did not continue his education after high school and is working a low-paying, laborious job in a local manufacturing company. Jane's mother tries to help with child care responsibilities. Nevertheless, Jane depends more and more on a day care center for her children.

As Jane approached her twenty-seventh birthday, she decided to fulfill her lifelong dream of becoming a dental hygienist. Jane was not academically prepared for the rigors of the hygienist program, however, and was required to take several prerequisite courses her first year.

During this first year of college, Jane's life is very complicated. She has very little time for her children, her husband, or herself. She cuts many corners, including some that affect the basics of good health. She is cutting back on her work hours but cannot give up working altogether. She gets up early in the morning and goes to bed late at night. She eats almost exclusively at fast-food restaurants. With no time for exercise, no time for adequate rest, no time for well-balanced meals, and no time for family, friends, or church, Jane is beginning to reach the point of total exhaustion.

Jane has resorted to drinking coffee or soft drinks to get the stimulating effects of caffeine. She uses coffee to wake up in the morning, and that is usually all she has for breakfast. She also uses coffee to keep her awake late at night to study. Jane is also smoking as a way to relax a few minutes between classes or when going from class to work.

After two successful semesters in the dental hygienist program at the local community college, Jane is mentally, physically, and spiritually drained. One day during a class clinical, Jane passed out and was hospitalized. Jane is ignoring the importance of the harmony of her mind, body, and spirit. And now, she will have to repeat a semester while taking time to recuperate from her rundown condition. ■

The management of your health is just as important as the management of your time. Health and wellness go hand in hand and require a certain amount of planning, implementation, and follow-up. ■

> Look to your health; and if you have it, praise God, and value it next to a good conscience; for health is the second blessing that we mortals are capable of; a blessing that money cannot buy.
> —Izaak Walton

Objectives

THIS CHAPTER is designed to help you understand the importance of health and wellness and to learn to manage your own health to ensure a well-balanced approach to wellness.

After reading this chapter and completing the exercises, you will be able to do the following:

- Understand the concept of *wellness* by identifying your strengths and weaknesses relative to health and wellness.
- Understand the eight components of the NEWSTART Lifestyle Program.
- Identify the stressors in your life and determine ways to cope with them.

- Determine if you have an addiction and understand how to address addictive behavior.
- Understand how to develop and implement a wellness program.
- Develop and maintain a well-balanced mental, physical, and spiritual life.

Where Are You Now?

Using the Milestones checklist, take a few moments and determine where you stand in relation to making health and wellness decisions.

Answer each statement by checking "Y" for Yes, "N" for No, or "S" for Sometimes.

1. I know how to develop a wellness plan.	Y	N	S
2. Eating well-balanced meals is important to me.	Y	N	S
3. I get adequate rest each day.	Y	N	S
4. I drink six to eight glasses of water each day.	Y	N	S
5. I understand the importance of getting adequate but not excessive sunshine.	Y	N	S
6. Exercising on a regular basis is important to me.	Y	N	S
7. Moderation and temperance in food and drink is important to me.	Y	N	S
8. Getting fresh air is important to me.	Y	N	S
9. Believing in a supreme being is important to me.	Y	N	S
10. I understand that being healthy helps me be a better student.	Y	N	S

If you have more "No" and "Sometimes" than "Yes" answers to these statements, do not be too concerned at this point. This chapter is designed to address each component of an effective wellness program and to provide you with valuable lessons and tools for becoming better balanced mentally, physically, and spiritually.

IDENTIFYING HEALTH AND WELLNESS STRENGTHS AND WEAKNESSES

Are you healthy? How do you know? Do you see a physician every year? Do you eat right? Do you get enough sleep, water, fresh air, sunshine, and so on?

These and other questions have been integrated into an assessment exercise (Exercise 10.1) designed to identify your strengths and weaknesses in terms of health and wellness. Completing this assessment will take about 25 minutes.

Exercise 10.1 is a three-step exercise. The first step is to read each question and assign it a score of 1 to 5 (with 5 being the highest). The next step is to add these numbers to compute an overall score. In the final step, transfer or record the 25 individual question scores from the top of page 218 to the

> Nobody can be in good health if he does not have all of the time, fresh air, sunshine, and good water.
>
> —Flying Hawk

Exercise 10.1 Identifying Health and Wellness Strengths and Weaknesses

Answer the following questions by writing in a score of 1 to 5, with 5 being the highest or most truthful on the "yes/no" spectrum.

_____ 1. Do you know what your blood pressure is?

_____ 2. Do you exercise at least three to five times a week for 30 minutes?

_____ 3. Most people need six to eight glasses of water each day. Do you get your share?

_____ 4. Do you eat and drink in moderation?

_____ 5. Do you have a positive spiritual life?

_____ 6. Do you know what your HDL and LDL cholesterol levels are?

_____ 7. Most adults need seven to eight hours of sleep each night. Are you getting adequate sleep?

_____ 8. Are you getting enough vitamin D–producing sunlight each week?

_____ 9. Are you a nonsmoker?

_____ 10. Do you pray or meditate on a daily basis?

_____ 11. Do you know your ideal body weight?

_____ 12. Do you take a daily break from technology (e-mail, cell phone, beeper, etc.)?

_____ 13. Are you getting enough fresh air each day?

_____ 14. Are you a nondrinker?

_____ 15. Do you support others through prayer or meditation?

_____ 16. Do you have a family doctor, and do you get an annual physical?

_____ 17. Do you practice positive self-talk?

_____ 18. Do you have one indoor plant in each room of your house and workplace?

_____ 19. Do you know that caffeine addiction has been linked to health problems?

_____ 20. Do you trust in a divine power?

_____ 21. Do you know what causes diabetes, cancer, and heart disease?

_____ 22. Weight-resistance exercise is good for all adults. Do you include it in your exercise program?

_____ 23. During the summer, do you take steps to prevent getting sunburned?

_____ 24. Are you aware of the problems of prescription and over-the-counter drug abuse?

_____ 25. Are you growing spiritually?

_____ Total Score

Health Status	Exercise & Rest	Water, Air, & Sunlight	Temperate, Drug-Free	Spiritual Well-Being
1. _____	2. _____	3. _____	4. _____	5. _____
6. _____	7. _____	8. _____	9. _____	10. _____
11. _____	12. _____	13. _____	14. _____	15. _____
16. _____	17. _____	18. _____	19. _____	20. _____
21. _____	22. _____	23. _____	24. _____	25. _____
Total Scores				
_____	_____	_____	_____	_____

corresponding question numbers on the bottom of page 218. For example, transfer the score for question 1 to 1 under the "Health Status" column. Transfer the score for question 2 to 2 under the "Exercise & Rest" column.

After identifying your strengths and weaknesses and determining ways to build on your strengths and improve on your weaknesses, the next step is to develop a lifelong plan. You will use this plan on a daily basis to ensure that you live a healthy and productive life.

An overall score of 100 to 125 is outstanding. It indicates that you have very effective health and wellness habits and skills. An overall score below 75 indicates that you may have one or more areas that need improvement. But which areas are strong and which are weak?

This section provides you with an indication of your strong areas, in which you have effective health and wellness skills or habits, and your weak areas, which need some improvement. As mentioned earlier, transfer the 25 scores on the top of page 218 to the corresponding question numbers on the bottom of page 218.

A score of 20 or higher in any of the five areas indicates strength in that area. A score of 15 or higher indicates a strong area that can be improved on. A score of less than 14 indicates a weak area that needs improvement.

Once you have identified your strong and weak areas, you can return to the 25 questions to look for solutions or ways to improve on any area of strength or weakness. For example, question 2 and every fifth question thereafter deals with exercise and rest and their impact on health and well-being. If you scored low in "Exercise & Rest," questions 2, 7, 12, 17, and 22 provide effective practices of good health that, when implemented, will improve overall wellness.

COMPONENTS OF A HEALTHY LIFESTYLE

In 1978, the Weimar Institute of Health and Education, a nonprofit organization, began fulfilling its mission to serve the needs of others in health improvement and quality education. The institute established the NEW-START Lifestyle Program, and in its residence program in California, it has taught thousands of people to become healthier and to maintain a wellness lifestyle. However, you do not need to travel to California to benefit from this very effective health and wellness program. The eight components of the NEWSTART program are:

1. Nutritious food
2. Exercise
3. Water
4. Sunlight
5. Temperance
6. Air
7. Rest
8. Trust

Exercise, fresh air, nutrition, and rest are all important components of overall health and wellness.
Source: SHUTTERSTOCK

MATH — the four-letter word!

Is math relevant to health and wellness? Absolutely! Math and numbers are extremely important in an effective health and wellness program. Calories, body mass index, and timing of specific exercise programs all generate important numbers and math computations for students who are serious about their health.

BMI, or *body mass index*, is a measure of body fat that applies to adult men and women. BMI is useful in evaluating whether someone is overweight or obese. It is an estimate of body fat based on the person's height and weight. BMI is also a good gauge for measuring risk for diseases that can result from having excess body fat. The higher your BMI, the higher your risk for heart disease, high blood pressure, type-2 diabetes, gallstones, breathing problems, and certain cancers.

How can you calculate your BMI? Divide your weight in pounds by your height in inches squared, and multiply that figure by 703. Here is the formula:

$$[\text{Weight [in pounds]}/\text{Height}^2 \text{ [in inches]} \times 703]$$

Here is an example of calculating BMI for a female college student:

Gwen, from the case study, is 5´ 5´´ and weighs 165 pounds. She completed the formula as follows:

1. Gwen figures out that her height in inches is 65´´.
2. She calculates that 65´´ squared (65 times 65) equals 4,225.
3. She divides her weight, 165, by 4,225, which equals 0.0391.
4. She multiplies 0.0391 by 703, which is 27.4873.
5. The resulting number, which is rounded to 27.49, is Gwen's BMI.

So, what does Gwen's 27.49 BMI indicate about her health? Here are the BMI categories:

Underweight < 18.5
Normal weight = 18.5–24.9
Overweight = 25.0–29.9
Obesity = 30 or greater

By looking at this list, Gwen is just over the midpoint of the "Overweight" category. She is not far from the "Obesity" category. Gwen needs to make some changes in her life and lifestyle, if she is to take a preventive approach to the diseases mentioned earlier.

Use the formula and steps in the example and calculate your BMI.

$$[\text{Weight [in pounds]}/\text{Height}^2 \text{ [in inches]} \times 703]$$

_____

_____

_____

What is your BMI category?

_____

To check your answer, use your computer or smart phone and go to the Internet. Find a BMI calculator, and key in your numbers. Your BMI will automatically be calculated. Does it match your calculation? If not, try again.

You should recognize these eight components as the basis for the health and wellness assessment you completed in Exercise 10.1. The following sections touch on each of these areas, providing information and an understanding of the concept, as well as an approach that can fit into your wellness plan.

Nutritious Food

Food is the foundation for any health and wellness program. There are literally hundreds of diet programs on the commercial market today—each promising a well-balanced, nutritious diet. Where do you start to ensure that your diet is nutritious and enjoyable?

The U.S. Department of Agriculture (USDA) developed what has become known as the food pyramid, which was their guide for a well balanced diet. In 2011 it was replaced with the MyPlate concept.

The purpose of these food pyramids and MyPlate is to provide a pictorial representation of how much you should eat from each food group to have a balanced daily diet.

You should plan your meals following a well-thought-out plan to ensure a nutritionally balanced diet.

Recent studies have shown that Americans consume less than the minimum servings recommended for the fruit, dairy, grain, and vegetables and exceed the recommended ranges for fats and sugars. Is it any wonder that the United States leads the world in a number of lifestyle conditions and diseases such as obesity, cancer, diabetes, high blood pressure, and heart attacks?

As a student with many different responsibilities (college, work, family), you are likely find it difficult to plan your meals each day. This difficult task can be simplified, however, by using the inverted food pyramid as a guide.

Figure 10.1 is an inverted food pyramid that we have developed to assist you in your daily meal planning emphasizing the importance of fruits, vegetables, whole grains, and nuts in your diet. You should have a good portion of your diet come from these other food groups. Most Americans have too much meat and dairy in their diets.

Over the past 15 years, studies have identified foods that lead to longevity, as well as so-called perfect foods. Use these foods when planning your meals each day, and take advantage of the most nutritious foods that have been identified.

Listed in no particular order, these foods include soy protein powder, soymilk, and tofu; whole grains and whole-grain and enriched cereals; lowfat milk and yogurt; nuts and legumes; tomatoes and tomato sauce; citrus fruits and juices; broccoli; spinach; red grapes; blueberries; garlic; olive oil; green tea; and water.

Let nutrition be your medicine.
—Hippocrates

If we could give every individual the right amount of nourishment and exercise, not too little and not too much, we would have found the safest way to health.
—Hippocrates

Figure 10.1 Inverted Food Pyramid

FOOD GROUPS	EXAMPLES
Eat All You Want of Any Whole, Unrefined, Plant-Based Food	
Fruits	orange, okra, kiwi, red pepper, apple, cucumber, tomato, avocado, zucchini, blueberry, strawberry, green pepper, raspberry, butternut squash, pumpkin, blackberry, mango, eggplant, pear, watermelon, cranberry, acorn squash, papaya, grapefruit, peach
Vegetables	broccoli, cauliflower, cabbage, Swiss chard, collard greens, celery, asparagus, mustard greens, Brussel sprouts, turnip greens, beet greens, bok choi, basil, cilantro, parsley rhubarb, spinach, artichokes, kale, lettuce, potatoes, beets, carrots, turnips, onions, garlic, ginger radish, rutabaga, green beans, soybeans, peas, peanuts, beans (all kinds), mushrooms.
Nuts	walnuts, almonds, macadamias, pecans, cashews, hazelnuts, pistachios
Whole grains	wheat, rice, corn, rye, oats, barley, buckwheat, millet
Minimize Your Consumption of These Foods	
Refined	pastas except whole-grain varieties
Carbohydrates	white bread, crackers, sugars, and most cakes and pastries
Oils	corn oil, peanut oil, olive oil, vegetable oil
Fish	salmon, tuna, cod
Avoid or Eat as Little as Possible of These Foods	
Meat and poultry	steak, hamburger, lard, chicken, turkey
Dairy	eggs, milk, yogurt, and products with high egg content (such as mayonnaise, egg salad, etc.)

These recent studies have also created lists of super foods. These foods contain more nutrients per calorie than most other foods, and consuming them on a regular basis can help you maintain your weight, fight off disease, and live longer. Best of all, you will look and feel better. Here is a list of superfoods:

Raw, unsalted almonds, walnuts, and flax seeds: Help you maintain a healthy heart

Beans: High in protein and fiber and help you cut calories without feeling deprived

Blueberries: Packed with antioxidants that protect cells from damage and have anti-inflammatory properties

Broccoli: Helps fight cancer and boosts the immune system

Garlic: Might help improve poor cholesterol levels and lower blood pressure

Whole-grain oats: Can help reduce cholesterol when part of a regular diet

Spinach: Helps maintain eye health

Tomatoes: Contain the antioxidant lycopene, help stimulate the immune system, and might slow degenerative diseases

Exercise

What is involved in an exercise program? There are really three components to an effective exercise program: stretching, weight-resistance training, and cardiovascular training.

To begin any exercise program, you must warm up the major muscle groups of your body. Stretching is the best way to warm up your muscles and get into the mode of exercising. Weight-resistance training or weight lifting provides strength and muscle tone. The body functions better when it maintains adequate muscle mass. After age 30, an average adult who does not follow a proper exercise program loses about 1 percent of his or her muscle mass each year and gains additional fat. If you are counting calories, keep in mind that muscle burns more calories than fat.

To prevent heart disease and obesity, cardiovascular exercise is essential. You need at least 30 minutes of cardiovascular exercise three times a week to strengthen your heart and respiratory system. To lose weight, you need to do between 45 to 60 minutes of cardiovascular exercise five times a week.

Where do you start? Naturally, you should talk to your doctor before starting any exercise program. After you have your doctor's okay, see what programs and facilities are available at your college. If you are able to pay a monthly fee, join a health club, YMCA, or a hospital-based wellness center. Most of these facilities have discounts for students and employ professional trainers. Walking, running, or bicycling are good programs to start independently.

All forms of exercise and activity are beneficial. Make some form of exercise and activity a part of your daily routine. *Source:* SHUTTERSTOCK

To acquire and maintain good health, exercise must be a part of your daily routine. It helps you feel good. It lowers your blood pressure. It lowers your LDL cholesterol, the bad cholesterol, and often raises your HDL, the good cholesterol. Exercise even lifts depression and relieves anxiety and stress.

Make exercising a fun and natural part of your life and find an exercise partner.

HELP!
I Need A Job

Jon Maynell is the program manager for Lite Machines Corporation, of West Lafayette, Indiana. Lite Machines develops, manufactures, markets, and supports unmanned aerial vehicle (UAV) platforms and control systems for military, law enforcement, and civilian/industrial applications.

We asked Jon to answer the following questions about potential employees. After reading each of Jon's comments, answer the question addressed to you as a prospective employee.

1. WHAT DO YOU LOOK FOR IN AN EMPLOYEE?

"Beyond the obvious straightforward analysis of skill set and experience relative to job requirements, we look heavily at how personable they are, how seasoned they are, specifically trying to find those skilled workers that seem open minded/flexible enough to perhaps adopt new ideas and methods within their discipline."

What can you do to be the prospect Jon is looking for in an employee?

_____

_____

_____

2. WHY WOULD YOU HIRE ME?

"Because you would have demonstrated not only a complimentary skill set and level of experience, but you're seasoned, which means you've lived through a few projects/assignments so you know how they can differ in their techniques and approaches, and you've demonstrated throughout the interviewing process that you're openminded and flexible enough to embrace any methods or workflow that we'll be presenting you with within your discipline."

What can you do to make Jon want to hire you?

_____

_____

_____

3. HOW CAN I GAIN A COMPETITIVE EDGE?

"The qualities outlined in question 2 are not exhibited by very many candidates. Someone who embraces new ideas, or better yet, has a history of embracing new methods and ideas, or who is continually looking for new and better ways of doing something would definitely have an edge over the vast majority of the candidate base."

What can you do to gain the competitive edge for a job at Lite Machines?

_____

_____

_____

4. WHAT ROLE WOULD MY EDUCATION PLAY IN BEING ABLE TO GET A JOB WITH YOU?

"Education plays a role, but it definitely just gets you in the door—into an interview. From there, it's your 'personability' and willingness to try new methods and embrace new ideas that will set you apart from the sea of other candidates."

How can you demonstrate that your education is relevant and competitive?

_____

_____

_____

5. WHAT VALUE CAN I BRING TO YOUR COMPANY?

"If you're openminded enough and motivated to continually try to find new and better ways of doing things, your biggest value to us would be two-fold: (A) We'd be confident that we could entrust you with our proprietary methods for designing/prototyping/manufacturing aerial robotic systems, and (B) we might be able to look forward to some new ideas from you on how we might even improve the status quo here in terms of workflow and efficiency."

How can you convince Jon that you would be a valuable employee at Lite Machines?

_____

_____

_____

What would you include in your résumé that will address Jon's comments about prospective employees?

_____

_____

_____

How could you use your cover letter to demonstrate your strengths relative to the job description?

_____

_____

_____

Water

Water, the third component of NEWSTART, plays an important role in every bodily function. Your body cannot function without water. It makes up almost 70 percent of your body. Water eliminates body heat through sweat; carries oxygen, carbohydrates, and fats to muscles; flushes waste products from your body; lubricates your joints; curbs your appetite; and assists in your digestion process. You need about 8 to 10 cups of water each day to maintain good health, more if you are exercising or the weather is very hot or cold. One simple axiom is to drink enough water to keep your urine pale.

Soft drinks, tea, coffee, and alcoholic drinks do more harm than good when it comes to adequate water intake. If you are thirsty, you have already lost 1 percent of your body's water. Your best choice of drinks to quench that thirst is water.

How can you get enough water into your body each day? The best thing to do is to drink two to three glasses of water at the start of the day. Remember that your body has had no food or water for 8 hours. Drink water during breaks, just before lunch and dinner and when you are exercising. Following this routine is a great way to ensure you are getting plenty of water. Try not to drink too much during a meal, however. Water can dilute saliva and stomach acids and prevent food from being digested properly.

How can you remember to drink water and to stay on a routine? One suggestion to help keep you on track is to carry a bottle of water wherever you go. Remember that water is nature's perfect beverage.

Sunlight

Is the fourth component of NEWSTART a friend or foe? Sunlight is both a friend and an enemy to the body. We know that excessive exposure to sunlight causes sunburn, wrinkles, and eventually skin cancer. However, adequate sunlight provides the body with that much-needed vitamin D, which enables the body to pick up calcium from the intestines for use in building healthy bones.

Sunlight can also help your body's immune system, alleviate arthritic joint pain, lowers blood cholesterol levels , and it is a great germ killer.

A few minutes of sunshine on your face and hands each day or as little as 15 minutes three times a week is all the sunlight you need. Modest tanning can be protective. Always use sunscreen if you are going to be exposed to direct sunlight for more than 15 minutes. Just remember that you should never get sunburn.

Temperance

Have you ever heard the sayings "Everything in moderation" and "Live a balanced life?" What do they really mean, and what impact do they have on our health?

It is no secret that Americans eat and drink too much. We indulge in the finer things of life. Too much of a good thing can be a bad thing, however, when our health is concerned. Surveys show that the majority of older Americans—those that live into their 80s and 90s—do not smoke or consume alcoholic drinks.

One of the problems experienced by Jane, in our story at the beginning of this chapter, was a dependence on coffee and soft drinks to get through each day. She really needed more sleep, but instead, she depended on a drug, caffeine, to help keep her alert.

The key is balance and avoiding unnecessary stimulants. NEWSTART is a program designed to create a balanced, healthy lifestyle. Once you have started a wellness program, stick with it for 30 days, then review your progress. That good feeling of well-being will be enough to keep you on track.

Air

Air? What does air have to do with wellness? *Air* is "the breath of life." Oxygen in air is essential for well-oxygenated cells and contributes to our overall well-being. It is vital for each cell in our bodies.

Air pollution has become a problem in many of our buildings and in many big cities. But what can we do to ensure having a good source of fresh air and oxygen for our bodies and minds? One of the first things is to exercise on a regular basis, following a program that includes deep breathing. In addition, several times during the day, take several deep-breathing breaks. It will energize and refresh you. We can also use houseplants which are powerful natural air cleaners.

Houseplants have been shown to remove nearly 87 percent of indoor air pollutants within a 24-hour period. A simple rule for houseplants is to have one plant for every 100 square feet of floor space. This simple rule applies for your work area, as well. To ensure having fresh, oxygenated air, make sure you have at least one houseplant for each room of your house and one for your office or workspace. The best indoor house plants that help provide clean air are English ivy; spider plant, peace lily; Chinese evergreen; bamboo palm; snake plant; heartleaf and elephant ear philodendron; cornstalk dracaena; Janet Craig dracaena; weeping fig; and golden poths.

Plants are the lungs of the world!
—Dewitt S. Williams

Rest

In the story at the beginning of this chapter, inadequate rest (primarily, sleep) was Jane's biggest health problem. It is a problem for many of us in today's fast-paced world. Surveys of high school students have shown that A- and B-grade students usually get 7.5 hours or more of sleep each night. Once they fall below this average, their grades begin to decline.

Sleep, the seventh component of the NEWSTART Lifestyle Program, is the time when your body rests and restores its energy. It is also an active state that is critical to good health. But how much sleep do we need? Young children need 10 to 12 hours of sleep each night, whereas adults need 7 to 8 hours. It varies a great deal among adults, but 7 to 8 hours is a good benchmark.

To get a good night's sleep, try the following suggestions.

- Try to go to bed at the same time every night and to get up at the same time every morning.
- During the day, get exposure to natural outdoor light.
- Make sure that your bedroom is cool, dark, and quiet.
- Eat your evening meal at least four hours before you go to sleep. Having your stomach at rest is conducive to getting a good night's sleep.
- Use a daily planner to maintain a regular schedule of going to bed, getting up, eating, and exercising.

The body responds better to regularity and good habits of wellness. Sleep habits, like all habits, are created through repetition.

Trust

In recent years, several research studies have shown that hospitalized patients who believed in a divine power, prayed on a regular basis, and had a circle of friends praying for them had a shorter time in recovery. In the book *The Stress Solution*, Miller, Smith, and Rothstein (1994) state, "Having trust in a higher power decreases feelings of isolation and abandonment and gives life a sense of meaning and purpose. Developing a source of guidance in your life will help put stressful events in perspective."

Having trust in a divine power and praying are important parts of a balanced wellness plan. During the Vietnam War, American prisoners of war who survived captivity in North Vietnamese prison camps testified that it was their strong faith that kept them alive. All of us can learn from men and women of strong faith.

Dr. Dale Matthews, in his book *Faith Factor, Proof of the Healing Power of Prayer* (1999), after reviewing more than 200 studies on the connection between health and faith in a supreme being, concluded that a weekly observance of faith is good medicine. In his studies, faith had a very positive effect on individuals' ability to deal with drug abuse, alcoholism, depression, cancer, high blood pressure, and heart disease.

The ultimate wellness plan is one that is not just designed for mental and physical health but that includes spiritual health, as well. True wellness involves spiritual growth that brings quality, fulfillment, and hope for the present and the future.

Early to bed and early to rise, makes a man healthy, wealthy, and wise.
—Benjamin Franklin

A cheerful heart does good like medicine, but a broken spirit makes one sick.
—Proverbs 17:22

Stress is the human response to overstimulation: sensory overload—noise, TV, lights, movies; information overload—TV, videos, newspapers, magazines, radio, computers, phones; and decision overload—assaulted with 360 advertising messages a day.
—Alvin Toffler

SOCIAL MEDIA . . .

Making Connections!

Social media includes Myspace, Facebook, YouTube, blogging, interactive video gaming, and virtual reality. There are also e-mail, texting, webcams, and the like, which are accessible via your cell or smart phone. We need to look at both the positive and negative effects of social media on your time and health.

One of the greatest advantages of using social media is the time you save communicating with classmates, your employer, your family, friends, and so on. Texting is an excellent way to use today's technology to make your life easier. However, like the technology of the past, social media can become a financial drain as well as a tremendous time drain, leading to unnecessary stress. It can also be similar to an addiction and take on a life of its own.

There does not seem to be a clear definition of what some psychiatrists refer to as "Internet addiction." The American Psychiatric Association's newest release of the *Diagnostic and Statistical Manual of Mental Disorders* (*DSM*) does not include Internet addiction as a disorder.

What we have seen over the past few years is that many students have become obsessed with cell phones, video gaming, or the wonders of virtual worlds to the extent they have lost touch with their responsibilities as students.

Complete the following questionnaire to determine if you have a problem with social media.

1. Do you feel happy when you are online or gaming and get easily angry when you stop? YES or NO

2. Do you think about gaming or going online when you should be focused on your college work? YES or NO

3. Do you spend more time on your computer online or gaming than you spend with your friends? YES or NO

4. Do you lie or make excuses about how much time you spend gaming or online? YES or NO

5. Do you find it hard to sleep at night and get up in the middle of the night to check e-mails, text messages, or Facebook? YES or NO

Answering "yes" to any of these questions may indicate dependence to one or more kinds of social media.

Being addicted to video gaming or virtual worlds, which can give you a high similar to a drug addict, can be much more problematic than spending too much time text messaging. When you are in a virtual world or playing a video game, your brain can produce endorphins. Your brain can also produce the same sensations experienced by a drug addict, such as a sense of urgency to use social media that is similar to withdrawal symptoms, anxiety, feelings of irritability, and the like.

Here are the symptoms of gaming or virtual world addiction:

- Spending most noncollege hours in a virtual world or on computer gaming

- Falling asleep in a college class

- Missing college assignment due dates

- Failing grades

- Lying about the time spent on computer games or in virtual worlds

- Being short tempered when not playing games or in a virtual world

- Having headaches, backaches, or neck aches

- Having no regular schedule for meals or personal hygiene

If you have one or more of the symptoms, you may need to seek professional help. Several good websites deal with video gaming and virtual world addiction and treatment. This website—www.video-game-addiction .org—has several articles about addiction and treatment.

If you feel that you need help, talk to your parents or contact your advisor, a college counselor, or a professional therapist. Seek their advice.

 **STRESS**

People often refer to stress using expressions such as "burned out," "overloaded," "exhausted," and "overwhelmed." Most students define *stress* by the problems that confront them and the concerns they have to confront. Stress occurs in any situation that requires making a change.

Researchers have developed ways to measure stress or stress levels. For example, researchers Holmes and Rahe (1967) developed the *social readjustment rating scale* to help people understand and cope with life's many stressors. This scale lists common life events and provides a corresponding stress value for each event. For example, the death of a spouse is the highest-rated stressor with a rating of 100. The lowest-rated stressor on the scale is 11 for minor violations of the law. For college students, the stressors of beginning or ending college have a rating of 26, a change in colleges has a rating of 20, and a change in work hours or conditions has a rating of 20. Taken together, these stressors can add up to a high score.

To read the review or take the social readjustment rating scale, go to your favorite search engine and key in "Homes and Rahe social readjustment rating scale" (or go to www.mindtools.com/pages/article/newTCS_82.htm). According to Holmes and Rahe, a student accumulating 200 or more points at any given time runs a 50 percent chance of becoming ill.

Do not let your hearts be troubled.
—John 14:1

What Can We Do about Stress?

The first step in dealing with stress is to recognize and identify the significant stressors in your life. Being aware that the stressor and the stress response are not identical is critically important.

Take a few minutes, and list some of the leading stressors in your life. Identifying these stressors opens the door for you to begin planning a process to cope with them.

_____

_____

_____

_____

Coping with Stress

In the book *Health Power: Health by Choice, Not Chance,* Luddington and Diehl discuss many techniques for coping with stress. Here are some of the key techniques, which you can apply (pp. 225–226):

- *Healthy adaptation* means that you recognize the stressor and do something positive about it.

- *Proper planning and organization.* Plan and organize a project to determine what it will take to accomplish the task before you begin.

- *Positive mental attitude.* Do not be anxious or worrisome about the future. Take one day at a time. Worry tends to incapacitate, but seeing the problem as a challenge tends to motivate.

- *Commit to a cause that helps others.* By helping others you forget about your own problems or causes of stress and you get a positive sense of accomplishment. Students that engage in voluntary work report greater feelings of well-being and satisfaction than students who do not.

- *A healthy lifestyle.* You can help protect your body against the harmful effects of stress with these simple stress inoculations:

  - Regular active exercise for at least 30 minutes a day. Exercise produces endorphins. Sunshine and fresh air also produce endorphins, so outdoor exercise is doubly beneficial.

  - A simple, whole-foods, plant-based diet. The body easily handles such a diet. The result is increased energy, efficiency, and endurance.

  - No cigarettes, alcohol, caffeine, or other harmful drugs. These substances all chalk up substantial "pay later" debts, often beginning the next day.

  - Adequate rest. This rest includes a good night's sleep and regular times for relaxation and recreation.

  - Liberal use of water, inside and out. Drink enough water to keep the urine pale (six to eight glasses a day). Taking a hot and cold shower each morning starts your day off right.

- *Stable life anchors.* Trust in a higher power or a religious faith, a loving home, a college that cares for and takes care of their students, a job that makes you feel worthwhile, inspiring friends, a purpose for living—these are all vaccines against stress.

ADDICTIONS: ALCOHOL, DRUGS, FOOD, CAFFEINE, AND TOBACCO

Students are addicted to everything from energy drinks to food, cigarettes, video gaming, illegal and prescription drugs, and Americans' favorite drug: alcohol.

Addicts are compulsive people. A student is probably an addict if he or she is compulsively seeking and using any one or more of these substances (or even food) despite having negative consequences come from it. Common consequences of addiction include the following:

- Excessive class absences or tardiness
- Failing tests, exams, or classes
- Having debt problems
- Being late for or missing work
- Family problems

The physical signs of being an addict can vary, depending on the student and what he or she is abusing.

Recognizing Addiction

Usually, addicted people are compulsive about their addiction to the detriment of themselves, their friends, and their family. If you feel you are compulsive about food, alcohol, tobacco, energy drinks, or some other substance, answer the following questions to see if this compulsion has become an addiction. For each question, write the name of the substance that is problematic or troubling for you. Make sure you fill in the question with only one substance—for example, alcohol. If you feel compulsive about more than one substance, answer the entire set of questions several times—once for each substance.

Answer each question with a "yes" or "no" answer.

Have you ever felt you should reduce the _____?

For example:

- **Number of cigarettes you smoke each day**
- **Amount of alcohol you drink each day**
- **Number of soft drinks or cups of coffee you drink each day**
- **Number of snacks you eat each day**

Have people ever annoyed you by criticizing your use of _____?

For example: energy drinks, alcohol, tobacco, or snack foods

Have you ever felt bad or guilty about your use of _____?

For example: illegal drugs, prescription drugs, food, or soft drinks

Have you ever _____ first thing in the morning to steady your nerves?

For example: drank alcohol, taken a drug, smoked a cigarette, drank coffee, or drank an energy or soft drink

Are you a compulsive _____? That is, do you _____ to feel better?

For example: eater/eat, smoker/smoke, or drinker/drink

If you answered "yes" to one or more of these questions, then you are probably addicted to one or more of these substances.

If you feel you have an addiction, you need to seek professional help. As the first step, you can talk to your friends, your college advisor, or even your college counseling service. But doing that is only the first step.

Students cannot treat themselves. It is important to seek help, if you feel overwhelmed by any compulsive behavior.

A WELLNESS PLAN: PUTTING IT ALL TOGETHER

Putting it all together is not as difficult as it might seem. You must begin with a goal.

For example, the first question on the goal-setting sheet is "What do you value most in life?" Once you have determined your goal, follow the questions on the goal-setting sheet to create your plan of action—your wellness plan.

The next question on the goal-setting sheet is "Where are you going in life?" Where are you going with your wellness plan?

The third question is "How are you going to get there?" What specific steps are you taking to achieve your goal?

Finally, include the eight components of the NEWSTART Lifestyle Program in your wellness plan. Incorporating these components as you answer the questions in your goal-setting sheet will help you pull it all together and will lead you to a more balanced and healthy life.

If you have not had an annual or general physical examination in the last 12 to 18 months, see your doctor before you start finalizing your wellness program. If you are under a doctor's care, it is even more important to see him or her before you start. It is also important to your health to find a doctor who uses nutrition along with medication, if necessary, to prevent and treat conditions such as obesity, diabetes, and hypertension.

Educate yourself, as well. Do your own research on health and wellness. Key in "NEWSTART" or "Weimar Institute" into your computer's browser to start your research. You will find well-researched and beneficial information about health and wellness. A well-educated patient with a well-educated doctor is a great combination.

> Physical fitness isn't enough. You need balance in your life, spiritual balance.
> —Donna Richardson

Milestones

Now That You Are Here...

Now that you have completed reading this chapter on health and wellness, take a few minutes to complete the Milestones checklist again.

Answer each statement by checking "Y" for Yes, "N" for No, or "S" for Sometimes.

1. I know how to develop a wellness plan.	Y	N	S
2. Eating well-balanced meals is important to me.	Y	N	S
3. I get adequate rest each day.	Y	N	S
4. I drink six to eight glasses of water each day.	Y	N	S
5. I understand the importance of getting adequate but not excessive sunshine.	Y	N	S
6. Exercising on a regular basis is important to me.	Y	N	S
7. Moderation and temperance in food and drink is important to me.	Y	N	S
8. Getting fresh air is important to me.	Y	N	S
9. Believing in a supreme being is important to me.	Y	N	S
10. I understand that being healthy helps me be a better student.	Y	N	S

Did any of your "No" and "Sometimes" answers become "Yes" answers as a result of reading and completing the exercises in this chapter? Hopefully, you will begin using the strategies presented to develop your health and wellness plan. Your wellness plan can be an excellent tool that you can use the rest of your life.

TIPS FOR SUCCESS

To live a healthy life based on wellness principles, you need to . . .

- Regularly **check** blood pressure, cholesterol, height, and weight.
- **Exercise** three to five times a week for 30 to 60 minutes.
- Drink eight glasses of **water** each day.
- Get 15 minutes of **sunlight** three times a week.
- Eat and drink in **moderation**.
- Get eight hours of **sleep** each night.
- Have one indoor **plant** in each room of your home and workspace.
- Practice positive **self-talk** each day.

APPLYING WHAT YOU KNOW

Now that you have finished this chapter on health and wellness, refer back to the Case Study about Gwen at the beginning of this book. Based on Gwen's situation, answer the following questions:

1. How will Gwen's situation affect her health and wellness if she does not take appropriate action?

2. What health and wellness strategies or techniques should Gwen follow?

3. How can Gwen use the eight components of the NEWSTART Lifestyle Program to assist her in reaching her goals?

GETTING THERE ON TIME

With today's technology, it is much easier to "get there on time" than it was in the past. We want you to use the most current technology at hand. Consider the technology you have access to: your computer, cell phone, smart phone, or electronic pad or notebook. Then answer the following questions:

1. How can you use your planner, cell or smart phone, or other technology to implement a physical fitness program?

2. How can you use technology to implement a meal-scheduling program?

3. What are the benefits of integrating your wellness plan into your daily schedule and available technology?

JOURNAL

The purpose of this journal exercise is to give you a chance to think about what you have learned from this chapter about health and wellness. Consider what you have learned, and comment on your newly found knowledge. List the steps you are going to take to implement your new health and wellness skills.

As a result of reading this chapter and in preparing for my journey, I plan to

_____

_____

_____

_____

_____

_____

_____

_____

_____

_____

_____

_____

_____

_____

_____

_____

_____

_____

_____

chapter 11

CAREER PLANNING, MARKETABILITY, AND DIVERSITY

REACHING YOUR DESTINATION

Grace was 56 when she first entered college, and her life had been anything but normal. She had two grown children, had gone through a divorce, lost a home to a fire, and one week before classes began, moved to a new home from 1,500 miles away. Needless to say, Grace was dealing with a great deal of stress in her life, but she was determined to become a nurse. That had been her lifelong dream.

Grace did not go to college after high school but got married and settled down to raise her family. When her children were older, she studied for the real estate exam and became an agent in Texas, where she and her family were living at the time. For several years, Grace did very well. One year, she made more than $100,000 selling real estate. However, as the market changed and the real estate in Texas got tough, she lost her job and eventually moved back home.

Grace could have continued in real estate, but her heart was not in it. She had always wanted to have a career in nursing. She enrolled in the nursing program at a local technical college and was devastated to find two major roadblocks to her dream. First, her SAT scores and admissions test indicated that she was not academically prepared to enter the nursing program. And second, there was a three-year waiting list to get into the two-year nursing program.

After much thought and consideration, Grace began traveling the road to her dream by deciding to enroll in the transitional studies program at the college. She also put her name on the waiting list for the nursing program and began to take courses that would upgrade her basic skills in math, reading, and vocabulary. Over the next two years, Grace hired tutors, went to study sessions, and stayed up into the late hours of the night studying. Then finally, she passed all of the tests to admit her into the associate degree nursing program.

The phone rang one day, and the nursing department at the college told Grace that there was an opening in the program. She was admitted almost one year earlier than she had expected! Her first course was very demanding. The subject was calculating drug doses for patients. To continue in the program, students *had* to pass the first test on mathematical calculations. Failing the first test meant not only being removed from the class but from the entire nursing program.

Grace failed the first test! She was asked to leave the nursing program.

Refusing to be beaten, Grace enrolled in a developmental math course and studied harder, stayed up longer, hired more tutors, and finally passed the course. Then she enrolled in another math course and continued to build her math skills for the nursing curriculum. One year later, Grace was invited to rejoin the nursing program. She enrolled in the same drug dosage calculation class. She passed the first test. She passed the second test. And she passed the course.

Two years after readmission, Grace walked down the aisle of the local civic center to be "pinned" as a nurse. Five years after beginning her journey to fulfill her dream, she was living that dream. There were countless times when Grace's life and experiences would have made most people quit, but Grace was determined to have a career in nursing. She knew in her heart what she wanted to be "when she grew up." ■

It is easy to live for others. Everybody does. I call on you to live for yourselves.
—Ralph Waldo Emerson

Objectives

AFTER READING this chapter and completing the exercises, you will be able to do the following:

- Understand the value of your career daydreaming.
- Identify the seven steps to career decision making.
- Recognize how valuable a mentor can be.
- Develop a personal success plan.
- Understand diversity in the workplace.

Milestones

Where Are You Now?

Take a few moments and determine where you stand in relation to making career decisions by completing the Milestones checklist.

Answer each statement by checking "Y" for Yes, "N" for No, or "S" for Sometimes.

1.	I have a good idea of what I want to be after I graduate.	Y	N	S
2.	I know how to find a mentor.	Y	N	S
3.	I think about my career daily.	Y	N	S
4.	I would consider seeking advice from an advisor or counselor.	Y	N	S
5.	I use the *Dictionary of Occupational Titles*.	Y	N	S
6.	I daydream about my career.	Y	N	S
7.	I know how to research a career.	Y	N	S
8.	I understand how job shadowing works.	Y	N	S
9.	I understand the nature of a diverse workforce.	Y	N	S
10.	I understand the difference between *diversity* and *affirmative action*.	Y	N	S

How did you in completing the questions in Milestones? If you do not have a good idea of what you are interested in doing for your life's work, do not worry. If you read this chapter carefully and complete the exercises, your career decision-making skills will be enhanced.

So, what do you want to be when you grow up? Have you been asked this question before? Do you know the answer?

You probably have given some thought to the question. Maybe you have even imagined yourself doing different jobs. The process of career selection can be lengthy, but it is by far one of the most important things you can do for yourself.

The key phrase here is *for yourself. You* are in charge. No one else can make this decision for you. The world of technology and information is changing so rapidly that most people will change careers at least once in their lives. This was not true of your parents. It is estimated that today, three out of every four workers will need retraining for the new jobs of this century!

The decisions you make about your career choices and the roads that you take to get there are *yours*. They belong to no one else. ■

DAYDREAMING

Do you like to daydream? Daydreaming can be fun and exciting. Think about how relaxing it can be to let your mind wander—perhaps taking you on trips to different places or having dinner with a favorite movie star or singer. As children, many of us told our friends that we were going to be doctors, lawyers, football players, or nurses. In the movie *A River Runs through It,* two brothers are lying on the bank of the river, thinking about their lives. One asks the other, "What are you going to be when you grow up?" "A professional boxer," comes the reply. "How about you?" After some thought, the first brother says, "A fly fisherman."

Very few people actually end up doing the work of their childhood dreams—whether boxing, fishing, dancing, acting, or being a fireman. Those dreams may come true for people who do not change their minds, but most of us eventually modify our aspirations. Doing so is natural. However, there are those people who want to do only one thing from childhood—and they do it!

Take a moment and clear your mind. Allow yourself to think about your first-grade classroom. Do you remember your teacher? Do you remember talking to your friends about what you would be when you grew up? List the different occupations you may have mentioned as a child. Enjoy the journey!

1. _____

2. _____

3. _____

Now, think about what you have just written. Why did you, even as a child, select the occupations you listed? Take a minute and write down why you wanted to be these things.

I went into the woods because I wished to live deliberately, to front only the essential facts of life, and see if I could not learn what it had to teach, and not, when I came to die, discover that I had not lived.

—Henry David Thoreau

For Occupation 1 _____

_____

_____

For Occupation 2 _____

_____

For Occupation 3 _____

_____

_____

Now, think for a moment about the present. What are your daydreams like now? What occupations do you see yourself doing? If you could do one thing for the rest of your life, what would it be? Think about that question.

List one or more occupations you dream about doing. You may only have one, and that's fine.

1. _____

2. _____

3. _____

Next, you need to take a strong look at your answer(s) and determine if you want to *do* something or to *be* something.

SOCIAL MEDIA . . .
Making Connections!

Today, with the Web and social networking, there is really no excuse for a student not to be able to research a potential job, community, or even housing. Finding a job, or even finding a career, depends on relationships and networking. Social networking can quickly move the relationship phase of this process to a new level.

Some of the most popular social media/social networks include LinkedIn, Twitter, and state-specific websites for job postings. Think of a position or job that really interests you, and go to www.monster.com, www.careerbuilder.com, or another job-posting site. Then key in the job title and your location—city and state. Review the job positions in your city, identify one that interests you, and find the following information:

1. Job description:

   _____

   _____

   _____

2. Education requirements:

   _____

   _____

   _____

3. Work experience:

   _____

   _____

   _____

4. Are you qualified for this position? If not, what do you need to do to become qualified?

   _____

   _____

   _____

DO YOU WANT TO DO SOMETHING OR BE SOMETHING?

If you were to ask people on the street the simple question "What do you do for a living?" most of them would respond, "I'm a welder," or "I'm an engineer," or "I'm a teacher," and so on. Most people would answer the question without ever thinking about what is really being asked.

This is one of the first questions you will need to examine when deciding on a career: Do I want to *do* something, or do I want to *be* something? A person may be called a "welder," an "engineer," or a "teacher," but the title alone does not necessarily confer his or her identity. To *be* something, you have to make a philosophical decision regarding your future. You have to ask two questions: How do I want to spend my time? and What is my purpose in life? As an individual, you can *do* almost anything. You can *do* the work of medicine, you can *do* the work of upholding the law, and you can *do* the work of instruction. But to *be* a doctor, lawyer, or teacher, you have to want to *become* the epitome of that profession. *Doing* the work is not enough to bring fulfillment to your life. In fact, doing is the easy part. *Being* the person who heals, protects justice, or teaches will bring you joy.

There is an old story about a stranger who was walking down the road when he came upon three men cutting stone. He stopped to ask the first man what he was doing. The man said, "I'm cutting these rocks in half. Can't you see that?" The stranger approached the second man cutting stone and asked him what he was doing. "I'm shaping these stones into blocks. Can't you see?" said the man. Finally, the stranger came upon the third stonecutter and stopped to ask him what he was doing. Replied the last stonecutter, "I'm building a cathedral. Can't you see?"

Where it takes only physical strength to *do* something, it takes vision to *be* something. So, what do you want to *be?* Have you decided? If not, help is available for the undeclared.

> Not all those who wander are lost.
> —J. R. R. Tolkien

Use some of your college electives to delve into new areas of interest. You may find that taking an elective will change your career direction.
Source: ANNIE FULLER/PEARSON

HELP ME! I'M UNDECLARED!

Being undeclared is not a fatal disease. Nor is it a disgrace or a weakness. It is a temporary state of mind, and the best way to deal with it is to stop and think.

A person should never declare a major simply because he or she is ashamed to be undeclared. Also, no one should succumb to pressure to declare a major. You can, however, take certain measures to work toward declaring a major and be satisfied with the decision you make.

Seven Steps to Career Decision Making

STEP 1: DREAM! As was asked earlier, if money was not a concern, what would you do for the rest of your life? If you could do anything in the world, what would you do and where would you do it? These are the types of questions you should ask yourself as you try to select a major and a career. Write down your dreams. In the words of Don Quixote, "Let us dream, my soul, let us dream."

STEP 2: TALK TO YOUR ADVISOR. Your academic advisor is there to help you. First, always make an appointment to see an advisor. Always call in advance. But when you have an appointment, make that advisor work for you. Take your college catalog with you, and ask probing questions.

Also use students in your program as advisors. They will prove to be invaluable to you as you make your way through the daily workings of the college. They can even help you join and become an active member of a pre-professional program.

STEP 3: USE COLLEGE ELECTIVES. Most accreditation agencies working with your college require that you be allowed at least one free elective in your degree program. Use your electives wisely! The wisest students use their electives to delve into new areas of interest or take a block of courses in another area that might enhance their career decision. Be creative, be courageous, be wild, but do not play it safe. Take a chance. It can be the best thing that ever happened to you. One of these electives might hold the key to choosing your career.

STEP 4: GO TO THE CAREER CENTER. Even the smallest colleges have some type of career center or career counselor. *Use them!* The professionals in the college career center can show you information on a variety of careers and work fields. They can also perform certain interest and personality inventories that can help you make good career decisions.

STEP 5: READ! READ! READ! Nothing will help you more than reading about careers and majors. Gather information from colleges, agencies, associations, and places of employment. Then *read it!*

STEP 6: DO JOB SHADOWING. *Job shadowing* is a term used to describe the process of following someone around on the job to see what he or she does. You might call an engineering office and ask if you can sit with several of their engineers for a day over spring break.

Job shadowing is the very best way to get firsthand, honest information about a profession you might be interested in. You might ask questions such as these: Why do you do this for a living? What training do you have? How long did you go to school to get this job? What is the salary range for this job? Is there room for growth? What is your greatest achievement on this job? What was your weakest moment?

STEP 7: JOIN PREPROFESSIONAL ORGANIZATIONS. One of the most important decisions you will make as a college student is to get involved in organizations and clubs on campus that offer educational opportunities, social interaction, and hands-on experience in your chosen field. Preprofessional organizations can open doors that will lead you to make a career decision, grow in your field, meet professionals already working in your field, and eventually get a job.

What Is a Mentor?

Another important aspect of studying and researching a career is finding a mentor you can work with and shadow. A *mentor* is a trusted advisor or guide. A mentor provides guidance and shares knowledge based on his or her experience and training.

The thoughts expressed by Jimmie in the following box demonstrate what a mentor can mean to a student. The concept of a *mentor* has been around for ages. A mentor can be anyone that you admire professionally, personally, intellectually, or socially.

Jimmie's Story

"I remember my first mentor, a gentleman who served as provost at the college I attended. Dr. Thomas was everything I wanted to be—successful, self-assured, intelligent, and fun loving. He had achieved much in his career, traveled widely, yet never lost the 'common touch.' He could relate to almost anyone on any level and was an excellent judge of character. I soon realized that not only was he my professional mentor but also my mental and emotional mentor, as well. I depended on his advice and his friendship. I find myself wishing that he was still alive today to offer advice about my career and about my life in general."

A mentor should be someone you feel comfortable with and that you can trust. When you become successful, you will be a professional peer to this individual, if your career follows the same course. A mentor does not necessarily have to be a lot older than you. People can be mentors at any age. Likewise, you are never too old to have a mentor.

It is important that you eventually let the mentor know that you perceive him or her as such. By doing so, you let this person know that you value his or her character and achievements.

Think for a moment about mentors in your life, and write down their names. For each mentor, explain why you admire him or her.

1. _____

Why do you admire this person?

_____

_____

2. _____

Why do you admire this person?

_____

_____

3. _____

Why do you admire this person?

_____

_____

Make the decision right now that you will let the people you listed know that you admire them. You will be surprised at the reactions it may elicit! You may very well be making the first professional contacts of your career—contacts that can help you find jobs as your career progresses.

Now, reflect on all of the responses you listed. Are you being influenced by another person or by an idea about a career? How much *original* thought have you given to career selection? Many people end up majoring in a certain discipline because a friend is majoring in that field or because a parent or grandparent majored in that field.

Remember, one of the most important decisions you will *ever* make in your life is choosing a career. The decision should be your own.

What Is a Career Counselor?

A career counselor could be viewed as a "career travel agent" of sorts. This person can help you understand the variety of options you might have and can help you "map" your way. They will assist you with the processes outlined previously, but you must remember that ultimately, *you* are in charge.

You may want to ask your counselor to administer the Myers-Briggs Type Indicator (MBTI) instrument or the Campbell Interest and Skill Survey (CISS) to assist you with this process. Each of these instruments gives you an idea of who you are and for what type of work you are best suited. If your counselor or college cannot provide this kind of assistance to you, look for private companies in your area that can.

ONCE YOU KNOW WHERE YOU ARE GOING, HOW DO YOU GET THERE?

The next step in this process is *research*. This is where *you* come in. Deciding to do the research will yield remarkable results. This process is lengthy, and if done correctly, it can take *lots* of time, especially if you want to examine several careers.

Here are some things you need to do:

1. Spend some time listing the careers identified by the career interest inventories or personality inventories you completed at your

school's career center. If you have not completed these kinds of inventories, look back at your mentor list and your "dream" list. Develop a list of careers that you want to explore.

2. After you have identified a career you are interested in, begin doing research. Look at the *Dictionary of Occupational Titles (DOT)*. It is usually available in the reference section of the library. Look up the careers you have selected, and *read every bit of information you can on them. Also take notes.*

DEVELOP A PERSONAL SUCCESS PLAN

Now that you have all of your directions, write them down in a place where you will be able to refer to them often. For example, file them behind the planner in your binder. Some career consultants suggest using the format described in the box that follows as a personal success plan.

Finally, you should realize that there are numerous places to find information about careers, majors, professions, and the world of work. Listed here are just a few of the places you should look when examining careers: college counseling centers; *Dictionary of Occupational Titles (DOT)*; *Guide for Occupational Exploration*; *What Color Is Your Parachute?*, by Richard Bolles; *The Three Boxes of Life,* by Richard Bolles; U.S. Armed Forces; Self-Directed Search (SDS), developed by John Holland; Myers-Briggs Type Indicator (MBTI); computer databases, such as SIGI, SIGI Plus, and DISCOVER; social media sites, such as LinkedIn and Twitter; and search engines to research professions and careers (Google, Bing, etc.).

MY PERSONAL SUCCESS PLAN: CAREER RESEARCH

Use the questions on the bottom of page 249 as a guide for developing your own personal success plan. For each career you are interested in, complete the following activity:

Write a paragraph in response to each question. Be sure to keep all of your answers in one place, such as your three-ring binder. This section in your binder will then become your Personal Success Plan Research Diary. By referring to this diary, you can compare careers, and the process will hopefully allow you to make more informed decisions about the world of work. Also include in your binder a copy of your current résumé. Techniques for creating a résumé will be discussed later in this chapter.

HELP!
I Need A Job

 Progress Energy Progress Energy Carolinas provides electricity and related services to nearly 1.5 million customers in North Carolina and South Carolina. The company is headquartered in Raleigh, NC, and serves a territory encompassing more than 34,000 square miles, including the cities of Raleigh, Wilmington, and Asheville in North Carolina and Florence and Sumter in South Carolina.

Lloyd Yates is president and chief executive officer for Progress Energy Carolinas. He has more than 28 years of experience in the energy business, including nuclear and fossil generation, and in energy delivery.

The quotations that follow present Yates's comments about what he looks for in a Progress Energy employee.

1. WHAT DO YOU LOOK FOR IN AN EMPLOYEE?

"Generally, we are looking for a person who is intelligent, a good communicator, well-rounded, and versatile. Gone, for the most part, are the days when employees were hired for a single position and retired in that same position 30 years later. Successful employees today must be flexible, willing to work in a team environment, able to learn new technologies and processes, and committed to our company's core values, including safety, high performance, and outstanding customer service."

What can you do to be the prospect Yates is looking for in an employee?

_____

_____

_____

2. WHY WOULD YOU HIRE ME?

"Hiring managers ask a number of questions about prospective employees. What do you bring to our company that sets you apart from other candidates? What skill or experience do you possess that can help the company achieve its goals and be successful? Are you a good collaborator? We are interested in people with both technical skills and relationship building skills."

What can you do to make Yates want to hire you?

_____

_____

_____

3. HOW CAN I GAIN A COMPETITIVE EDGE?

"Again, by looking for ways to differentiate yourself from the competition. For many jobs, most candidates have similar technical skills. What sets candidates apart are attributes such as character, communication skills, the ability and desire to collaborate with peers, leadership skills, and the like."

What can you do to gain the competitive edge for a job at Progress Energy?

_____

_____

_____

4. WHAT ROLE WOULD MY EDUCATION PLAY IN BEING ABLE TO GET A JOB WITH YOU?

"Education is very important, as energy jobs are often technical and require an understanding of complex concepts. But your education doesn't end with your degree. A career in energy requires ongoing learning that constantly builds upon your initial skill set. Likewise, our craft and technical employees are held to the same standard of continuing education to remain current on trends, as well as new processes and technologies. We are committed to continuous improvement, and we expect the same from our employees and those seeking employment with the company."

How can you demonstrate that your education is relative and competitive?

_____

_____

_____

5. WHAT VALUE CAN I BRING TO YOUR COMPANY?

"The value you bring to the company is a combination of your experience and expertise, and how well those attributes can help the company achieve its goals. We value the contributions of all our employees and work to create an environment in which diversity, collaboration, and multiple perspectives are appreciated and can flourish."

How can you convince Yates that you would be a valuable employee at Progress Energy?

_____

_____

What would you include in your résumé that will address Yates's comments about prospective employees?

_____

_____

_____

How could you use your cover letter to demonstrate your strengths relative to the job description?

_____

_____

_____

Success Plan Outline

- Write down your goals.
- Make an appointment to see an advisor (counselor).
- Visit your school career center.
- Research your interests at the library and online.
- Read about your interests.
- Take classes that interest you as electives.
- Find someone to job shadow.
- Tell others about your dreams.
- Review your goals.

Career to Be Researched:

Why am I interested in this career?

Will I work with people or things?

How much training is required?

How much money will I likely make?

Whom do I know already working in this field?

What has this person said about this profession?

Will I work indoors or outdoors?

Will the work be mental or physical?

Where will I live while doing this work?

Will this work involve much travel?

What is the best thing I have found out about this career?

What is the worst thing I have found out about this career?

Whom did I interview about this career?

What sources did I use for my research on this career?

ROAD PLAN DECIDED?
WHERE DO I GO FROM HERE?

Suppose you have taken all of the advice provided so far and you are ready to meet the real world head on. You have decided what career is best for you, you have selected a college and major to get you to your final destination, and you are suddenly faced with the stark reality of *finding a job!* Where should you turn?

First, turn to your college placement office. This resource can be invaluable in helping you with writing your résumé and putting together a logical, coherent, and effective cover letter. The staff members of your college placement office are professionals who understand what you are going through. They can help you land a job that will enhance your career and provide you with invaluable experience.

RÉSUMÉ WRITING

Before you begin your job search process, you must first learn to write a professional and effective résumé. A *résumé* tells prospective employers who you are and what you know. It gets your "foot in the door," so you can get an interview and a chance to demonstrate your potential value as an employee. Think of a résumé as a sales plan. Then, after you get your foot in the door (through an interview), you have a chance to really shine and close the sale.

Effective résumé writers all say basically the same thing: Be brief, positive, action oriented, honest, and precise, and use some basics of presentation and style. *Above all else, make sure that your résumé is flawless, typographically and grammatically!*

By being brief, we mean you should list all relevant job experience (in order of current or most recent job to earliest job) and the corresponding dates of employment. It is important that you highlight (possibly with bullets) some of the relevant experiences you had with each job. This is where you need to be especially brief. Do not go on and on about mundane tasks you did at each job. Highlight the tasks you were responsible for, rather than the tasks you were required to do.

Prospective employers want to hire individuals who did an excellent job at mundane or routine tasks and so were given more responsibilities. Employers look for potential employees who can accept responsibility and get the job done. Highlight any experiences you have had that reflect this kind of work.

Be action oriented in your choices of verbs. Instead of writing "I did X," write "I was responsible for assuring X was completed." This is where your career counselor can be *most* helpful: by turning your passive

> "People are always blaming their circumstances for what they are. I don't believe in circumstances. The people who get on in this world are the people who get up and look for the circumstances they want, and, if they can't find them, they make them."
> —George Bernard Shaw

verbs into active verbs, which will get employers' attention. Above all else, keep the discussions simple. Potential employers do not want to read extensive biographies!

Be honest and truthful when you write your résumé. Do not attempt to exaggerate your qualifications. Honesty really is the best policy here. There have been documented cases in which an employee lied on his or her résumé or application, and when the employer found out, the employee was fired immediately and legal proceedings were initiated. In short, *do not lie* on your résumé.

Regarding presentation, there are some basic and simple rules. *Always* have your résumé neatly typed and printed on the best-quality paper you can afford. A tip here is to share costs with friends and buy high-quality paper (25 percent rag bond) and envelopes. Generally, subdued, neutral colors are best for a résumé: tan, gray, or white. Avoid colors such as pink, yellow, green, or blue. You want

When writing your résumé, be truthful and accurate. Customize your résumé, and highlight experience and education that are relevant to the position you seek. *Source:* ANNIE FULLER/PEARSON

your résumé to stand out among a sea of other résumés—but you do not want it to scream!

With the advent of word processing, spell checking, and grammar checking, there is *absolutely no reason* for a résumé to contain any errors. If your résumé does have errors, it will stand out for all of the wrong reasons. Have a friend or relative (someone you trust) proofread your résumé and cover letter before you mail them. It is better to delay mailing by one day than to have a résumé or letter with an obvious error.

To assist you in answering some basic questions about résumé writing, a sample résumé is provided in Figure 11.1. Generally speaking, it is a good idea to keep your résumés to one page or at most two pages.

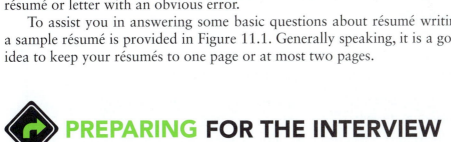

PREPARING FOR THE INTERVIEW

Once you have been called for an interview, it is time for you to aggressively approach learning more about the company. It is perfectly appropriate that you will dig into many aspects of the company to find out more about its operation. An excellent place to find this information is on the Internet.

You should also tap into your network of friends and relatives. Perhaps you know someone who works with the company, or you "know someone who knows someone." Use this resource, but be careful that you accept only factual information from these sources.

As you prepare for an interview, consider appropriate clothes and hygiene. Basic daily hygiene and conservative, understated clothing are appropriate for any interview.

𝓕igure 11.1 **Sample Résumé**

Jane Doe

138 Brentwood Ave.   (333) 555-4568
Any City, USA 12345   doej@internetprovider.com

OBJECTIVE   Meaningful employment in the career service field

QUALIFICATIONS
- Strong written and oral communication ability
- Excellent computer skills
- Outstanding interpersonal skills
- Part-time experience in career services field

EDUCATION   Bachelor of Science, Business Administration (5/11)
XYZ University, Anytown, USA

- Concentration in Personnel and Human Relations
- 3.05 GPA
- Full-time Trustee Scholarship

Associate of Applied Technology (5/09)
USA Community College, Anytown, USA

- Phi Theta Kappa National Honor Society Member
- 3.895 GPA

RELEVANT
EXPERIENCE   University Career Center, Anytown, USA
As a part-time college employee, I was responsible for:

- Designing and implementing Web pages for the center and for individual students.
- Helping to conduct resume critiques, workshops, and seminars.
- Helping students to complete online research and prepare for college-based interviews.

OTHER
EXPERIENCE   Peace Corps Volunteer (2006–08)
Served in Shanghai, China, for one year, helping to teach English as a second language and working with fish-farming enterprises.

REFERENCES   Available upon request.

Follow this simple list of "Dos and Don'ts" for interviewing:

Do:

- Spend an appropriate amount of time on grooming. A bath or shower, fresh haircut, clean nails, and freshly brushed teeth are appropriate.

- For men, if you are not clean shaven, make sure your beard or facial hair is neatly trimmed and clean.

- Dress in a manner appropriate to the position you are interviewing for. But it is always a good idea to be a little overdressed. If you are uncertain what to wear, wear a business suit.

- Always wear shoes that will "hold a shine," and make sure they are well shined.

- Wearing some jewelry (a watch, ring, and necklace for women) is appropriate.

- As soon as possible after the interview, write a thank-you note to the person, expressing gratitude for his or her time and the opportunity to learn more about the company.

- *Be on time.*

Don't:

- Wear gaudy or revealing clothing.

- Wear excessive cologne, makeup, or jewelry. (Individual expressions of style are fine but not for a job interview. Leave nose rings and lip rings at home.)

- Wear clothing that will distract the interviewer from you, your qualifications, or your abilities.

- Chew gum during an interview.

- Use tobacco products during an interview.

- Bring spouses, children, or significant others to an interview.

- *Show up late.*

Many of the items on these lists may seem obvious or elementary, but some job hunters do not know these behaviors are either expected or considered taboo. A good rule of thumb is that when you are in doubt, err on the side of being conservative. You will not be viewed as a prude but as a professional.

THE IMPORTANCE OF DIVERSITY IN THE WORKPLACE

Diversity is the acknowledgment of humanity within ourselves.
—D. Thoreson

As you begin a new position or even a new career, you may be more aware of diversity and be asked to appreciate differences among people. *Diversity* and *diversity training* are often confused with *affirmative action.*

You are likely to encounter individuals from all parts of the world in your college classes. Take the opportunity to learn from them and benefit from the diversity that surrounds you.
Source: SHUTTERSTOCK

Understanding Diversity

Are you a fan of vegetable soup? On a chilly autumn day, a bowl of hot, steamy vegetable soup can do more than satisfy your hunger. It can also give you a sense of comfort.

We usually find comfort in things that we know well—an old pair of sneakers, a favorite shirt, or a faded pair of jeans. Soup and some other foods, as well, can evoke those same feelings of comfort.

Have you ever considered how different all of the vegetables are that are key ingredients in vegetable soup? Tomatoes have a far different consistency than corn or beans. In fact, if you look at these three vegetables, you will find there is more different about them than similar. Yet when they are combined and seasoned with pinches of salt and pepper, these vegetables take on an entirely different flavor and taste. Collectively, they are the basis for good, homemade, comforting vegetable soup.

Primary and Secondary Dimensions of Diversity

Why all of this talk about soup and vegetables? Because in life, just as in soup, individual items with unique characteristics make up a wonderful mix, when combined.

These differences are what characterizes diversity. Diversity comprises several *primary dimensions*—factors that can be seen and that potentially can lead to discrimination. The primary dimensions of diversity include the following: age, ethnicity, gender, physical ability, race, and sexual orientation.

When we observe people with physical characteristics other than those we are familiar with, we have the potential to discriminate. You are probably thinking to yourself that you would never discriminate against anyone based on any of the characteristics just listed. In fact, in U.S. society, discrimination based on many of these characteristics is not only frowned on socially, but it is also illegal.

Sometimes, however, people use more subtle dimensions of diversity to discriminate against others. These more subtle characteristics, or *secondary dimensions* of diversity, include the following: educational background, geographic location, income, marital status, military experience, parental status, religious beliefs, and work experience.

These dimensions of diversity can cause people to act and react in particular situations based on their beliefs and assumptions they have about these dimensions. For example, some people may assume that someone from the South who speaks with a distinct southern accent is less intelligent, less well read, less traveled, or less cultured than others. That may or may not be the case.

As with each of these dimensions, we cannot judge others until we know them individually. When we begin to assign traits to certain categories of people, we begin to *stereotype* individuals. We often misjudge people and do not give them a chance to let us know who they really are.

Think of a time you might not have had an open mind and misjudged someone whom you later learned to like and respect. What were your first impressions of that person?

_____

_____

Were your impressions based on what you observed or based on what someone else told you about this person?

_____

_____

Often, we are not even aware of some of the biases we have when we meet people. In some cases, we automatically begin thinking of reasons we do not like a person and are not aware of the basis of our prejudice. Prejudice exists in modern society, regardless of what one would like to believe.

This has never been more apparent than with the use of *profiling*. Many times, law enforcement personnel determine what the profile of a particular criminal might be based on the characteristics of former criminals. This method may be helpful for law enforcement, but it can cause true agony among citizens. Clearly, an entire culture cannot be judged by the actions of a few. To be truly educated is to know there are many ways of viewing a problem or situation. See Exercise 11.1 to explore the diversity around you.

> You are not educated as long as you have prejudices against anyone for any reason other than his or her character.
> —Martin Luther King Jr.

Exercise 11.1   Exploring Diversity

Find at least one person in your class or school who is of a different religious faith than you. Spend some time talking about his or her faith and what the faith means.

Do you feel comfortable? Do you feel uncomfortable? Why do you feel the way you do?

_____

_____

_____

_____

Is this an easy exercise or one that you find difficult? Why?

_____

_____

_____

_____

_____

MATH —the four-letter word!

As you know, everyone must be proficient in mathematics to secure a job in today's competitive job market. When deciding what career you plan to pursue, you should also identify the math course(s) that will be required to earn your degree. In this activity, you will look at various careers and identify the math that someone in each career uses every day.

Use your college website and the Internet to answer the following questions:

1. What math course(s) does your college require to earn a degree in nursing? In what ways does a nurse use math?

_____

_____

_____

2. What math course(s) does your college require to earn a degree in computer technology? In what ways does a computer technician use math?

_____

_____

_____

3. What math course(s) does your college require to earn a degree in accounting? In what ways does an accountant use math?

_____

_____

_____

4. What math course(s) does your college require to earn a degree in dental hygiene? In what ways does a dental hygienist use math?

_____

_____

_____

5. What math course(s) does your college require to earn a degree in automotive technology? In what ways does an automotive technician use math?

_____

_____

_____

6. What math course(s) does your college require to earn a degree in engineering technology? In what ways does an engineering technician use math?

_____

_____

_____

 # CULTURE

According to the dictionary, _culture_ is defined as the set of customs, values, and beliefs that characterize a particular group of people. A key aspect of culture is that those customs, values, and beliefs are shared by members of the group—whether a religious group, a racial or ethnic group, or even the members of a company or other organization.

Culture plays an important role in any situation involving diversity. Culture allows us to be ourselves, based on our shared past and our beliefs, and to call on problem-solving techniques that have proven to work for us in the past. A person's culture can help to predict how he or she may react to certain situations.

Some Asian cultures, for example, stress honor and loyalty. Should an individual act in a way that is not within the cultural expectations, then harmony is interrupted and confusion may occur. In the Japanese business culture, for example, if you are presenting your business card to another individual, you should do so using both hands to demonstrate that this "gift" has some level of importance. By the same token, if you are handed a business card, you should not immediately place the card in your suit pocket. You should spend a moment to acknowledge the card and then read its contents before putting it away. It is a sign of disrespect in both situations for you to dismiss the card—either as the giver or the receiver.

Working with and getting along with others is not always easy. This is especially true when we factor in the many cultural differences that exist in any group. Our families, the various roles we play in them, and the hierarchies within them all contribute to our belief system. In addition, our language, how we use it, and the communication breakdowns that are bound to occur can affect our ability to get along with one another. These factors, along with our religious differences and our race or ethnicity, all present challenges when trying to deal with one another.

Appreciating various cultures enables us to see the world as a mosaic and challenges us to think of diversity as something that is to be valued. Harmonious cultural diversity goes beyond merely understanding someone else's belief system and the way he or she has been raised. In addition, it allows us to celebrate and embrace the differences that are inevitable.

We are a nation of communities, . . . a brilliant diversity spread like stars, like a thousand points of light in a broad and peaceful sky.
—George H. W. Bush (written by Peggy Noonan)

DISCRIMINATION

Would you ever purposely exclude someone based on the color of his or her skin, hair, or eye color? Probably not. We have all been taught that discrimination has no place in our society. The US government has enacted legislation to prevent discrimination in certain situations, including the Civil Rights Act, the Americans with Disabilities Act, and affirmative action.

Often, our uninformed and misguided thoughts and prejudices cause us to incorrectly judge other people. If we exclude certain classes of people from our social and business settings, if we stereotype people based on an incorrect set of assumptions, or if we assume that certain groups of people, based on their language, are "less than . . . ," then we are discriminating. Learning to be aware of our own biases and then learning to eliminate them from our actions leads to greater inclusion and acceptance.

Think about this: How often do we "uninvite" others with our actions and our words? This is not intended to be a discussion about who our friends are or how they get invited to parties. Rather, the discussion is intended to raise our awareness that regardless of our situation, we are always "inviting" or "uninviting" others based on our actions.

Learning to embrace a more "inviting" philosophy should make us more aware of discriminatory acts. In addition, it should enable us to include more people in our circle of friends and acquaintants. See Exercise 11.2 to investigate your experiences with discrimination.

AFFIRMATIVE ACTION

Often, when people talk about diversity, culture, and discrimination, the notion of affirmative action finds its way into the conversation. Just what is *affirmative action*?

It is a deliberate process designed to remedy the effects of past discrimination, eliminate present discrimination, and prevent future discrimination. It is a law (Executive Order 11246), and it has stirred quite a number of public and private debates about both the concept and how the law should be defined.

An affirmative action plan will likely be in place in one or more of the places you might eventually work. That plan should be specific about what is to be accomplished and should be designed to correct statistical differences caused by discrimination. Ultimately, affirmative action should be used as a tool to reach the goal of fair employment.

There are a number of myths and misconceptions about affirmative action:

- *Affirmative action* is another name for a *quota system*.
- African Americans are the only previously oppressed group that benefits from affirmative action.

Exercise 11.2 Exploring Discrimination

Think of a time when you were not invited to a party or social event.

How did it make you feel to know that others were invited and you were not?

_____

_____

_____

Why do you think you were not included on the guest list? Were you discriminated against? If so, why?

_____

_____

_____

In what situations have you unintentionally discriminated against someone?

_____

_____

_____

- Affirmative action programs are not really needed—not in this day and time.
- Minorities are stealing jobs and opportunities from qualified majority applicants.

In reality, affirmative action plans are designed to do the following:

- Prohibit the use of quotas.
- Prohibit employers from hiring unqualified people.
- Involve proper training of employees and an awareness of fairness issues in the workplace.
- Demonstrate a good-faith effort on the part of the employer to ensure that barriers to employment, education, and the like have been removed.

Affirmative action programs demonstrate a good-faith effort on the part of employers to ensure that barriers to fair employment are removed.
Source: SHUTTERSTOCK

Another popular and often-misunderstood term in the world of work is *equal opportunity*. Equal opportunity is applicable to *all* citizens—not just groups that have been discriminated against historically. Likewise, it is not applicable only to minorities and to females, and it is certainly not a social program.

Equal opportunity means just what it says: providing equal consideration for *all* applicants for a particular job. Even so, equal opportunity is not a guarantee of a job.

Both affirmative action and equal opportunity make sure that in the world of work and education, every citizen—regardless of race, creed, sexual orientation, and so on—is given equal and fair treatment.

In conclusion, we all enjoy working and learning in an environment that respects us for who we are. We must all become more aware of one another and know that diversity exists among all groups of people. One of the most important life skills that a student can develop is to be tolerant of other individuals and their ideas. Having open and honest communication with our coworkers, fellow students, and friends is vital.

The "golden rule" is still appropriate today: "Do unto others as you would have them do unto you." We should treat people as we would like to be treated and learn to enjoy and appreciate the mosaic of life.

Milestones

Now That You Are Here...

Now that you have read this chapter, complete the Milestones checklist again.

Answer each statement by checking "Y" for Yes, "N" for No, or "S" for Sometimes.

1.	I have a good idea of what I want to be after I graduate.	Y	N	S
2.	I know how to find a mentor.	Y	N	S
3.	I think about my career daily.	Y	N	S
4.	I would consider seeking advice from an advisor or counselor.	Y	N	S
5.	I use the *Dictionary of Occupational Titles*.	Y	N	S
6.	I daydream about my career.	Y	N	S
7.	I know how to research a career.	Y	N	S
8.	I understand how job shadowing works.	Y	N	S
9.	I understand the nature of a diverse workforce.	Y	N	S
10.	I understand the difference between *diversity* and *affirmative action*.	Y	N	S

As a result of reading this chapter, do you feel that you know more? Are you better equipped to research a particular career, and do you know what is involved on a daily basis? Career decisions are some of the most important decisions you will ever make, so do not take this process lightly. The time you spend now researching, reading, investigating, questioning, and learning is minimal compared to the time you will spend earning the appropriate degree, diploma, and certificate for your chosen career.

TIPS FOR SUCCESS

To have a clearer understanding of your future career path, spend a few minutes considering each of the following questions:

- Will I **work** with people, things, or ideas?
- How much **training** am I going to need to do this job?
- How much **money** will I make in this profession?
- Do I know **anyone** who already works in this profession?
- Will I work **indoors** or outdoors?
- Will the work be **mental** or physical?

- Where will I **live** while doing this job?
- Will I **travel** with this job?
- Do I want to do this for the rest of my **life**?

These are important issues and questions that you must answer when researching and considering a career. Take time to answer these questions about your life's work.

APPLYING WHAT YOU KNOW

Now that you have completed this chapter, refer to the Case Study about Gwen at the beginning of this book. Based on Gwen's situation, answer the following questions:

1. Gwen actively researched a career in the medical field, based on a broad category identified with a variety of assessments. How have your career goals been shaped by the research you have done?

   _____

   _____

   _____

2. Given what you know about the value of "dreaming" and setting goals, where do you see yourself in five years? Ten years?

   _____

   _____

   _____

3. How might you apply what you learned in the Seven Steps to Career Decision Making section to your own situation?

   _____

   _____

   _____

GETTING THERE ON TIME

1. How will your career choice affect the amount of personal time you will have?

   _____

   _____

   _____

2. How much time outside your education will be expected for you to be successful in your career?

   _____

   _____

   _____

3. Describe the importance of time as it relates to getting a job.

   _____

   _____

   _____

4. How long will it take you to achieve your career goal?

   _____

   _____

   _____

JOURNAL

The purpose of this journal exercise is to give you a chance to think about what you have learned from this chapter about careers, marketability, and diversity. Consider what you have learned and comment on your newly found knowledge. Also, complete the following sentence:

As a result of reading this chapter and in preparing for my journey, I plan to . . .

UNDERSTANDING THE ROAD SIGNS

"COLLEGEEZE": THE LANGUAGE OF SUCCESS

I can remember going to my first day of college and walking into the auditorium for orientation. I was excited and afraid, but I knew the information I would get in the orientation session would ease my fears. I was wrong! When I left that auditorium, I felt as if I had gone to another country and had understood nothing of what had been said.

We were to register for 15 semester credit hours, use appropriate prefixes, choose one elective outside the curriculum or discipline, and take our registration forms to be keyed. We were not to co-op our first semester, nor were we to audit, because we could ruin our GPA and not be on the dean's list. If we did that, we would have to go to the provost or the registrar!

Now, I certainly did not know what my GPA was, but I knew that I did not want it ruined. Would it be painful? And who was this registrar? Rumor had it that it hid under the main building and would eat freshmen who were on Pell Grants.

It was not that bad, but I did not know the terminology or the lifestyle of college students or where to go to find the answers. It took me over a year to come to grips with the new language of college. This glossary is intended to assist you in learning the basic terminology of college life to empower you to do your best when you arrive on campus.

The very first difference that you will notice is the amount of freedom and time that you have compared to high school. You decide, with the assistance of your advisor, what your schedule will entail. If you want to come to school at 8:00 a.m., you will be able to do so. If you prefer that your classes begin at 10:00, that can be arranged, also.

Although all colleges have attendance policies, it will be up to you to attend your classes. If you do not attend, that is your business. No teacher will call your parents and tell them that you were not in class. No attendance report will be sent to your parents' address. In fact, the Family Educational Rights and Privacy Act (FERPA) of 1974 prohibits this from happening.

Because of the freedom you will have in college, you will have the best of times and the worst of times. You will have hours during the day you might not be in class. You can use this time to study, work on college co-curricular activities, or catch a nap. That decision is up to you. One of your first challenges in college will be to make use of Chapter 3 in this book, which is on time management. Your new life will be filled with many exciting and wonderful events and people, but your studies *must* come first.

Another great difference between high school and college will be the attitude and behavior of your instructors. In high school, there is an assumed line between the student and the instructor, and that line is seldom crossed. In college, you can visit with your professors, go to their offices, or go to lunch with them. It is not even uncommon for a professor to have a group of students come to his or her home. The student/teacher relationship is based on a more open set of standards.

It might be quite possible, however, that as a freshman or sophomore, you will have a graduate assistant teach one of your classes. A graduate assistant is a student—one who is in graduate school seeking a master's or doctorate degree—who also teaches classes to undergraduate students. The graduate assistant, or teacher's assistant (TA), works under the direction of a full professor, but seldom, if ever, will you see the professor. Graduate and teaching assistants usually teach only at larger institutions, where master's and doctorate degrees are awarded.

Another interesting aspect of college is the number of co-curricular activities available. You could become involved with a sorority or fraternity; work on the college newspaper, yearbook, or literary magazine; or join an organization directed toward a social cause. You might also join the student organizations of professional scholars, such as the Student Psychological Association of America or the Student Speech, Language, and Hearing Association. These organizations allow you to be involved in activities related to your field of study. You will also find activities related to specific matters, such as religious organizations. You are encouraged to find an organization in which you can grow and learn. Participating in co-curricular activities is a wonderful way to meet new people and broaden your horizons.

Research has proven that students who join organizations on campus are more likely to complete their degrees. You must remember, however, that your academic performance *must* come first. In fact, some organizations have a grade requirement just to be a member.

 ## QUESTIONS **ABOUT TERMS**

You may have questions about some of the terms used in this book. The following section is a glossary of terms, which will provide you with a working knowledge of the language of college when you arrive on campus.

Academic freedom This is a term used by professors in institutions of higher education. Having academic freedom allows them to conduct research and then teach that research, regardless of its controversial issues. Professors have the freedom to teach certain aspects of materials that might not be allowed in high schools.

Accreditation Most high schools and colleges in the United States are accredited by a regional agency. This agency is responsible for ensuring that all the institutions that are members of the accreditation agency meet a minimum set of standards. The Southern Association of Colleges and Schools is one accreditation agency.

Adding This term is usually used during registration periods or during the first week of classes. When a student adds a class, it means he or she is adding another class to his or her schedule.

Administration The administration of a college is usually made up of nonteaching personnel who handle all of the administrative aspects of the college. The administration is headed by the president and vice presidents. The structure of the administration at each college varies.

Advising To make sure you know what classes to take and in which order, you will be assigned an advisor when you arrive on campus. This advisor will usually be with you the entire time you work on your degree. He or she is responsible for guiding you through your academic work at the college. Your advisor is most often a faculty member in your discipline or major.

Alumna, alumni, alumnus These terms are used to refer to students who hold degrees from a college. The term *alumna* refers to women and *alumnus* refers to women and men. The term *alumni* is the plural form.

Articulation An articulation agreement is a signed document between two or more institutions guaranteeing that the courses taken at one college will transfer to another college. For instance, if Oak College has an articulation agreement with Maple College, it means the courses taken at Oak will be accepted toward a degree at Maple.

Associate's degree Several types of degrees can be earned in college. An associate's degree is a two-year degree that usually prepares the student to enter the workforce with a specific skill or trade. The associate's degree is also offered to students who have completed the first two years of a bachelor's, or four-year, degree. Not all colleges offer associate's degrees.

Attendance Each college has an attendance policy, such as "A student can miss no more than 10 percent of the total class hours, or he or she will receive an F for the course." This policy is followed strictly by some professors and on a more lenient basis by others. You should *always* know the attendance policy of *each* professor you are studying with.

Auditing Most colleges offer a choice of enrolling in a course or auditing a course. If you enroll, you pay the entire fee, attend classes, take exams, and receive credit. If you audit, the fee is usually less, you do not have to take exams, and you *do not* receive credit. Course auditing is usually done by people who are having trouble in a subject or who want to gain more knowledge about a particular subject. Some colleges charge full price for auditing courses.

Baccalaureate The baccalaureate degree, more commonly called the bachelor's degree, is a four-year degree in a specific field. Although this degree can be completed in as few as three years or as many as six years, traditionally, the amount of academic work required is four years. This degree prepares students for careers such as teachers, social workers, engineers, journalists, and fine arts personnel. Graduate work is also available in these fields.

Board of trustees The board of trustees is the governing body of the college. At a public college or university, the board is appointed by government officials (usually, the governor) of each state. The board hires the president and must approve any curriculum changes in degree programs. The board also sets policies for the college.

Catalog The college catalog is a book issued to you at the beginning of your college career. It is one of the most important tools you will use in developing your schedule and completing your degree. This catalog is a legal, binding document stating what your degree requirements are for the duration of your studies. You will need to obtain and *keep* the catalog for the year in which you entered college.

Certificate A certificate program is a series of courses, usually one year in length, designed to educate and train an individual in a certain skill or trade, such as welding, automotive repair, medical transcription, tool and die, early childhood, physical therapy assistant, or fashion merchandising. Although these programs are certified and detailed, they are not degrees. Often, associate and bachelor degrees are offered in these areas, as well.

CLEP The College Level Examination Program (CLEP) is designed to allow students to "test out" of courses. CLEP exams are nationally normed and often more extensive than a course in the same area. If you CLEP a course, it means you passed the exam and do not have to take the course. Some colleges have limits on the number of hours that can be earned by CLEP.

Cognate A cognate is a course (or set of courses) taken outside your major. Some colleges call this a *minor*. For instance, if you are majoring in English, you may wish to take a cognate in history or drama. A cognate is usually in a field close to the major. A student would not likely major in English and take a cognate in pharmacy, for example.

Communications College curricula often state that a student must have nine hours of credit in communications. This most commonly refers to English and speech (oral communication) courses. The mixture of these courses is usually English 101 and 102 and Speech 101. This varies from college to college.

Continuing education Almost every college in the United States offers continuing education or community education courses. These courses are not offered for college credit, but continuing education units are awarded in many cases. These courses are usually designed to meet the needs of specific businesses and industries or to provide courses of interest to the community. Continuing education courses range from small engine repair to flower arranging, from stained glass making to small business management.

Counseling Most colleges have a counseling center on campus. Do not confuse *counseling* with *advising*. Trained counselors are at the college to assist you with problems that might arise in your personal life, with your study skills, or with your career aspirations. Academic advisors are responsible for your academic progress. Some colleges do combine the two, but in many instances, the counselor and the advisor are two different people with two different job descriptions.

Course title Every course offered at a college has a course title. You may see something in your schedule of classes that reads ENG 101, SPC 205, or HIS 210. Your college catalog will define what this means. ENG 101 usually stands for "English 101," SPC could be the heading for "speech," HIS could mean "history," and so forth. Headings and course titles vary from college to college.

Credit A pay-later system, in which someone is granted money or the use of money, usually for the purchase of merchandise, with the promise to repay the money in the future.

Credit hours Credit hours are the amount of credit offered for each class you take. Most classes are worth three credit hours. Science courses, foreign language courses, and some math courses are worth four credit hours, because a lab is required for the class. If a class carries three credit hours, it usually means the class meets three hours a week. This formula will vary greatly during the summer or a midsession.

Curriculum The curriculum is the area of study you are engaged in. It is the set of topics you must study and classes you must take to earn a degree.

Dean The word *dean* is not a name but a title. A dean is usually the head of a division or area of study. Some colleges might have a dean of arts and sciences, a dean of business, and a dean of mathematics. The dean is the leader of a division. He or she is the policymaker and usually the business manager and final decision maker of an area of study. Deans usually report to vice presidents.

Dean's list The dean's list contains the names of students who have achieved at least a 3.5 (B+) grade-point average (GPA) on a 4.0 scale. (See the entry for GPA for the meanings of these numbers.) This achievement may vary from college to college, but generally speaking, the dean's list comprises students in the top 5 percent.

Degree When a student completes an approved course of study, he or she is awarded a degree. The title of the degree depends on the college, the number of credit hours in the program, and the field of study. A two-year degree is called an associate's degree, and a four-year degree is called a bachelor's degree. These degrees usually take two and four years to earn, respectively. If a student attends graduate school, he or she may receive a master's degree (approximately two to three years) or a doctorate degree (anywhere from three to ten years). Some colleges even offer postdoctorate degrees.

Diploma A diploma is awarded when an approved course of study has been completed. The coursework for a diploma is not as detailed or comprehensive as that for an associate's degree. It usually consists of 8 to 12 courses specific to a certain field.

Dorms Dorms are residential facilities on campus where students live. Dorms can be single sex or coeducational. If a student lives in another state, he or she may opt to live "on campus." The college usually staffs each dorm with a full-time supervisor and a director of student housing. Each dorm usually elects a student representative to be on the student council.

Dropping When a student decides that he or she does not enjoy a class or will not be able to pass the class because of grades or absenteeism, he or she may elect to drop it. This means the class will no longer appear on the student's schedule or be calculated in his or her GPA. Rules and regulations on dropping vary from college to college. All rules should be explained in the catalog.

Elective An elective is a course that a student chooses to take outside of his or her major field of study. It could be an area of interest or an area that complements the chosen major. For example, an English major might choose an elective in the field of theater or history, because these fields complement each other. However, a student majoring in English might also elect to take a course in medical terminology because he or she is interested in that area.

Emeritus, emerita, emeriti This Latin term is assigned to retired personnel of a college who have performed exemplary duties during their professional careers. For example, a college president who obtained new buildings, added curriculum programs, and increased the endowment might be named *president emerita* upon retirement. *Emeriti* is plural.

Evening college An evening college program is designed to allow students who have full-time jobs or are full-time homemakers to obtain college degrees by enrolling in classes that meet in the evenings. Some colleges offer entire degree programs in the evenings; others only offer some courses.

Faculty The faculty of a college is the body of professionals who teach, do research, and perform community service. Faculty members have prepared for many years to fulfill the responsibilities conferred by this title. Many have attended school for more than 25 years to obtain the knowledge and skill necessary to train students in specific fields.

Fees Fees refer to amounts of money charged by colleges for specific items and services. Some fees may be tuition, meal plans, books, health, and activity fees. Fees vary from college to college and are usually printed in the catalog.

Financial aid If a student is awarded money from the college, the state, the federal government, private sources, or places of employment, he or she is receiving financial aid. Financial aid can be awarded on the basis of need or the basis of merit. Any grant, loan, or scholarship is formally called financial aid.

Fine arts Many people tend to think of fine arts as drawing or painting, but in fact, the fine arts encompass a variety of artistic forms. Theater, dance, architecture, drawing, painting, sculpture, and music are considered areas of the fine arts. Some colleges also include literature in this category.

Foreign languages Almost every college offers at least one course in a foreign language, and many colleges offer degrees in this area. For schools in the United States, foreign languages include Spanish, French, Russian, Latin, German, Portuguese, Swahili, Arabic, Japanese, Chinese, and Korean.

Freshman This is a term used by high schools and colleges to refer to a student in his or her first year. Traditionally, a college freshman is someone who has not yet completed 30 semester hours of college-level work.

GPA (grade-point average) The GPA is the numerical grading system used by almost every college in the United States. The level of a student's GPA determines whether he or she is eligible for continued enrollment, financial aid, or honors. Most colleges operate under a 4.0 system. This means that all A's earned are worth 4 quality points, B's are worth 3 points, C's are worth 2 points, D's are worth 1 point, and F's are worth 0 points. To calculate your GPA, multiply the number of quality points by the number of credit hours carried by the course, and then divide the total points by the total number of hours carried.

Example: Suppose a student is taking English 101, Speech 101, History 201, and Psychology 101, and all these courses are worth three credit hours each. If the student makes all A's, he or she will have a GPA of 4.0. If the student makes all B's,

he or she will have a GPA of 3.0. However, if the student has a variety of grades, the calculation is as follows:

Course	Grade	Credit Hours	Quality Points		Total Points
ENG 101	A	3	×4	=	12 points
SPC 101	C	3	×2	=	6 points
HIS 201	B	3	×3	=	9 points
PSY 101	D	3	×1	=	3 points

The total of 30 points divided by 12 hours results in a GPA of 2.5 (or a C+ average).

Grant A grant is usually money that goes toward tuition and books and does not have to be repaid. Grants are most often awarded by the state and federal governments.

Health Health is the overall condition of the student at a given time. It is soundness of the body and mind. It is the freedom from disease and a condition of optimal well-being.

Higher education This term is used to describe any level of education beyond high school. All colleges are called institutions of higher education.

Honors Academic honors are based on a student's GPA. Each college usually has many academic honors, including the dean's list, the president's list, and departmental honors. The three highest honors awarded, however, are summa cum laude, magna cum laude, and cum laude. These are awarded at graduation to students who have maintained a GPA of 3.5 or better. The GPA requirement for these honors varies from college to college. Usually, they are awarded as follows:

3.5 to 3.7	cum laude
3.8 to 3.9	magna cum laude
4.0	summa cum laude

Honors college The honors college is usually a degree or a set of classes offered for students who performed exceptionally well in high school.

Humanities The humanities are sometimes as misunderstood as the fine arts. Courses in the humanities include history, philosophy, religion, and cultural studies, and some colleges also include literature, government, and foreign languages. The college catalog will define what your college has designated as humanities.

ID card Having an identification (ID) card is essential for every college student. Some colleges issue IDs for free, but some charge a small fee. A college ID card allows the student to use the college library, participate in activities, and use physical fitness facilities, and it may allow the student to attend college events for free. College IDs are also useful in the community. Movie theaters, museums, zoos, and other cultural organizations usually charge less if a student has an ID, and many events will be free. Having an ID card also allows the student to use most area library facilities with special privileges.

Independent study Many colleges offer courses by way of independent study, meaning that there are no formal classes and no classroom teacher. The student works independently to complete the course under the general guidelines of a department and with the assistance of an instructor. Many colleges require that a student maintain a certain minimum GPA before enrolling in independent study classes.

Junior This term refers to a student who is enrolled in his or her her third year of college or a student who has completed at least 60 credit hours of study.

Learning management system (LMS) A learning management system is a software application for the administration, documentation, tracking, and reporting of college credit courses, not for credit training programs, e-learning programs, and training content.

Lecture The word *lecture* refers to the lesson given by an instructor in a class. The term usually refers to the style in which material is presented. Some instructors have group discussions, peer tutoring, or multimedia presentations. In the lecture format, the professor presents most of the information.

Liberal arts A liberal arts program or college involves a student in a series of courses that go beyond training for a certain vocation or occupation. For instance, a student at a liberal arts college might be majoring in biology but will also have to take courses in fine arts, history, social sciences, math, and the "hard" sciences. The liberal arts curriculum ensures that the student is well educated, because he or she has been exposed to a variety of information and cultural experiences.

Load A student's load is the amount of credits or the number of classes he or she is taking. The normal load for a student is between 15 and 18 hours, or five or six classes. For most colleges, 12 hours is considered a full-time load, but a student can take up to 21 hours for the same amount of tuition.

Major A major is the intended field of study for a student and refers to the amount of work completed in one field. In other words, the majority of the courses have been in one field, such as English, engineering, medicine, nursing, art, history, or political science. A student is usually required to declare a major by the end of the sophomore (or second) year.

Mentor A mentor is someone students can call on to help them through troubled times, assist them in decision making, and give advice. Mentors can be teachers, staff members, outstanding classmates, or upperclassmen. Mentors seldom volunteer for this role. Usually, they fall into the role of mentoring because they are easy to talk with, knowledgeable about the college and the community, and willing to lend a helping hand. You may, however, be assigned a mentor when arriving on campus.

Minor A student's minor consists of the courses he or she takes that complement the major, in most cases. The minor is usually six to eight courses in a specific field. If a student is majoring in engineering, he or she might minor in math or electronics—something that would be beneficial in the workforce.

Natural sciences Natural and physical sciences refers to a select group of courses from biology, chemistry, physical science, physics, anatomy, zoology, botany, geology, genetics, microbiology, physiology, and astronomy.

Orientation Every student is requested and many are required to attend an orientation session. This is one of the most important steps a student can take when beginning college. Important information, such as the material covered in this book, will be presented at orientation. Details concerning individual colleges and their rules and regulations are also discussed.

Planner or time-management system A planner is a systematic approach to time management using a commercially produced system. It usually includes a yearly calendar, a monthly calendar, a daily schedule, and a to-do list.

Prefix A prefix is a code used by the office of registrar to designate a certain area of study. The prefix for English is usually ENG, religion is REL, theater is THE, history is HIS, and so forth. Prefix lettering varies from college to college.

Preprofessional programs Preprofessional programs usually include majors that *require* advanced study to the master's or doctorate level to be able to practice in the field. Such programs include law, medicine, dentistry, psychiatry, nursing, veterinary medicine, and theology.

Prerequisite A prerequisite is a course that must be taken *before* another course. For example, most colleges require that English 101 and 102 (Composition I and II) be completed before *any* literature class is taken. Therefore, English 101 and 102 are prerequisites to literature. Prerequisites are always spelled out in the college catalog.

President The college president is the visionary leader of an institution. He or she is usually hired by the board of trustees of a college. Primary responsibilities include financial planning, fundraising, community relations, and maintaining the academic integrity of the curriculum. Every employee at the college answers to the president.

Probation This term is used when a student has not performed well in his or her academic studies and is being put on notice, essentially, that improvement is needed. Many times, a student who has a GPA below 2.0 in any given semester or quarter is placed on academic probation for one semester. If that student continues to perform below 2.0, suspension may be in order. The rules for probation and suspension *must* be displayed in the college catalog.

Professor Many people believe that all teachers at the college level are professors, but this is *not* true. A full professor is someone who has been in the profession for a long time and usually holds a doctorate degree. The hierarchy of positions or system of promotion for college teachers is as follows: adjunct instructor, instructor, lecturer, assistant professor, associate professor, full professor (professor).

Provost The provost is the primary policymaker at the college with regard to academic standards. He or she usually reports directly to the president. Many colleges do not have a provost but instead have a vice president for academic affairs or a dean of instruction.

Readmit When a student has dropped out for a semester or two, he or she will usually have to be readmitted to the college. This term does *not* apply to a student who elects not to attend summer sessions. Usually, there is no application fee for a readmitted student, and he or she does not lose previously earned academic credit, unless that credit carries a time limit. For example, some courses in psychology carry a 5- or 10-year limit, meaning that if a degree is not awarded within that time, the course must be retaken.

Registrar The registrar has one of the most difficult jobs on any college campus. He or she is responsible for all students' academic records. The registrar is also responsible for entering all grades, recording all drops and adds, printing the schedule, and verifying all candidates for graduation.

Residency requirement Many colleges have a residency requirement, meaning that a certain number of hours must be earned at the home institution. For many two-year colleges, at least 50 percent of the credits put toward graduation must be earned at the home college. For four-year colleges, many require that the last 30 hours be earned at the home college. All residency requirements are spelled out in the college catalog.

Room and board Students who live on campus are charged a fee for this service that is often called room and board. It typically includes a place to stay and food to eat. Many students may opt to buy a meal plan along with their dorm rooms. These issues are usually discussed during orientation.

Scholar A scholar is usually someone who has performed in a superior manner in a certain field of study.

Section code At many larger colleges, many sections of the same course are offered. The section code tells the computer and the registrar the hour and instructor assigned to a particular class. When you see a schedule, it may look something like this:

English 101   01   MWF   8:00–8:50   Smith

English 101   02   MWF   8:00–8:50   Jones

English 101   03   T TH   8:00–9:15   McGee

The number 01, 02, or 03 refers to the section of English in which the student wishes to enroll.

Senior The term *senior* is used for students in their last year of study for an undergraduate degree. The student must have completed at least 90 credit hours to be a senior.

Social media Social media refers to the use of forms of electronic communication, web sites, cell phones, iPads, etc., for social networking to turn communication into an interactive dialogue. Social media are media for social interaction that users can use to create online communities to share information, ideas, personal messages, and other content such as videos.

Social sciences Social sciences are courses that involve the study of or interface with society and people. Social science courses may include psychology, sociology, anthropology, political science, geography, economics, and international studies.

Sophomore The term *sophomore* refers to students who are in their second year of study. A student must have completed at least 30 credit hours to be a sophomore.

Staff Personnel in the college setting are usually divided into three categories: administration, staff, and faculty. The staff are responsible for the day-to-day workings of the college. Usually, people in admissions, financial aid, the bookstore, housing, student activities, and personnel hold staff titles. The people heading up these departments are usually in administration.

Student loan Unlike a grant, a student loan *must* be repaid. A student loan is usually offered at a much lower rate of interest than a bank loan. For most student loans, the payment schedule does not begin until six months after graduation. This allows the graduate to find a job and become secure in his or her chosen profession. If a student decides to return to school, he or she can get the loan postponed, with additional interest, until a graduate degree has been completed.

Syllabus In high school, you may have been given a class outline, but in college, you are given a syllabus. This is a legal, binding contract between the student and the professor. This document contains the attendance policy, the grading scale, the required text, the professor's office hours and phone number(s), and important information regarding the course. Most professors also include the class operational calendar as a part of the syllabus. This is one of the most important documents you will be issued in a class. You should take it to class with you daily and keep it at least until the semester is over.

Tenure You may hear someone call a college teacher a *tenured* professor. This usually means the instructor has been with the college for many years and has performed in a manner that ensures him or her lifelong employment.

TOEFL TOEFL is an acronym for the Test of English as a Foreign Language. Passing this test allows students whose native language is not English to use English as their foreign language requirement.

Transcript A transcript is a formal record of all work attempted or completed at a college. If a student attends more than one college, he or she will have a transcript from *each* college. Many colleges have a policy that all classes, completed or not, remain on the transcript. Some colleges allow D's and F's to be removed if the student repeats the course and earns a better grade. Many colleges, however, leave the old grade *and* continue to count the D or F in the GPA. Rules regarding transcripts vary from college to college. Many employers now require prospective employees to furnish their college transcripts.

Transfer This term may refer to coursework or a student. If a student enrolls in one college and then decides to go to another, he or she is classified as a transfer student. The coursework completed at one college and moved to another is called transfer work. Many colleges have rules regarding the number of credit hours that can be transferred. Most colleges will not accept credit from another college if the grade on the course is below a C.

Transient A transient student is someone who attends another college to take one or two courses. If a student comes home for the summer and wants to enroll in a college near home *but* maintain student status at his or her chosen college, the student is a transient.

Transitional studies Many colleges have an open-admission policy, meaning that the door is open to any student. In these cases, the college usually runs a transitional studies program to assist the students in reaching their educational goal. A student who has not performed well in English, math, or reading may be required to attend a transitional studies class to upgrade basic skills in that area.

Veteran affairs Many colleges have an office of veteran affairs to assist those students who have served in the military. Many times, a college will accept the credit earned by a veteran while in the service, and most of the time, the veteran's financial package is different because of the G.I. Bill.

Vice president Many colleges have several vice presidents that serve under the president. Vice presidents are senior-level administrators that assist with the daily operations of the college. Most colleges have vice presidents of academic affairs, financial affairs, and student affairs.

Volumes This term is used by most libraries in the nation. A *volume* is a book or a piece of nonprint material. You may see that a college library has 70,000 volumes. This means the library has 70,000 books and other pieces of media. Many colleges have volumes that range in the millions.

Wellness This is the enjoyment of good health and vigor of body, mind, and spirit. A student needs to develop a wellness plan to reach good health and vigor.

Wellness plan A wellness plan is a plan based on a student's goal for lifelong good health. It should be designed according to the eight components of the NEWSTART Lifestyle Program or another similar approach.

Who's Who This is a shortened title for the national *Who's Who in American Colleges and Universities*. Students are nominated for this honor by their colleges because of their academic standing and their achievements in co-curricular activities and community service.

 **CONCLUSION**

College will be one of the, if not *the*, most exciting and rewarding times of your life. If you ask anyone who has attended college "When were you happiest?" most will reply "During my college years."

Sometimes, however, college can be a cruel and harsh place for even the best-prepared student, let alone an unprepared student. Doing well in college requires commitment and dedication. It requires that you surrender yourself to the notion of change and growth. It demands that you reevaluate all that you know and hold to be true. College should not be the end of your formal education but the beginning of your pursuit of lifelong knowledge.

"The knowledge of words is the gate of scholarship."

—John Wilson

References

Adler, R., Rosenfeld, L., & Towne, N. (1989). *Interplay: The Process of Interpersonal Communication* (4th ed.). New York: Holt, Rinehart and Winston.

Barefoot, B. O., & Gardner, J. N. (2008, February). *The "First-Year Experience": A Foundation for Achieving the Dream.* Policy Center on the First Year of College Presentation: Achieving the Dream Strategy Institute, Atlanta, GA.

Barranger, M. (1994). *Understanding Plays* (2nd ed.). Boston: Allyn & Bacon.

Bennett, W. (1993). *The Book of Virtues.* New York: Simon & Schuster.

Bits and Pieces, vol. N, no. 2. Fairfield, NJ: Economic Press.

Bolles, R. N. (1978). *The Three Boxes of Life: And How to Get Out of Them.* Berkeley, CA: Ten Speed Press.

Bolles, R. N. (2011). *What Color Is Your Parachute: A Practical Manual for Job-Hunters and Career-Changers,* 2011 ed. Berkeley, CA: Ten Speed Press.

Carper, J. (1999, July 2–4). "10 Foods for Longevity." *USA WEEKEND.*

Chappell, C. (1938). *If I Were Young.* Nashville, TN: Abingdon Press.

Clark, K. (1999, February). "Perfect 10: The Best Foods to Eat for Peak Fitness and Health," *Muscle & Fitness.*

Corliss, R. (2002, July 15). "Should We All Be Vegetarians?" *Time,* pp. 48–56..

Douglass, M. E., & Douglass, D. N. (1993). *Manage Your Time, Your Work, Yourself.* New York: American Management Association.

Ellis, D., Lankowitz, S., Stupka, E., & Toft, D. (1990). *Career Planning.* Rapid City, IA: College Survival.

"Food Facts: What We Eat in America." (2000, June). *Muscle & Fitness.*

Gardner, J., & Jeweler, J. (1995). *Your College Experience.* Belmont, CA: Wadsworth.

Gross, S. J. (2006). *How to Raise Your Self-Esteem.* Retrieved from http://psychcentral.com/lib/2006/how-to-raise-your-self-esteem/

Hill, N. (1992). *Think and Grow Rich.* New York: Fawcett Crest. (Original work published 1937)

Holmes, T. H., & Rahe, R. H. (1967, August). "The Social Readjustment Rating Scale." *Journal of Psychosomatic Research,* Volume 11, Issue 2, pp. 213–218.

Lakein, A. (1973). *How to Get Control of Your Time and Your Life.* New York: Signet.

Luddington, A., & Diehl, H. (2005). *Health Power: Health by Choice, Not Chance.* Hagerstown, MD: Review and Herald, pp. 225–226, 245–248.

Matthews, Dale A. (1999). *Faith Factor: Proof of the Healing, Power of Prayer.* New York: Penguin, pp. 192–194.

Miller, L., Smith, A., & Rothstein, L. (1994). *The Stress Solution.* New York: Pocket Books.

Pauk, W. (1997). *How to Study in College.* New York: Houghton Mifflin.

Index